Reading Early American Handwriting

Reading Early American Handwriting

Kip Sperry

GENEALOGICAL PUBLISHING Co., Inc

Second printing, 1999
Third printing, 2001

Published by Genealogical Publishing Co., Inc.
1001 N. Calvert St., Baltimore, Md. 21202
Library of Congress Catalogue Card Number 97-77226
International Standard Book Number 0-8063-0846-X
Made in the United States of America

Contents

Preface

This guidebook focuses on how to read and understand early American handwriting. Also covered are techniques for reading early American documents, the illustration of alphabets and letter forms, definitions and terminology, interpreting terms and abbreviations, and tips and suggestions for reading early American handwriting. Representative examples of various early American documents, such as town, church, court, land, and probate records, are reproduced in this work, along with transcriptions for each document. By studying and transcribing each document, the reader will become familiar with the various early handwriting styles, letter forms, abbreviations, and terminology used in American records.

One of the best ways to begin a study of paleography is to read facsimiles of documents and then transcribe them word for word, letter for letter. This book will assist the reader in those tasks; however, it covers only early American handwriting written in English. Foreign language documents, French, Spanish, German script, Gothic script, Latin, etc., are not covered.

Included in this work is an annotated bibliography of articles and books that will be of particular interest to American genealogists and historians. Supplemental references are included which will be of interest to those who wish to study older handwriting, especially British handwriting. These additional titles will interest researchers who study seventeenth-century and earlier English and Scottish handwriting. Because the handwriting found in many early American records is not much different from handwriting found in British records, an understanding of early British handwriting is helpful. Excluded from the bibliography are references to most foreign language paleography texts and related works.

Source references to "FHL" in the transcriptions refer to the microfilm number at the Family History Library™ in Salt Lake City, Utah. In most cases these microfilms may be borrowed and used at their over 3, 000 Family History Centers™ (branch libraries) located throughout the world.

Acknowledgments

I wish to thank the following organizations for use of documents from their collections and publications: Association for the Preservation of Virginia Antiquities, Richmond, Virginia; Brigham Young University, Harold B. Lee Library, Provo, Utah; Everton Publishers, Logan, Utah; Family History Library, Salt Lake City, Utah; Genealogical Publishing Company, Baltimore, Maryland; Indiana Historical Society, Indianapolis, Indiana; Massachusetts Historical Society, Boston, Massachusetts; National Archives and Records Administration, Washington, D.C.; National Society Daughters of the American Revolution, Washington, D.C.; North Carolina State Archives, Raleigh, North Carolina; Presbyterian Church (U.S.A.), Department of History and Records Management Services, Philadelphia, Pennsylvania; Surry County Historical Society, Elkin, North Carolina; and Western Reserve Historical Society, Cleveland, Ohio.

I would like to express thanks to archivists, librarians, historians, and other individuals who alerted me to early American documents. Vicki Standing served ably as a research assistant. Heartfelt thanks go to Marta M. Smith for her secretarial services. I am grateful to Brigham Young University for providing research support and editorial assistance.

Appreciation is extended to the following individuals for reading the manuscript and offering valuable suggestions: Professor David H. Pratt, Ph.D., AG, Department of History, Brigham Young University (BYU); Elizabeth Shown Mills, CG, CGL, FASG, FNGS; Professor Don E. Norton and Vanessa Christenson of the English Department, BYU; Michael Tepper, Ph.D., Genealogical Publishing Company, Baltimore, Maryland; and Jimmy B. Parker, AG. Professor Raymond S. Wright III, Ph.D., AG, Department of Church History and Doctrine, BYU, provided a great deal of support and offered helpful suggestions. Sincere thanks for their contributions to this work.

Kip Sperry
Associate Professor of family history, Brigham Young University, Provo, Utah
Certified Genealogist
Accredited Genealogist
Fellow, American Society of Genealogists
Fellow, National Genealogical Society
Fellow, Utah Genealogical Association

Reading Early American Handwriting

Chapter 1

Reading Early American Handwriting

"Adopt the pace of Nature: her secret is patience."

— Ralph Waldo Emerson

Paleography, the study of early handwriting, or the rules of reading old handwriting, is an essential element in genealogical and historical research. The experienced researcher not only needs to be able to read old documents, but also requires the ability to interpret the value and significance of the content of records. The researcher must be able to analyze documents and their relationship to other records.

Paleography also refers to the study of the history of early scripts and the analysis of handwriting and inscriptions; it can be used to date early documents. The paleographer may be able to date a manuscript by studying handwriting styles and comparing features of a manuscript. A knowledge of paleography is useful to both genealogists and historians. C. Trice Martin observes that "paleography is the foundation of all history."[1] Codicology, a related historical and paleography subject, is the study of manuscripts as cultural artifacts for historical purposes.

Generally speaking, the further back you go toward the early seventeenth century, the more difficult the old handwriting becomes. The reader would do well to study the first nineteenth- and eighteenth-century documents in the Documents and Transcriptions section at the end of this book where the handwriting is easier to read, and then work toward the end of that section where seventeenth-century handwriting will be much more difficult to interpret.

Although compiled sources (such as family histories, genealogies, Ancestral File™, etc.), indexes, computer databases (such as the International Genealogical Index®), and the Internet are a basic part of the research process, genealogists and historians should spend much of their time searching original records—either original records in courthouses, archives, libraries, or historical

---

[1]C. Trice Martin, in E. E. Thoyts (Emma Elizabeth Cope), *How to Read Old Documents* (1893; reprint, Christchurch, England: Dolphin Press, 1972), p. vi.

societies, or microfilm or microfiche copies of original records, such as vital records, church registers, probate records, military records, land records, court records, and so forth.

The ability to read old script, interpret abbreviations, and understand terminology is an important dimension in the research process, as well as understanding the proper use of indexes and printed sources. After indexes, printed sources, and compiled databases have been exhausted, it is always wise to search original records and primary sources in genealogical and historical research to verify the accuracy of the extracted data and glean other details that the extractor(s) may have omitted. Indexes and the Internet are tools to help you locate the original source. It is critical to search the original source whenever possible.

Reading Documents

For those just beginning their study of paleography, reading old handwriting styles may not be easy, especially when abbreviations and terminology must be interpreted. For some, reading colonial handwriting is much like learning a new language.

There are four considerations when reading early American documents:

1. Make a correct analysis and interpretation of the handwriting, and understand the terms and abbreviations used.

2. Make a proper abstract, transcription, extract, or translation of the document.

3. Evaluate and analyze the document for its genealogical value and the proper interpretation of the document. Identify genealogical clues in the document.

4. Devise a research plan identifying genealogical sources to search, listing indexes and personal name finding aids, printed works, and especially original records.

Writing Implements, Ink, and Paper

Writing implements, such as the quill pen, and parchment and paper were much different from the pens and paper used today. Quill pens were often made from the primary feathers of common birds, most often geese, but sometimes turkeys, swans, and hens. Quills were used from the colonial period until the nineteenth century. Although a functional and inexpensive writing instrument, quills may have been of poor quality. Quills were sharpened to a specific angle with a "penknife." Quill pens did not hold a great quantity of ink and were eventually replaced during the nineteenth century by pens with steel nibs and better quality ink.

The quality of ink used in early American documents was often poor. In addition, ink fades over the years, often taking on a yellowish or brownish appearance. Faded handwriting may be the result of poor ink or inferior paper. The paper may have been damaged by insects, water, or fire. These are some of the reasons many old records are difficult to read. Paper was expensive and not readily available during the colonial period. An important study of early American writing instruments is found in an article by Maygene Daniels and published in *The American Archivist*.[2]

Handwriting Styles

Many of the colonial American handwriting styles passed through several phases, deriving principally from secretary hand and court hand used in Great Britain during the sixteenth and seventeenth centuries.[3] Other influences were from the Italic hand and Latin script. Many of these styles and old scripts were mixed hands, and may have included some court hand or other variations. Sometimes the scribe or clerk alternated between secretary hand, anglicized versions of Italic hand, and mixed hand.

Overall, the greatest influence on American handwriting was from secretary hand and Italic hand. These styles were used for church registers, correspondence, wills, deeds, and the like. Although colonial Americans were aware of the more complex handwriting used in England, they tended to simplify their own handwriting styles.

The standard penmanship texts for cursive writing were handwriting copybooks which

---

[2]Maygene Daniels, "The Ingenious Pen: American Writing Implements from the Eighteenth Century to the Twentieth," *The American Archivist* 43 (Summer 1980), pp. 312-24. Also useful for a study of writing and writing instruments is Donald Jackson, *The Story of Writing* (New York: Taplinger Publishing Co., 1981).

[3]For a valuable history of handwriting, see Noel Denholm-Young, *Handwriting in England and Wales*, 2nd ed. (Cardiff, Wales: University of Wales Press, 1964), as well as other titles cited in the bibliography later in this guidebook.

consisted of handwriting specimens.[4] Writing masters, schoolmasters, and professional writers published and taught from copybooks showing how letters were to be formed.

Although some consistency may be seen in colonial American documents, handwriting styles varied in different parts of the country and for different time periods. National origins of early Americans tended to influence handwriting styles and abbreviations, but in general, early American handwriting was highly individual, and varied according to the scribe—thus the challenge of deciphering old documents. We usually refer to our modern cursive script handwriting style as the round hand or modern hand (that is, mixed hand).[5]

The percentage of the early American population that could read and write was small compared to today. Perhaps Richard Bushman said it best: "a good hand was necessary to grace a genteel correspondence."[6] This literate population included scribes, clerks, court clerks, lawmakers, clergymen, and professional writers. More adults could read than could write, and most were men.[7] Sometimes a person signed a document with the mark *X*, usually because he or she could not read, was unable to write, or was very elderly.

Transcribing Documents

It is important for researchers to transcribe documents and include abbreviations, capitalization, punctuation, original spellings, and marginal additions exactly as they appear in the original. It is acceptable and recommended that you place your interpretation or explanation within square brackets [ ], not parentheses, or use footnotes.

The transcriber should copy personal names and place names exactly as they are written.

---

[4]Tamara Plakins Thornton, *Handwriting in America: A Cultural History* (New Haven, Conn.: Yale University Press, 1996), pp. 9, 22. Thornton's work is also useful for a study of early writing instruments used in America.

[5]For a history of early American writing, see Ray Nash, *Some Early American Writing Books and Masters* (Hanover, N. H.: The author, 1942).

[6]Richard L. Bushman, *The Refinement of America: Persons, Houses, Cities* (New York: Vintage Books, 1993), p. 92.

[7]Thornton, *Handwriting in America*, pp. 4-5.

This is especially important for genealogical and historical purposes. You must be alert to spelling variations, copying personal names exactly as they are written, including abbreviated given names and surnames.

Always identify and document the type of record and provide complete citations. Identify the date of the document in the abstract, extract, or transcription. If the provenance of the document is known, it should be stated, along with other details regarding the record. If the provenance is not known, an explanation should be given. Some researchers copy information onto a printed form, while others use standard word processing programs. Some researchers number the lines in the transcription to match the lines in the original document.

It is recommended that punctuation be copied exactly as used in the original document. Adding punctuation may alter the meaning of the original record. Capital or lower-case letters should be copied as closely as possible, although these may sometimes be difficult to determine and may vary within a document. Some transcribers modernize capital and lower-case letters to follow how they might be written today.

Three ellipsis . . . are recommended to indicate the omission of letters or words, or if dark ink spots on the page cover up the handwriting. Sometimes the word "illegible" within brackets [illegible] or a question mark [?] are used in the transcription if the original record is difficult to read. The expression [*sic*], set in italics and inserted in brackets, may be used when transcribing documents to indicate that the word has been transcribed exactly as written, or that the original was misspelled. However, overuse of the word *sic* in transcribing old documents is not encouraged. Writing, editing, and indexing procedures are described in detail in *The Chicago Manual of Style*.[8]

It is recommended that the interpretation of a word, such as *ye*, by placing the meaning [the] in brackets, should be used only once in a transcription to prevent overuse. Otherwise the overuse of an interpretation in brackets will be redundant.

The long *s* should be modernized as a regular *s*. Thus what appears as *Maps* or *Mafs* should be copied as *Mass*. The letters *ff* meant a capital *F* and may be transcribed as a capital *F*, or as *ff*. This author prefers that *ff* be transcribed as *ff*.

You may wish to add a footnote or introduction that explains what rules were used to transcribe the document, or cite any manuals or other references you used. Words and sentences

[8]University of Chicago Press, *The Chicago Manual of Style*, 14th ed. (Chicago: University of Chicago Press, 1993).

should not be rearranged when transcribing. This is especially true for the arrangement of personal names.[9] A valuable guide to source citation used in genealogy and family history is Elizabeth Shown Mills, *Evidence! Citation & Analysis for the Family Historian.*[10]

The documents in this guidebook have been transcribed letter for letter and word for word, and they follow capitalization used in the original document as closely as possible. In this way the author has attempted to retain the spelling, capitalization, and punctuation of the clerk or scribe as closely as possible.

It is realized that some words, letters, contractions, and abbreviations are difficult to interpret. For example, the small letter *a* and small letter *o* sometimes look very much alike. Sometimes the small letter *t* is not crossed. The old style small letter *e* and small *o* are sometimes difficult to interpret. The old style small letters *c*, *r*, and *t* present some problems in transcribing. It is sometimes difficult to see the difference between a capital *S* and a small *s*. The correct spacing between words is sometimes difficult to determine. The reader may, therefore, disagree with some of the transcriptions in this guidebook.

---

[9]See Elizabeth Shown Mills, "Skillbuilding: Transcribing Source Materials," *OnBoard* [Board for Certification of Genealogists Newsletter] 2 (January 1996), p. 8; and Elizabeth Shown Mills, "Skillbuilding: Producing Quality Research Notes," *OnBoard* 3 (January 1997), p. 8.

[10]Elizabeth Shown Mills, *Evidence! Citation & Analysis for the Family Historian* (Baltimore: Genealogical Publishing Co., 1997).

Chapter 2
Guidelines for Reading Old Documents

> "When it comes to early seventeenth century script, the differences from modern writing are so great that this is a study in itself. I have known first-class genealogists, even professional ones, who could not read that script with ease."
>
> —Donald Lines Jacobus

Included in this chapter are guidelines and general concepts for reading early American handwriting—methods for deciphering old documents. These principles will allow you to read even the most difficult colonial handwriting.

Before beginning the study of old handwriting it is important to realize that scribes, clerks, and church clergy did not write with the intent that researchers would be able to read their handwriting several hundred years later. In some cases the writer's objective may have been to create an impressive looking document. Regardless of the motives for writing, the scribe obviously had some latitude in using his own abbreviations, punctuation, and writing style.

Guidelines for Reading Old Documents

One of the most important fundamental principles in reading old handwriting is that it is always necessary to *compare*: compare or match unknown letters, characters, or doubtful words with letters you recognize in other words in the same document to determine if they are the same. Compare with words on the same page, and then look on the pages before and after the one in question. Compare with letters and words that are familiar to you. For example, if you think a letter looks like it could be an *i,* see how the scribe makes the letter *i* in other words on the same page and surrounding pages. Look through the record to determine how the writer forms the letter(s) in question in words you can read. Continue comparisons until you recognize the letter(s) you are studying. Look backwards and forwards in the record for similar words or letters. An unusual looking letter, word, personal name, or place name may occur in the record more than once.

Compare any letters in question with letters in the months of the year or other familiar words in the record. Most of the records used by genealogists and historians contain dates and the months of the year. For example, if you find an unusual looking letter that may be a capital *A*, look for the months April or August. Months are usually easy to read and contain many of the letters of the alphabet.

For those just beginning to read old handwriting, start your research in the more recent nineteenth-century handwriting and work backwards in time toward the colonial period. This way you will gradually become familiar with the older handwriting and abbreviations. With some practice, you will eventually be able to read seventeenth-century records with some ease. For records that have been microfilmed, this usually means beginning your research at the end of the roll if it contains more recent and easier to read handwriting.

Read the document through at a fast pace, identifying the letters and words you recognize. Note any unusual letters, words, or unique abbreviations, then read it again slowly, word for word. Look for familiar words and phrases. If necessary, read the document through a third and fourth time. You will eventually become familiar with the scribe's handwriting style and abbreviations. Do not spend too much time on one word. Rather, leave the word blank and transcribe the rest of the document, then go back and read the record for common sense. You should now be able to fill in the missing letters, word, or words.

Be aware of spelling variations, especially in records written before or during the Civil War, 1861-1865. There were no strict spelling rules in America until the nineteenth century. In 1806 Noah Webster published *A Compendious Dictionary of the English Language*, the first American dictionary which helped define correct spelling.

Spelling was not important to early Americans. Words were often written the way they sounded, phonetically, and often in local accents. For example, an individual's name might be spelled two, three, or more different ways in the same document, as is sometimes found in military records at the National Archives in Washington, D.C. Such documents with misspelled personal names are frequently found in Civil War pension files.

When you find a word you cannot decipher, place your fingers or thumbs over the word, covering all except the letter(s) in question. In this way you can study just one or two letters at a time and compare them with other letters in the same document. It may be helpful to transcribe the last letter of the word and move backward to the beginning.

Write out on a sheet of paper or note card the letters you can decipher, or use a personal computer and leave a blank space or dash for the part of the word(s) in question. Substitute letters, such as vowels, *a, e, i, o,* and *u,* for the missing letter(s). Every word has one or more vowels. Now read the sentence again for common sense.

Research Guidelines and Materials

A good quality magnifying glass is helpful to study old documents. It is advisable to take one with you when you research in courthouses, libraries, archives, and historical societies, since they are usually not available at such repositories. In the event that a magnifying glass is not available, enlarge a photocopy or microfilm/microfiche reader printer copy and carefully study the enlarged copy at that time or at a later date.

Microfilmed records are frequently copies of the original records, such as deeds and wills recorded in books on deposit in a county courthouse or other repository. The signatures in the book were often copied from the original by a clerk, recorder of deeds, or other official.

If you use a microfilm reader that projects the image onto a white sheet, place a piece of paper under the image and move the paper up and down. This may make the old handwriting easier to read. It is often helpful to place a piece of colored paper flat on the microfilm screen; the most helpful colors for some researchers are yellow and buff. Some researchers use yellow transparency film, or another color. It is recommended that you take colored paper with you when researching microfilmed records in libraries and archives.

If microfilm is used, it might be helpful to trace the word or words of interest onto a piece of white or colored paper. After you remove the paper, study the words and sentences. In this way you will be able to study the scribe's style of handwriting.

Microfilming is a valuable method of preserving original records, making them readily available to thousands of researchers in libraries, archives, and even their own homes. Sometimes pages were missed by the camera operator and may not have been microfilmed. Sometimes shadows may be seen, because poor lighting was used in the filming process. Film developing might have been inadequate. Microfilming may make faded brown ink appear even more faint. When possible, therefore, it is advisable to refer to the original records for transcription accuracy.

Guidelines for Reading in Context

- Read the document for common sense and for context in the original record. Words may be understood by their position in the text of the record. Reading sentences for common sense will help you understand the scribe's handwriting style. Study the handwriting carefully.

- Become familiar with standard phrases used in early records, such as church registers, probate records, deeds, and other similar documents. Some phrases are repeated throughout the record, so it will be helpful to study those words and letters. Look for familiar phrases in the record and then compare the letters with the ones you are studying.
- Sometimes an individual's occupation or title appears immediately after the surname. Do not mistake this for the surname. Examples of occupations that may look like surnames are baker, carpenter, clerk, cook, cooper, mason, and shoemaker. Consider the name "John Jones Baker." Is "Baker" his occupation or his surname? Again, read for common sense.
- If you search church records and find a personal name difficult to read in the marriages, look through the baptisms for the same church to determine how the names are spelled. Conversely, if you have difficulty reading a personal name in the baptisms in a church record, search the marriages for that same church and locality. If deaths or burials are available for the same church, these, too, may assist to decipher names.
- In addition to searching the same record for personal names, it may be helpful to look for those names in other types of records. For example, search land and probate records for names found in a church register for the same locality.
- A document, such as a will, may have been signed by a mark, an *X*, for example, or the person's initials. This was especially true for those who could not write or the elderly. Always copy the mark(s) exactly as they are written.
- Never accept a guess as correct until you have verified it. Be aware that some scribes used more than one form of the same letter.
- Understanding the geographical area of your research, terms and abbreviations used in that locality, language peculiarities, historical background, and ethnic and cultural background will be worth the effort.
- You should have an understanding of the method for recording the types of records for the time period and locality of interest. County and local histories, gazetteers, maps, and other geographical finding aids will provide useful background information.

Gazetteers and Maps

A gazetteer is a geographical dictionary of place names. Some gazetteers include maps, and some atlases include a gazetteer. Sometimes a place name or locality appears after an individual's surname. This may have been given for his place of residence; for example, "John Jones

Springfield," or "John Jones of Springfield." Springfield is the place name.

If you are uncertain of the spelling of a place name (the name of a geographical locality), such as the town or county, check a map, atlas, gazetteer, or local history to determine how that locality is spelled. Place names are usually listed in county histories or town histories. Two useful references for locating information about U.S. counties are the basic genealogical reference sources *Ancestry's Red Book: American State, County & Town Sources*,[11] and *The Handy Book for Genealogists*.[12]

A good, general United States gazetteer is needed to search for information on place names, or to verify the spelling of localities. Valuable American gazetteers include *Fanning's Illustrated Gazetteer of the United States*,[13] *The Cambridge Gazetteer of the United States and Canada: A Dictionary of Places*,[14] John Hayward, *A Gazetteer of the United States of America*,[15] Henry Gannett, *The Origin of Certain Place Names in the United States*,[16] Leo de Colange, *The National Gazetteer: A Geographical Dictionary of the United States*,[17] and George R. Stewart, *American Place-Names:*

---

[11]Alice Eichholz, ed., *Ancestry's Red Book: American State, County & Town Sources*, rev. ed. (Salt Lake City: Ancestry, 1992). Be sure to use the revised edition.

[12]*The Handy Book for Genealogists*, 8th ed. (Logan, Utah: Everton Publishers, 1991).

[13]*Fanning's Illustrated Gazetteer of the United States* (1855; reprint, Bowie, Md.: Heritage Books, 1990).

[14]*The Cambridge Gazetteer of the United States and Canada: A Dictionary of Places*, edited by Archie Hobson (Cambridge, England: Cambridge University Press, 1995).

[15]John Hayward, *A Gazetteer of the United States of America* (Hartford: Case, Tiffany and Co., 1853).

[16]Henry Gannett, *The Origin of Certain Place Names in the United States*, 2nd ed. (1905; reprint, Baltimore: Genealogical Publishing Co., 1973).

[17]Leo de Colange, *The National Gazetteer: A Geographical Dictionary of the United States* (Cincinnati: J. C. Yorston & Co., 1884).

A Concise and Selective Dictionary for the Continental United States of America.[18] A comprehensive bibliography of United States and Canadian gazetteers and place-name books and articles is Richard Burl Sealock, et al., *Bibliography of Place-Name Literature: United States and Canada.*[19]

Guidelines for Common Phrases

It will be helpful to look for common words and phrases in old records, and then compare letters in those phrases with words you are reading. Wills often begin with the standard phrase, "In the name of God Amen." Probate records may also include standard phraseology, such as "I give and bequeath to my beloved wife," "I give and bequeath unto..." or "my last will and testament." Look for key words in probate records and wills, such as "loving wife," "legacy," "legacies," or "testament."

Deeds often begin with a set phrase, such as "This indenture made this...[date]" or "This indenture made and entered into this ...[date]." Look for key words in deeds and land records, such as "appurtenances," "grantee," "grantor," and land description.

Other early American records may begin, "Know all men by these presents," "We whose names are underwritten," "To all Christian people to whom these presents shall come, greeting," or they may include the phrase (or similar phrase) "In witness whereof I have hereunto set my hand and seal this [date]," or "Signed sealed and delivered in the presence of [name]." Various words in these phrases may be capitalized, such as "Greeting," depending on the emphasis or style of the writer.

Court records often use similar legal phrases and standard openings. Repetitive phrases are frequently written, especially in legal documents, and are sometimes repeated within the same document. The same words may be used many times over.

Become familiar with set phrases and words in order to study the handwriting. A familiarity with such organization of words will be helpful in reading old records.

---

[18]George R. Stewart, *American Place-Names: A Concise and Selective Dictionary for the Continental United States of America* (New York: Oxford University Press, 1970).

[19]Richard Burl Sealock, Margaret M. Sealock, and Margaret S. Powell, *Bibliography of Place-Name Literature: United States and Canada,* 3rd ed. (Chicago: American Library Association, 1982).

Trouble Spots

Be on the lookout for letters, words, and numbers that bleed through from the back of the document, which may also be seen in a microfilm or microfiche copy. Note also that ink may have faded or smeared over the years, or there may be one or more ink spots on the document. A common adage in genealogical research is that if there is a large ink spot, it appears only on the page covering your ancestor's name or previous place of residence in the old country. Be on the lookout for words where ink has faded or flaked away. This may make a letter of the alphabet look like a different letter than the one intended. Examining the original record may show that the now missing ink actually eroded a tiny indentation in the paper leaving the complete outline of the letter or letters indistinct.

Be patient. One of the pitfalls in reading old handwriting and transcribing documents is to read a word and assume that it is the same word used today. Many researchers attempt to trace their pedigree too far, too fast, making overabundant use of computer databases of compiled genealogies, genealogies found on the Internet, and printed sources. Likewise, beginning researchers may be tempted to read a document too fast without studying all possible spelling variations and making a proper and correct abstract, extract, or transcription. Do not be in a hurry to transcribe old documents; you may make an incorrect deduction.

Ask an experienced genealogist, historian, archivist, or reference librarian, for assistance in reading the document in question. Sometimes another person will have success in deciphering a word, sentence, or document for you. Most archivists and historians are trained in or have had experience in reading old handwriting—many in foreign languages.

The Family History Library in Salt Lake City has a large staff of qualified employees and volunteers. Most of the professional staff at the Family History Library have been trained in reading old handwriting, and many read foreign languages, including Latin.

Practice is Important

Most of all, *practice* at reading old documents. It will greatly improve your paleography skills. Study the handwriting carefully and evaluate difficult words letter by letter. Practice transcribing documents for different time periods and localities in America. Patience, practice, and perseverance will pay off in big dividends when studying early American handwriting. Read and interpret the documents carefully. Getting used to old handwriting will come with experience and will become easier to those who persevere.

"One of the major challenges facing the genealogist in any language is learning to use and understand older language forms and handwriting styles. . . .The ability to read early records develops slowly and can only be obtained through actual experience. Do not try to absorb, in a single reading, all of the material written in the old script or unfamiliar [language, i.e., Spanish]. It is necessary, instead, to have available one or two of the reference works described while attempting to read an early record until an instinctive knowledge of the techniques develops.

"You can compensate for any deficiency in formal [foreign language] instruction by study, patience, and a determination to understand the records. Consulting a good beginning grammar book (and possibly one of the quick introductory [foreign language] courses) and always having a dictionary at hand will also help to compensate for any deficiency. Do not be discouraged from performing research by a lack of formal training in the [foreign] language."[20]

The purpose of this guidebook is to instruct the reader in reading and interpreting early American handwriting and to provide facsimiles of documents that may be used to practice reading and transcribing. Study each reproduction carefully. The more experience you have in reading and understanding old handwriting and abbreviations, the greater will be your confidence, and genealogical research will provide you with ever greater rewards.

Guidelines for Spelling Variants

Spelling was unsystematic until the nineteenth century. Donald Emery compiled a reference source entitled *Variant Spellings in Modern American Dictionaries*, which is useful to study variant spellings in English.[21] This work will assist those studying early American language.

Listed below are a few examples of common words with variant spellings found in old documents:

---

[20]Loretto Dennis Szucs and Sandra Hargreaves Luebking, eds., *The Source: A Guidebook of American Genealogy*, rev. ed. (Salt Lake City: Ancestry, 1997), p. 591.

[21]Donald William Emery, *Variant Spellings in Modern American Dictionaries*, rev. ed. (Urbana, Ill.: National Council of Teachers of English, 1973).

Old Documents	*Modern Equivalent*
akers	acres
alsoe/allso	also
att	at
behoof	behalf
caled	called
coppy	copy
coussen	cousin
deceised	deceased
doe	do
dollers	dollars
dyed	died
estimacon	estimation
eyther	either
fenc	fence
fowre	four
howse/hous	house
noate	note
ordayne	ordain
setle	settle
sole	soul
sume	sum
wagges	wages

Notice from this list that an ending *e* was sometimes added to words. Additional examples include *bee* [be], *mee* [me], *owne* [own], *shee* [she], *sicke* [sick], *soe* [so], *wee* [we], and *whoe* [who]. The letters *ie* may have been used instead of the letter *y*.

Vowels were often interchanged. Read the word out loud so you can hear the phonetic possibilities. For example, the given name Jonas might also be spelled Jones, Jonis, or Jonus. In addition, a badly misspelled word may have been written as it sounded to the scribe.

Sometimes two or more words were connected or run together by the writer; for example, "tobe" for "to be." Conversely, there was sometimes a wide space between letters —"Tar box" for the surname Tarbox, or "bap tized" for "baptized."

If you are unable to read a personal name or a place name, determine if there is an index to the record. The person who indexed the record may have known the local names. In addition, that person may have had access to the original record. The index may have been made contemporaneously with the record. This guideline will be especially useful when searching vital records, deeds, and probate records that are often well indexed by local people. Check the index to the record to help you determine how the name was written by the scribe. Naturally, because errors may sometimes be found in indexes, indexes need to be used with some caution.

It is very important to transcribe personal names (given names and surnames) exactly as they appear in the original record. For example, you may personally know someone with the given name of Elizabeth. Upon reading an old document where the given name is clearly spelled Elisabeth, it may be tempting for you to transcribe the name as Elizabeth because that is the name with which you are most familiar. Understanding spelling variations may be helpful in identifying a manuscript or when and where the manuscript was written.

Guidelines to Handwriting Variations and Transcribing

Sometimes a stroke, flourish, curl, swirl, squiggle, or loop was used by the writer and may change the appearance of a letter or word. For example, a capital *L* may look like a capital *D.* This may have occurred on the same line, or for words above or below the word, the flourish making the letter look like a different letter. For example, a stroke from another word through a small *l* might make the letter look like a *t*. The small letter *d* frequently had a backward flourish, sometimes connected to another letter. Some strokes may indicate the omission of a letter. Sometimes the ascenders or descenders are exaggerated. Ascenders or descenders, perhaps appearing as a "curlicue" extending above or below the writing line, may run into or connect to other letters, thus changing the appearance of those letters.

It may be helpful to make a sample alphabet of the hand a particular writer used. This is especially useful for difficult-to-read handwriting. Trace the writing of the scribe. When you have trouble reading a word, compare each letter with the alphabet you made. In this way you will be able to become familiar with the writer's style of writing and abbreviations.

For difficult-to-read documents, it is recommended that you transcribe the entire document, writing only the words and letters you can read, then go back and fill in the missing words and letters. Read the document for common sense and compare letters and words. It may also be helpful to read your transcription out loud or to another person. In this way you may be able to hear what the scribe meant to say in his writing.

It may be helpful to make a word-for-word transcription of the document in order to study the scribe's handwriting style and abbreviations. It is essential to transcribe the record accurately and not to omit any details. Use footnotes where necessary to document sources and clarify your transcription and interpretation.

Guidelines for Capitalization and Punctuation

The first word in a sentence may or may not begin with a capital letter. Likewise, words in the middle of a sentence may be capitalized. Capital letters are often used to place emphasis on a word, for example Born, Baptized, Married, or Died. There may be inconsistency in the use of capital letters. Sometimes personal names and place names (localities) are capitalized, while other times they are not. In addition, it is common to find proper names that begin with a lower case letter. Do not correct capitalization as shown in the original record in your transcription.

Be on the lookout for initials that were used for given names in old records, such as the 1850, 1860, 1870, and 1880 U.S. population census schedules. For example, the personal name "A.B. Smith" may be found in a census schedule or other record. Compare and study each letter with other words in the same record.

Punctuation may or may not be clearly seen in early American documents. Some sentences clearly end in a period, while others do not. Punctuation was not important to early American writers and was seldom used. Commas, colons, and semicolons were used haphazardly. A colon (:) was often used to denote an abbreviation. A dash (—) or equal sign (=) may frequently be seen indicating the end of a line or an abbreviation. Note that long dashes or other similar marks in a document are frequently ignored during transcription.

Be aware of symbols, wavy lines, and dots used for abbreviations or word divisions. A double hyphen similar to a modern equal sign (=) may have been used at the end of a line to divide a word carried into the next line. Sometimes a letter or word is repeated from the ending of a line to the beginning of the next line (which may appear on the next page), or the equal sign (double hyphen) is repeated at the beginning of a line.

Chapter 3

Abbreviations and Contractions

> Mr. Patrick Kelly, a native of Ireland, being tired of this
> Cold Country, put an end to his existence this morning
> by fastning [*sic*] a strong line one end round his neck
> and the other end to a spike. That is to say he hung himself.
> June 28th 1823.
>
> Eastport, Washington Co., Maine, Vital Records.

Many words were often abbreviated or shortened in old records, including given names, place names, months, phrases, and so forth. Contractions (a shortening of a word by the omission of certain letters) were often used indiscriminately. Scribes and clerks often used abbreviations, signs, and symbols as a type of shorthand, especially at the end of lines.

Abbreviations may have been used for several reasons, but for whatever reason, often to save time, effort, and space, it appears that some records were hastily written, the result being poor or difficult-to-read handwriting, including the frequent use of abbreviations.

Researchers today may have difficulty determining the exact meaning of some of the unorthodox abbreviations, contractions, flourishes, and marks. Some were taken from Latin words, while many were very common at the time, but no specific rule governed the use of abbreviations. Some of these abbreviations have become obscure. Abbreviations may or may not have periods, but they often have a colon. They may be above or below the line of writing. Months of the year were frequently abbreviated, such as *Feb*^{r} for February, or *ffebr.* for February, and *Dec*^{r} for December.

Many times given names (and even sometimes surnames) are abbreviated. For example, *Abr.*, *Danl.*, *Geo.*, and *Robt.* If you wish to include a personal interpretation of the abbreviation, brackets [ ] should be used. For example, *Abr.* should be transcribed as *Abr.*, but you may include your interpretation in brackets [Abraham]. It is sometimes difficult to interpret the correct meaning of all given name abbreviations, for example *Jno.* Would this be Jonathan or John?

States of the United States, Canadian provinces, and names of foreign countries were frequently abbreviated. Thus *Ills.* was for Illinois, and *Mass.* stood for Massachusetts. Some state and country abbreviations are not always clear. For example, *Ia* may have stood for Indiana or for

Iowa, depending on the record and time period.

Single letters in old records sometimes stood for an abbreviation. For example, a capital *P* or lowercase *p*, with a flourish or wavy line, or a crossed *P*, usually stands for *par*, *per*, or *pro*, but may have also stood for *pre*. *Per* or *pson* usually stood for person and *pfect* stood for perfect. An apostrophe may have been used to indicate such an abbreviation, thus *p'son* for person. Such abbreviations may or may not be spelled out by the transcriber. Sometimes vowels were dropped (*clk* may have been used as an abbreviation for clerk).

A wavy stroke, curl, or looped line was sometimes drawn above or through letters or words to denote an abbreviation, omitted letter(s), or a contraction. For contractions, an apostrophe or short line replaced the missing letters. A straight or crooked line over, through, or under a word probably meant an abbreviation. An abbreviated word might have a backward and upward stroke at the last letter of the word. *Ch* with a horizontal line drawn through it represented the word Church. Words may have been "suspended" by the omission of an ending.

Some representative abbreviations and shortened word forms found in early American records are listed below. Some abbreviations may or may not have periods in the original documents, and some may or may not have raised superscript letters.

Abbreviation	*Meaning*
acct/acco^{t}/acct^{s}	account/accounts
A.D.	*anno Domini* (in the year of the Lord)
admr./admin^{r}	administrator
admin^{x}	administratrix
admon.	administration
ae.	age/aged
afsd/aforesd	aforesaid
agt/agst	against
als	alias
b.	born
bapt./bp.	baptized
B.L.W./B.L.Wt.	bounty land warrant
bur.	buried
ca.	*circa* (about), approximately

Capt.	Captain
ch/chh	church
chr.	christened/christening
clk	clerk
co.	county; company
—con	tion [i.e., condicon means condition]
d.	died
dau.	daughter
dec./decd./deced.	deceased
div.	divorce(d)
do	ditto, the same as above (frequently used in U.S. census schedules or in personal name lists)
d.s.p.	died without issue
d.v.m.	died while mother was living
d.v.p.	died while father was living
E.D.	Enumeration District (found in U.S. census schedules)
Eod	*Eodem* (on the same date)
Esq./Esqr.	Esquire
exec./execr.	executor
$exec^{x}$	executrix
Gen^{all}	General
Gent.	Gentleman
gdn.	guardian
honble	honorable
Imp./Imp^{r}	*Imprimis* (in the first place)
inft.	infant
inst.	instant (same month; this immediate month)
int.	intestate; interred
inv.	inventory (such as a list of personal property)
J.P.	Justice of the Peace
Jr./Jun./Junr	Junior
lic.	license
m./md.	married

Maj.	Major
Matie	His/Her Majesty
M.G.	Minister of the Gospel
M^{r}	Mister or Master
M^{rs}	a title for women, but may have applied to both married and unmarried women
N.B.	take careful note; to mark well
N.S.	New Style (Gregorian) calendar (after 1752)
obit	newspaper obituary
o^{r}	our
O.S.	Old Style (Julian) calendar (before 1752)
o.s.p.	died without issue
par	parish
pay^{mt}	payment
pd	paid
per/pson	person
plt./pltf.	plaintiff
pr	per
pre/p^{r}sent	present
recd./rec^{d}	received
regr.	register
R.G.	Record Group (used in archives)
s	son
sd.	said
Sen./Senr	Senior
S^{r}	Sir
Ss	*supra scriptum* (as written above); a form of greeting; normally refers to a statement written above, aforementioned, afore written
test.	testify, testament, testate, testator
twp.	township
ult.	*ultimo* (last month; of or occurring in the preceding month)
unm.	unmarried

V.D.M.	minister of the word of God
viz.	namely
w.	wife or widow
warrt.	warrant
wch/w^{ch}	which
wd./wid./wido.	widow
Wit.	witness, witnesses
W.P.	will proved; white poll
w^{t}	what
wth/w^{th}	with
X	used for a person's mark, such as in a will; Christ
ye	the: *y* from Old English letter *thorn* for the pronunciation *th*
yeo.	yeoman
yor/y^{r}/yr.	your; year
yt	that (where *y* represents the *thorn*)
&	and (ampersand); derived from the Latin *et*
&c	and so forth (*et cetera*)
£, s., d.	pound(s), shilling(s), and pence

Some of the above are Latin abbreviations. While Latin is generally not seen in American records, perhaps with the exception of Catholic or Anglican Church registers and some colonial records, Latin abbreviations and terms may sometimes be found.[22]

Given name (first name) abbreviations (or other words) may be followed by a colon (:) in old

---

[22] Valuable Latin reference guides include Eileen A. Gooder, *Latin for Local History: An Introduction*, 2nd ed. (London: Longman Group Ltd., 1978); Denis Stuart, *Latin for Local and Family Historians: A Beginner's Guide* (Chichester, Sussex, England: Phillimore, 1995); Benjamin Hall Kennedy, *The Shorter Latin Primer*, rev. by J.W. Bartram (London: Longman Group Ltd., 1931); Ronald Edward Latham, *Revised Medieval Latin Word-List from British and Irish Sources* (London: Oxford University Press, 1965); and Charles Trice Martin, comp., *The Record Interpreter: A Collection of Abbreviations, Latin Words and Names Used in English Historical Manuscripts and Records*, 2nd ed. (1910; reprint, Dorking, Surrey, England: Kohler & Coombes, 1976; Chichester, Sussex, England: Phillimore, 1982).

documents, while other names and words may be followed by a period or no punctuation. A colon or period often was used to designate missing letters. Thus *Dan:* stood for Daniel.

It is very important that personal names be copied exactly as they appear in the record. The difference between *Ja.*, *Jas.*, and *Jos.* is critical for genealogical research.

While abbreviations were often used for given names, they were not as frequently used for surnames (last names). A scribe may have created his own abbreviations for given names. Sometimes these are difficult to interpret.

A few representative examples of how given name abbreviations may be written in early American documents are listed below:

Abra:/Abram./Abm./Ab:	Abraham
Alex^{r}	Alexander
And^{w}/And:	Andrew
Benj./Benja.	Benjamin
Cath./Cath^{ne}	Catherine or Catharine
Chs./Chas.	Charles
Danl.	Daniel
Ed./Edw./Edwd.	Edward
Elis./Eliz./Eliza.	Elisabeth/Elizabeth
Eph^{m}/Eph:	Ephraim
Fred^{k}	Frederick
Geo:	George
Hen:/Hen^{r}	Henry
Ja:/Jas.	James
Jer:/Jere:/Jereh	Jeremiah
Jno./Jno	Jonathan or John
Jos./Jos:	Joseph or Josiah
Margt.	Margaret
Matt^{w}	Matthew
Nathl./Nath:/ Nath^{ll}	Nathaniel
Nich^{o}/Nich^{s}/Nicol^{s}	Nicholas
Reb^{a}	Rebecca
Rich./Richd.	Richard

Robt.	Robert
Sam:/Saml./Samll.	Samuel
Sim^{n}	Simon
Tim:/Tim^{o}	Timothy
Tho/Thos.	Thomas
Wm./Willm	William
Xtoph./Xfher/Xo^{pher}	Christopher

Superscript letters or a single letter may be raised above the line of writing, such as a small *n*, *r*, *s*, *t*, or *th*, and may appear as an abbreviation. This is a form of contraction. A few examples include:

Chas	Charles
Esqr	Esquire
Govr	Governor
Jonath^{n}	Jonathan
Maj^{tie}	Majesty [Majestie]
M^{r}	Mister
rec^{d}	received
reg^{r}	register
Sam^{ll}	Samuel
s^{d}	said
serv^{t}	servant
S^{r}	Sir
th^{t}	that
w^{ch}	which
W^{m}	William
wth	with
y^{e}	the
y^{r}	your
y^{t}	that

Chapter 4
Terms

Departed this Life, having been instantly killed by
lightning at Bedford Forge, Caroline Spies, aged
14 years, 5 months, and 10 days.

Departed this Life, having been stabbed by Hen. [Henry] Dilling-
er and instantly killed by him in a fracas during Saturday night, October 10th A.D. 1857, James Fluck
Aged nineteen years and some months.

Register of Deaths, 1857, German Reformed Church, Yellow Creek,
Bedford Co., Pennsylvania, p. 115 (236).

Definitions

The following terms are used frequently when studying paleography and early American handwriting. They deserve a brief discussion here.

Abstract: An abridgement or summary of relevant information in a document. An abstract is a short form of a document, which gives the main points or most important information, and deletes repetitive language. Researchers usually make an abstract (summary) of such documents as wills and deeds. Many documents contain lengthy and superfluous words and phrases, thus the need to abstract pertinent information, such as personal names, relationships, occupations, dates, localities (place names), description of real or personal property, and names of witnesses.

Ascender: A part, stroke, or upstroke of a capital or lowercase letter which extends above the writing line. Examples include the lowercase letters *b*, *d*, *f*, *h*, *l*, and *t*.

Contraction: A shortening or abbreviating of a word. One or more letters are omitted in a word (for example, *p'sent* for present, or *pson* for person), usually in the middle of a word. A line may be drawn above the word for a contraction, or another graphic symbol may be used.

Descender: A part, stroke, or downstroke of a capital or lowercase letter which extends below the writing line. Examples include the lowercase letters *f*, *g*, *h* (mostly seventeenth century), *j*, *p*, *q*, and *y*.

Extract: An exact copy, word for word, of a portion of a document, such as an extract of a family from the 1850 U.S. census copied onto a census extract form. It is a quotation or part of a written document, as opposed to an abstract or summary.

Facsimile: An exact reproduction of a document, such as a photocopy or a reader printer copy (taken from microfilm or microfiche).

Ligature: Two or more letters or characters joined together, such as *ch, ff, sh, ss, st,* and *th*. Such letters were often run together and were used as a type of early shorthand.

Minim: A short up-and-down vertical stroke in a series usually formed by the lowercase letters *i*, *m*, *n*, *u,* and *w*. These letters frequently look alike when they occur side by side, such as *in* and *ni*, where it is difficult to determine where the dot appears. It is usually helpful to count the minim strokes individually in order to decipher the correct letters and then read for common sense.

Serif: A short cross-stroke at the top or bottom of ascender or descender letters. A serif may indicate an abbreviation or missing letters. It is often a tiny stroke or short horizontal line, but may be at an angle.

Superscript: A superior letter, symbol, or word written above a letter, word, or line of script. Often the last letter of a word is written raised or superscript. Thus ye represents *the*.

Suspension: The end of a word is abbreviated, or the final letter(s) of a word may be omitted. This may be indicated by a colon, a short stroke, a horizontal bar, or other graphic symbol.

Transcription: A letter for letter, word for word copy. It is an exact copy of a record. As much as practical, the documents in this text have been transcribed letter for letter, word for word, thus preserving the writer's handwriting style, abbreviations, and spelling. Some people number the lines in their transcription to match the lines in the original document.

Translation: A full copy of a document translated from one language to another, such as from German script to English, or from French to English.

Terms

A number of terms are found in old documents which may be unfamiliar to researchers. Dictionaries and reference guides are available which will help define these terms. Researchers need to become familiar with the terminology used in old records.

For court terms and legal terminology, one excellent source is *Black's Law Dictionary*.[23] Terms and occupations are defined in *The Oxford English Dictionary*.[24] Three useful genealogical dictionaries are *What Did They Mean by That?: A Dictionary of Historical Terms for Genealogists*,[25] *Ancestry's Concise Genealogical Dictionary*,[26] and the revised *A to Zax: A Comprehensive Dictionary for Genealogists & Historians*.[27] *A to Zax* is a valuable reference source for genealogists, historians, and reference librarians.

---

[23]Henry Campbell Black, *Black's Law Dictionary*, rev. ed. (St. Paul, Minn.: West Publishing Co., 1991). This dictionary is available in many libraries.

[24]*The Oxford English Dictionary*, 2nd ed., 20 vols. (Oxford, England: Clarendon Press, 1989). Also helpful is *Webster's Unabridged Dictionary*, available at most libraries.

[25]Paul Drake, *What Did They Mean by That?: A Dictionary of Historical Terms for Genealogists* (Bowie, Md.: Heritage Books, 1994).

[26]Maurine Harris and Glen Harris, comps., *Ancestry's Concise Genealogical Dictionary* (Salt Lake City: Ancestry Publishing, 1989).

[27]Barbara Jean Evans, *A to Zax: A Comprehensive Dictionary for Genealogists & Historians*, 3rd ed. (Alexandria, Va.: Hearthside Press, 1995).

A few selected common terms found in early American records are listed below:

Term	*Definition*
Administrator	A person appointed by a court to take care of the estate of an individual who died intestate
Annoque	And in the year
Appurtenance(s)	Term often found in land records; a right-of-way attached to property; rights and duties attached to land
Banns	Publication (announcement) of an intended marriage by engaged couples; often recorded in church records
Base-born	An illegitimate child
Bond	A contract, such as a marriage bond
Bounty land	Land given to an individual as reward for military service
Calendar	A summary of documents or list of court cases
Codicil	An addition or supplement to a will that changes the provisions of the will
Conveyance	The transfer of the title of land from one person to another
Cousin	In early American records this may have meant a niece or a nephew
Dower	A portion of a widow's entitlement to her husband's estate; her dower right (usually one-third of her husband's estate)
Emigration	To leave a country, place of origin, or residence
Enfeoff	A term usually found in deeds; the transfer of land from a person to a purchaser; to invest with a fee; the granting of use or authority over land
Entail	To restrict inheritance of land to an individual person or group
Esquire	Used as a title of courtesy (usually abbreviated as Esq. or Esqr. after a man's surname)
Executor	A person appointed by a testator to execute (carry out instructions) his will (an executrix is a woman)

Folio	Often refers to a large size book in a courthouse or archives; one leaf of a book (two pages—one recto and one verso)
Freeman	A man who was a church member and had the right to vote; a person having full rights of a citizen; in New England, church membership was a prerequisite for a freeman
Friend(s)	Quaker(s); Society of Friends; Religious Society of Friends
Gaol	Jail
Gazetteer	A geographical dictionary
Grantee	A buyer of property; a person to whom something is transferred by deed (purchased land)
Grantor	A seller of property; a person transferring land to another
Hereditament(s)	Property that may be inherited or passed on by inheritance
Holograph	A document written in the author's handwriting (for example, a holograph or holographic will written by the testator)
Homestead	Land obtained from the U.S. government
Illegitimate	A child born out of wedlock
Immigration	To come into a country or place of residence
Imprimis	In the first place (often introduces a list of items, such as found in a will or inventory)
Indenture	Often refers to a land deed; also refers to a contract where one individual works for another for a specified time
Intestate	The condition of dying without having made a valid will
Inventory	A list of personal property (such as a deceased person's property)
Issue	Children, offspring, progeny
Land records	Deeds; land and property records
Legacy/legacies	A gift of money or personal property left in a will
Liber/libro	Book or volume
Lis pendens	A pending lawsuit
Manuscript	Unpublished material, such as a diary or journal
Messuage	A large house; a dwelling house with surrounding land

Metes and bounds	Land description survey system identifying creeks, trees, and other natural features
Minor	A child under twenty-one years of age
Mulatto	A person of mixed African American and white race
Née	Born (usually used after a woman's surname to identify her maiden family name, e.g., Mrs. Mary Johnson, née Brown)
Nuncupative will	An oral will
Parchment	The skin of an animal used for writing, often a sheep or goat
Patronymic	The creation of a surname from the name of a father
Probate	The process of proving a will
Recto	A right-hand page; also refers to the front or top of a folio
Relict	Widow of the deceased
Testate	A person who dies and leaves a valid will
Testator	A person who makes a will
Verso	A left-hand page, or the back of a folio
Uxor	Wife
Yeoman	A farmer who cultivates his own land

Chapter 5
Numbers and Roman Numerals

"You can be a little ungrammatical if you come from the right part of the country."

—Robert Frost

Arabic numbers and roman numerals were sometimes written different than today and may be difficult to interpret. Over time arabic numbers replaced roman numerals. Arabic numbers can usually be deciphered from the context of the record and by comparing with other numbers in the record. Numbers, especially years, were sometimes linked together. A.D. is an abbreviation for *anno Domini* (in the year of the Lord), as used in era designations. Roman numerals were sometimes used in dates.

Many of the original records microfilmed by the Genealogical Society of Utah and held at the Family History Library™ in Salt Lake City and its Family History Centers™ have been filmed in chronological order, thus usually making it easier to decipher dates. This is also true for records microfilmed by the National Archives and Records Administration, historical societies, and similar archival agencies. Most of the dates in these records are written in the modern system of numbers.

A few examples of troublesome arabic numbers found in old documents are listed below:

1 might be connected to the next number, e.g., as in the year 1709
1 might look like a *2*, a *7*, or the letter *l*
1 may have a wavy line and look like a capital *S*
2 might look like a *4*
*2^d^* stands for *2nd*
4 might look like a *6* or a *7*
5 might look like a *6*
6 might look like a *4* or the letter b
7 might look like a *1*, *4*, or a *9*

8 might look like the number *6*
8 might be slanted or turned horizontally
8 might appear to be a capital *S*
9 might look like a *g*

Roman Numerals

In the roman numeral system, letters represent numbers. Roman numerals are frequently seen in early American documents and may also be found in printed sources, such as serials. They are written in either capital or small letters. The roman numerals 4 or 9 are written by placing a symbol of lesser value before one of greater value (thus *iv* is 4 and *ix* is 9).

A long minim in handwritten documents was frequently used at the end of roman numerals. Thus, *iiij* would be an arabic 4, and viiij would be an arabic 9. The last minim *j* in the roman numeral would be long and took the place of *I*.

Examples of some of the major roman numerals are:

Roman					*Arabic*
I	or i		or	j	1
II			or	ij	2
III			or	iij	3
IIII	or	IV	or	iiij	4
V					5
VI			or	vj	6
VII			or	vij	7
VIII			or	viij	8

IX	or	viiij	9
X			10
XI	or	xj	11
XII	or	xij	12
XIII	or	xiij	13
XIV	or	xiiij	14
XV			15
XVI	or	xvj	16
XVII	or	xvij	17
XVIII	or	xviij	18
XIX	or	xviiij	19
XX			20
XXI	or	xxj	21
XXIV			24
XXV			25
XXX			30
XXXII			32

XXXX	or	XL	40
L			50
LIV			54
LX	or	lx	60
LXV			65
LXX			70
LXXVI			76
LXXX	or	iiij^{xx}	80
LXXXX	or	XC	90
XCIX	or	iiij^{xx}xix	99
C			100
CI	or	cj	101
CII	or	cij	102
CLVI			156
CC			200
CCC			300
CCCC	or	CD	400

D	500
DC	600
DCC	700
DCCC	800
CM	900
M	1, 000
MD	1, 500
MCM	1, 900
MM	2, 000
MMM	3,000
$\overline{\text{V}}$	5, 000
$\overline{\text{X}}$	10, 000

A bar over a numeral multiplies it by 1, 000.

Example Roman Numerals

Examples of years written in roman numerals include the following:

MDCXLVI	1646
MDCCLII	1752
MDCCLXXVI	1776
MDCCCLXVIII	1868
MCMXVII	1917

Chapter 6
Dates and the Calendar Change

"Foreigners always spell better than they pronounce."

—Mark Twain

In 45 B.C. Julius Caesar, upon the advice of a Greek astronomer, declared that the Roman calendar should be 365 days, and one year in four 366 days (one day added to February every fourth year). This calendar became known as the Julian calendar and was used throughout the Middle Ages in Europe. It established the order of the months and days of the week, and is also known as the Christian calendar. As the centuries passed, it became apparent that the Julian calendar did not agree with the solar year, and the accuracy of the calendar needed improving.

In 1582 Pope Gregory XIII introduced a calendar correction which dropped ten days from the calendar and became known as the Gregorian calendar. It was adopted almost immediately by predominately Catholic countries.

The Gregorian calendar was eventually adopted in 1752 by Great Britain, the American colonies, and other British possessions, where it was termed the New Style calendar. In order to make an eleven-day adjustment in the calendar, 2 September 1752 was followed by 14 September 1752. People went to bed on 2 September and woke up on 14 September. In other words, what would have been 3 September was actually 14 September 1752. A child born on 2 September 1752 would be twelve days old on the next day, 14 September 1752 (the first day of the New Style calendar).[28] America and England converted from the old Julian calendar to the new Gregorian calendar in 1752. A day was added to the calendar each fourth year, known as Leap Year.

Dates in American colonies of British origins preceding the calendar change are known as O.S. (Old Style or Julian), while dates since 1752 are known as N.S. (New Style or Gregorian). Most dates in genealogical and historical research have been converted to the Gregorian calendar, or New Style.

Prior to 1752 the first day of the year was 25 March (ecclesiastical calendar). Thus New

---

[28]Donald Lines Jacobus, *Genealogy as Pastime and Profession*, 2nd ed. (Baltimore: Genealogical Publishing Co., 1968), pp. 109-13, 117-18.

Year's Day was 25 March in colonial British America and Great Britain. This fact was often reflected in church records. March 25th was sometimes known as Lady Day, Annunciation Day, or Annunciation of the Blessed Virgin Mary. The last day of the year was 24 March (before 1752).

Double dating was used in colonial British America and Great Britain before 1752 for dates occurring between 1 January and 24 March (dates between 1582 and 1752). When transcribing documents, it is important to record dates exactly as they are shown in the original record. Old style double dates are often seen as listed below and should be transcribed with a slash mark (/). For example,

15 January 1681/2	15 March 1700/1
15 February 1691/2	15 February 1750/1

Months ending in "ber" before 1752 may have been written based on the older Julian calendar (for example, December was formerly the tenth month of the year). The following months as number abbreviations will illustrate this situation:

7ber	September
8ber	October
9ber	November
10ber or Xber	December

With the calendar change, Great Britain adopted the first day of the year as 1 January, known as New Year's Day (historical calendar). The last day of the year of our modern calendar is 31 December. Double dating ended in 1752 with the adoption of the Gregorian calendar.

Quakers (Society of Friends) often followed the ecclesiastical calendar, thus March was the first month (O.S.) and February was the twelfth month (O.S.). Quaker records may show the name of the month in addition to the number, thus "4th month called June." Any date in March was considered as the first month. April was the second month, May the third month, etc. Under the New Style (N.S.) calendar, March is the third month and February is the second month.

George Washington was actually born on 11 February 1731 (1731/32) (O.S.). After the Gregorian calendar change, he rectified his birthdate to 22 February 1732 (N.S.). Thus if George Washington would have been born under the New Style calendar he would have been born on 22 February 1732.

Some events in colonial American records might be written in a *regnal year*, or year of the monarch's reign (i.e., reign of the king or queen). These records usually show "the reign of_____" (followed by the name of the king or queen, or reigning monarch).

Many of the dates used in genealogical and historical documents end with the Latin *anno Domini* (or a spelling variation thereof), meaning "in the year of the Lord" or "in the year of our Lord." This was frequently abbreviated A.D.

An Internet web site is available which will show you a monthly calendar for any given year, and will create a calendar for you which may be printed out:

http://www.presstar.com/w3magic/cgi-bin/homepage.cgi?calendar

The major reference guide for American genealogists wishing to understand dates and dating in old records is Kenneth Smith's *Genealogical Dates: A User-Friendly Guide*.[29] Smith's guide shows how to convert regnal years. A chart showing regnal years is included in Terrick V.H. FitzHugh, *The Dictionary of Genealogy*.[30] For additional examples of the calendar change see Donald Lines Jacobus, *Genealogy as Pastime and Profession*, Chapter 18, "Dates and the

---

[29]Kenneth Lee Smith, *Genealogical Dates: A User-Friendly Guide* (Camden, Maine: Picton Press, 1994). See also Leo H. Garman, "Genealogists and the Gregorian Calendar," *NEXUS* [New England Historic Genealogical Society] 6 (April 1989), pp. 61-62. Four additional titles of interest are Archibald F. Bennett, *A Guide for Genealogical Research* (Salt Lake City: Genealogical Society of the Church of Jesus Christ of Latter-day Saints, 1951); Christopher Robert Cheney, ed., *Handbook of Dates for Students of English History* (1945; reprint, London: Offices of the Royal Historical Society, 1961); John Richardson, *The Local Historian's Encyclopedia*, 2nd ed. (New Barnet, Herts, England: Historical Publications Ltd., 1986); and Clifford Webb, *Dates and Calendars for the Genealogist* (London: Society of Genealogists, 1994).

[30]Terrick V.H. FitzHugh, *The Dictionary of Genealogy*, 4th ed. revised by Susan Lumas (London: A&C Black Publishers Ltd., 1994).

Calendar."[31]

A perpetual calendar is helpful in determining the day of the week during a specific time period. Perpetual calendars may be seen at these Internet sites:

http://www.wiskit.com/calendar.html

http://users.mainlink.net/~sledford/cal/main.html

---

[31]Jacobus, *Genealogy as Pastime and Profession*, 2nd ed. See also Val D. Greenwood, *The Researcher's Guide to American Genealogy*, 2nd ed. (Baltimore: Genealogical Publishing Co., 1990), pp. 41-43, and Milton Rubincam, *Pitfalls in Genealogical Research* (Salt Lake City: Ancestry Publishing, 1987).

Chapter 7

Sample Alphabets and Handwriting Styles

"It's a poor mind that can only think of one way
to spell a word."

—Andrew Jackson

Both capital and lowercase letters are discussed in this chapter. Sometimes capital letters are more difficult to recognize than lowercase letters because of the flourishes and style of writing, while at other times lowercase letters are more difficult to interpret.

A summary of handwriting styles and letters of the alphabet to be aware of is given below:

Aa Small *a* may have its top flaked off, or may not have been rounded, making the letter look like a *u*. Small *a* may look like an *o*. Capital *A* may look like a capital *T* or *H*.

Bb Small *b* may look like an *f*, especially if it descends below the line, or it may look like an *l* or a *b*.

Cc Capital *C* often has a horizontal or slanted line drawn through it. A capital *C* may stand for *and*. Small *c* sometimes looks like a small *r*, or resembles an older style *t*. A small *c* may not be rounded at the top making the letter look like an undotted *i*.

Dd Small *d* was often looped to the left with a flourish. Small *d* may look like *el*. A looped small *d* may appear as an *O*.

Ee Small *e* may resemble a modern *o* with a loop or circle at the top. Sometimes a small *e* was written large and looks like an *l*. A small *e* may resemble a *d*. A final *e* may have a flourish or tail.

Ff Two small *ff*(s) were used to form a modern capital *F*. A small *f* or backward lower case *f* may look like an *s*. A capital *F* may be confused with a capital *H*.

Gg Small *g* may appear as a small *y* with a flat line on the top.

Hh Capital *H* and small letter *h* are often the most difficult to recognize because of the flourish or loop which often descends below the line. About one-half to three-quarters of the lowercase *h* may descend below the line (especially in colonial handwriting). An *h* may have both an ascender and a descender. To some people this may look like a large *E*.

Ii Letters *I* and *J*, *i* and *j*, were often used interchangeably and often appear identical. A small *i* may appear as a minim (an up and down stroke). A small *i* may or may not have been dotted over the letter. A capital *I* or *J* may look like a capital *F*.

Jj Letters *J* and *I* and *j* and *i*, were often used interchangeably.

Kk Capital *K* or small *k* may look like an *R*. A small *k* may look like a *t*.

Ll Capital *L* often looks like a capital *S*. Read for the context of the document.

Mm Letters *m* and *n* were often written as minims, or up-and-down strokes in a series. It is helpful to count each stroke when deciphering these two letters.

Nn It is important not to confuse the letters *n* and *m*. Also, sometimes *n* and *u* look alike. A small *n* may look like an *r*, for example, *on* and *or*. Read for common sense.

Oo Small *o* was often rounded to avoid confusion with the small letter *e*. A small *o* may look like an *a*.

Pp Small *p* may look like a *q* or a small *x*. The descender on a small *p* may have a wide space between the two lines, especially in colonial handwriting. A small *p* may have an ascender.

Qq Small *q* may look like a *p* or a *y*.

Rr Small *r* was often written upside down, especially during the colonial period. It may be written upside down and regular in the same word or on the same page. It may appear to be a small modern *w*. A small raised *r* may look like an *E*. A small *r* may look like a small *n*.

Ss What is often known as the old style *s*, long *s*, double *s*, or long-tailed *s* often looks like a backward lower case *f*, double *f*, double *p*, *fs*, *p*, or a backwards *s*. It frequently resembles the letter *p* or an *h*. This style *s* is seen even in records into the middle nineteenth century, including the 1850 U.S. census. It can be a troublesome letter for those beginning their research. The first *s*, or what is known as the leading *s*, was usually followed by a more regular looking or modern *s*. See, for example, *Mass*. for Massachusetts. But you can sort of see it in Mifsifsippi and Mifsouri. An *s* at the end of a word was sometimes round, as opposed to the long *s*. An ending *s* in a word may look like an *o*, or an *o* with an upward swirl, and may be a superscript letter; it may not be closed or rounded, and may look like a looped *o*. A small *s* in the middle of a word will appear different than at the end of a word. A capital *S* may look like a capital *L* or a capital *G*.

Some examples of the old style *s* are:

Appearance in Document	*Interpretation*
Jefsie/Jefse/Jepe	Jessie/Jesse/Jesse
Maps	Mass [Massachusetts]
Mifsifsippi	Mississippi
Mifsouri	Missouri
Rofs	Ross

Tt Small *t* and the small *c* often look like the same letter and may be difficult to distinguish. Read for context. A small half-crossed *t* at the end of a word is often called a "Palmer T" and is still used by some people today. A small *t* may not be crossed. A capital *T* may appear to be a capital *F*.

Uu The letters *U* and *V* and *u* and *v*, were often used interchangeably. Thus David may appear as Dauid and Upon may appear as Vpon. A small *u* may appear as a minim. Sometimes a small *u* looks like an *n* or an *s*.

Vv The letters *V* and *U* and *v* and *u*, were often used interchangeably. A small rounded *v* may look like an *o*.

Ww Capital *W* may appear as a capital *M*. A small *w* may appear as a double *v*. A capital *W* may appear as two *U* s.

Xx An *x* may appear as a *c* or two half circles connected. An *X* was frequently used as a mark in a document when an individual could not write his or her name.

Yy Small *y* may look like a *g* with a descender. A capital *Y* may be closed at the top.

Zz This letter appears infrequently and when it does appear is usually clearly written.

In summary, some of the most difficult letters to be aware of in old handwriting, especially during the seventeenth century, are the following lowercase letters:

c
e
h
r
s
t

The capitals of the above letters may also present problems in deciphering old handwriting. Also remember that the lowercase *d* was often looped back to the left, and *I* and *J* and *U* and *V* were used interchangeably.

If you can master these dozen or so more difficult or unusual looking letters, you should be ready to begin reading seventeenth and eighteenth-century American handwriting.

Sample Alphabets

Four sample alphabets follow. It is difficult to present alphabets that represent all handwriting styles and letter forms used in America since the early seventeenth century. However, these four alphabets represent many of the letters described previously and those seen in the documents reproduced in this manual.

All scribes did not write exactly alike, and even their own handwriting styles changed. It is more important to understand the concepts in reading old handwriting and to practice reading documents than to memorize alphabets. There were almost as many different styles of writing as there were writers.

1. The first alphabet, adapted from the Society of Genealogists, London, England, has been reproduced as a handout by Stevenson's Genealogical Center, Provo, Utah. See Archibald F. Bennett, *A Guide for Genealogical Research* (Salt Lake City: Genealogical Society of the Church of Jesus Christ of Latter-day Saints, 1951), p. 269. See also the Internet site *Examples of Letters of the 17th Century Found in Parish Registers:* http://www.rootsweb.com/~genepool/oldalpha.htm

2. The second alphabet, "Letter Forms Found in American Handwriting, 1640–1790," is from the booklet by Harriet Stryker-Rodda, *Understanding Colonial Handwriting*, rev. ed. (Baltimore: Genealogical Publishing Co., 1986), pp. 20-21, courtesy Genealogical Publishing Company, Baltimore, Maryland.

3. The third alphabet is reproduced from Kent P. Bailey and Ransom B. True, *A Guide to Seventeenth-Century Virginia Court Handwriting* (Richmond, Va.: Association for the Preservation of Virginia Antiquities, 1980), pp. 18-19, courtesy Association for the Preservation of Virginia Antiquities, Richmond, Virginia.

4. The fourth alphabet is reproduced from Andrew Wright, *Court Hand Restored, or the Student's Assistant in Reading Old Deeds, Charters, Records, etc.*, 8th ed. (London: John Camden Hotten, 1867), plate 18.

Concluding this chapter is a list of personal names, words, and abbreviations reprinted from *Kansas Review*, Kansas Council of Genealogical Societies, Topeka, Kansas, vol. 11, no. 3 (1986); and *CSGA Newsletter*, California State Genealogical Alliance, vol. 12, no. 2 (Feb. 1994), p. 34.

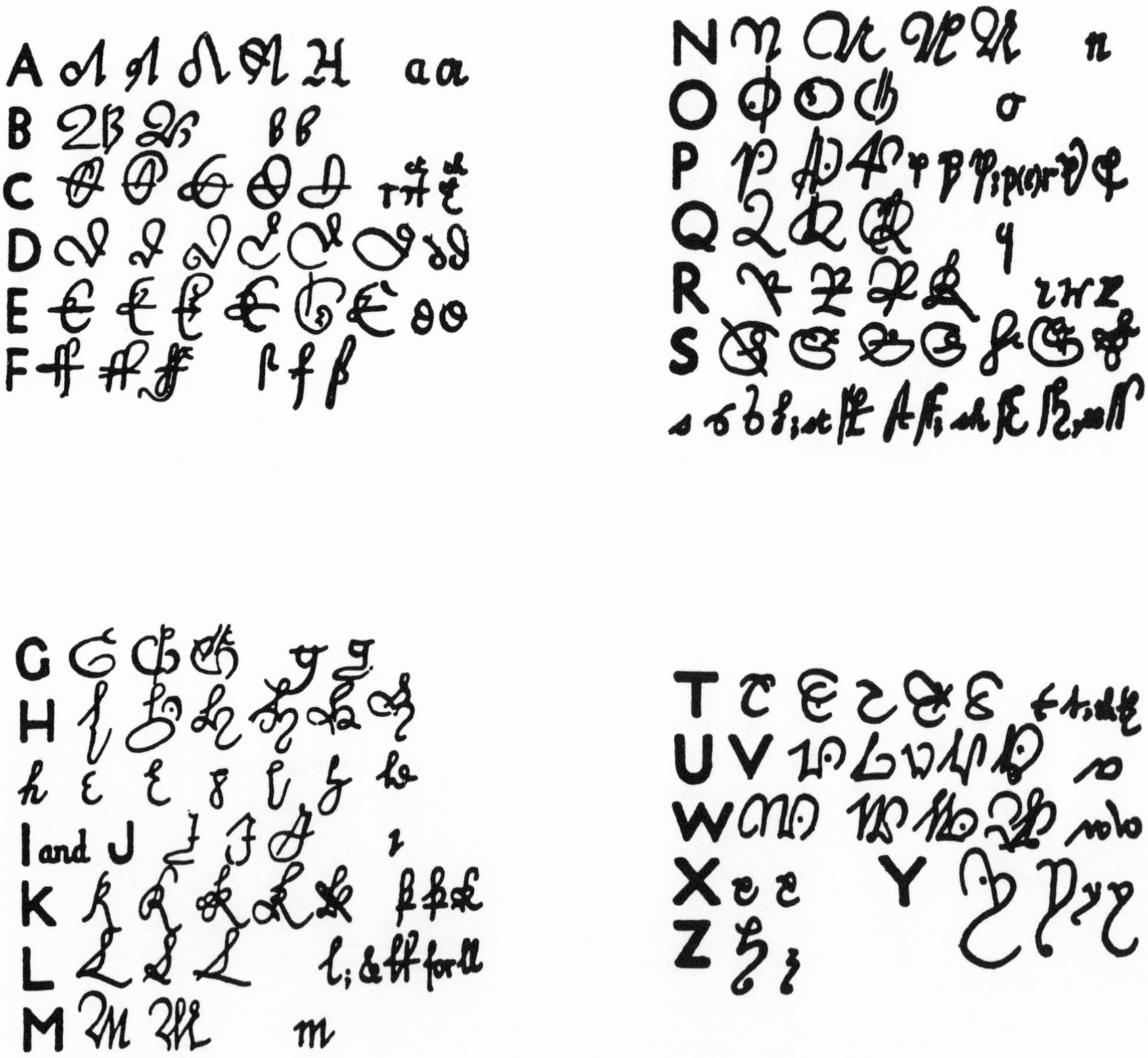

British and Early American Alphabet

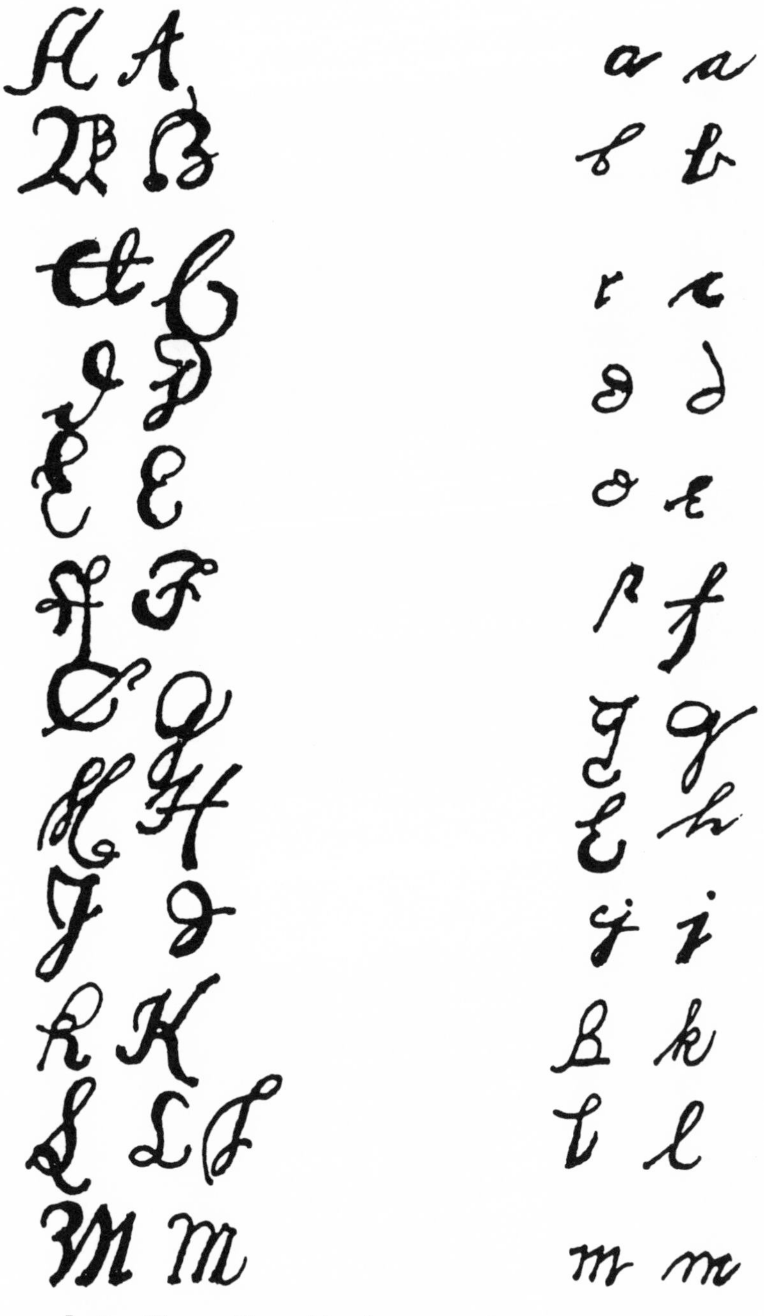

Letter Forms Found in American Handwriting, 1640-1790

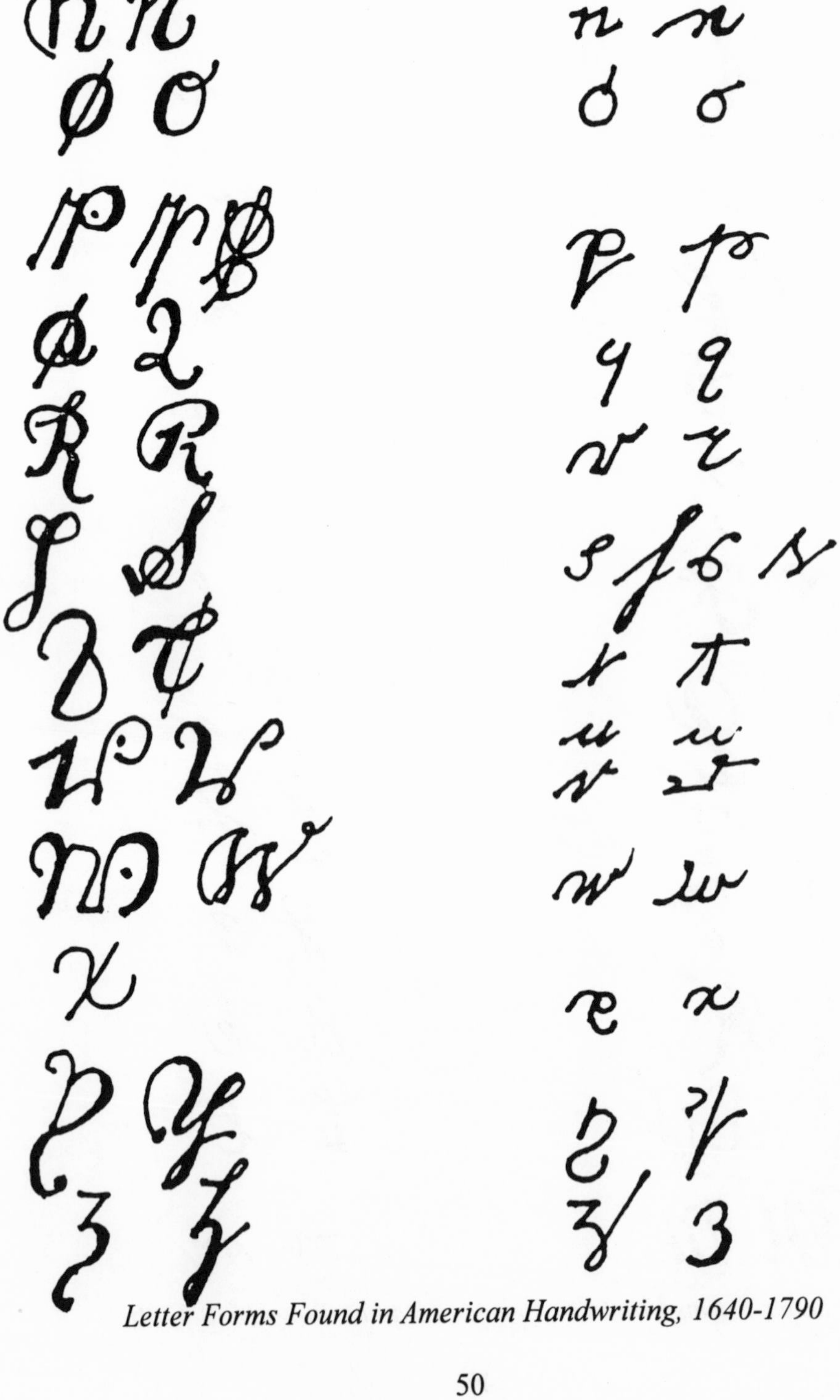

Letter Forms Found in American Handwriting, 1640-1790

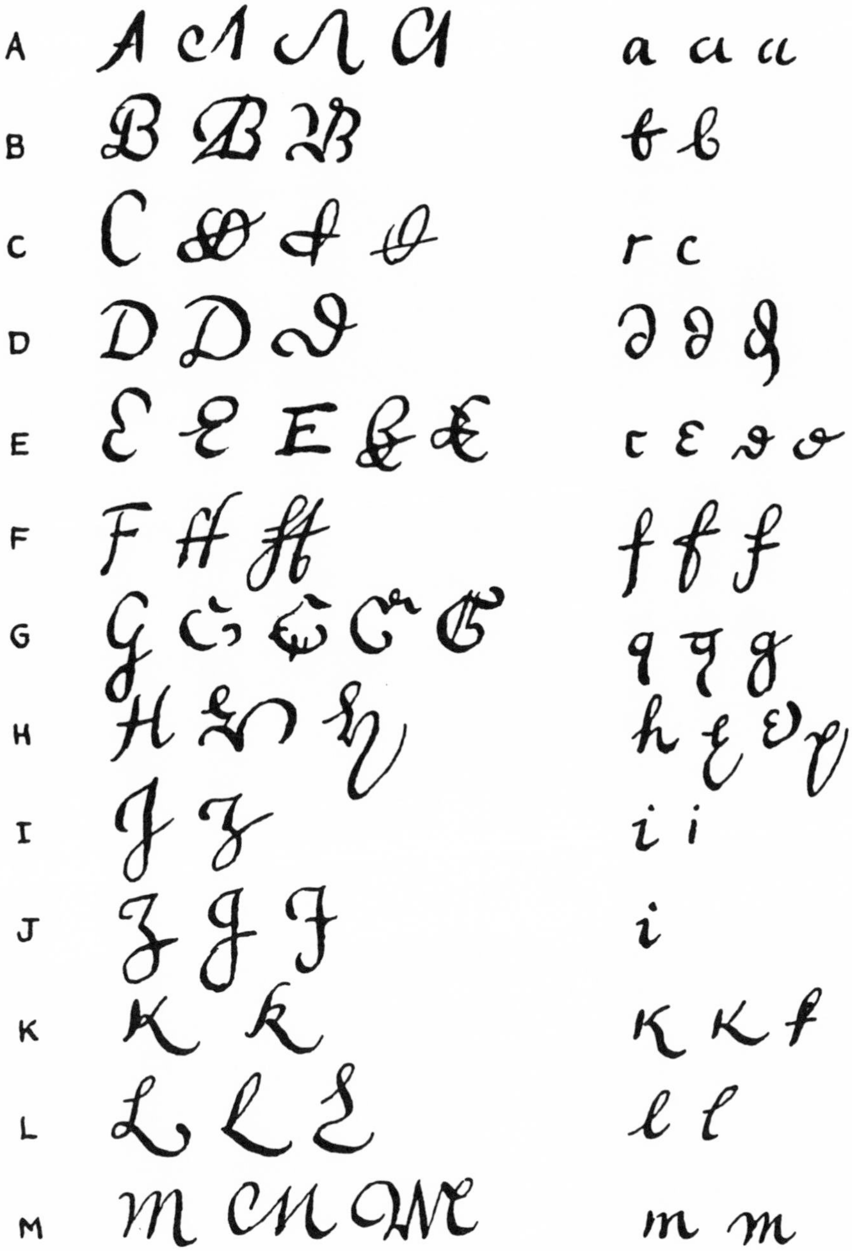

Seventeenth-Century Alphabet

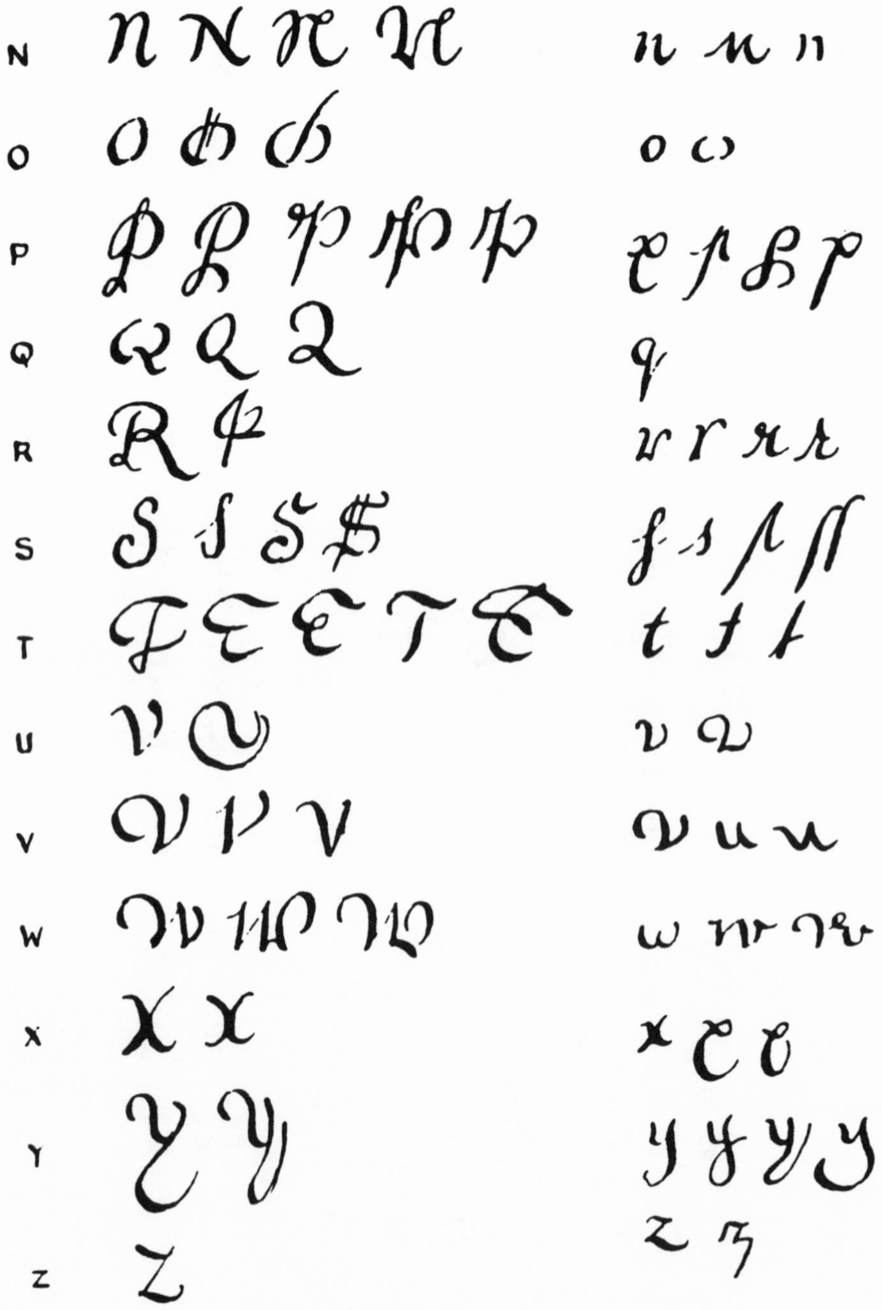

Seventeenth-Century Alphabet

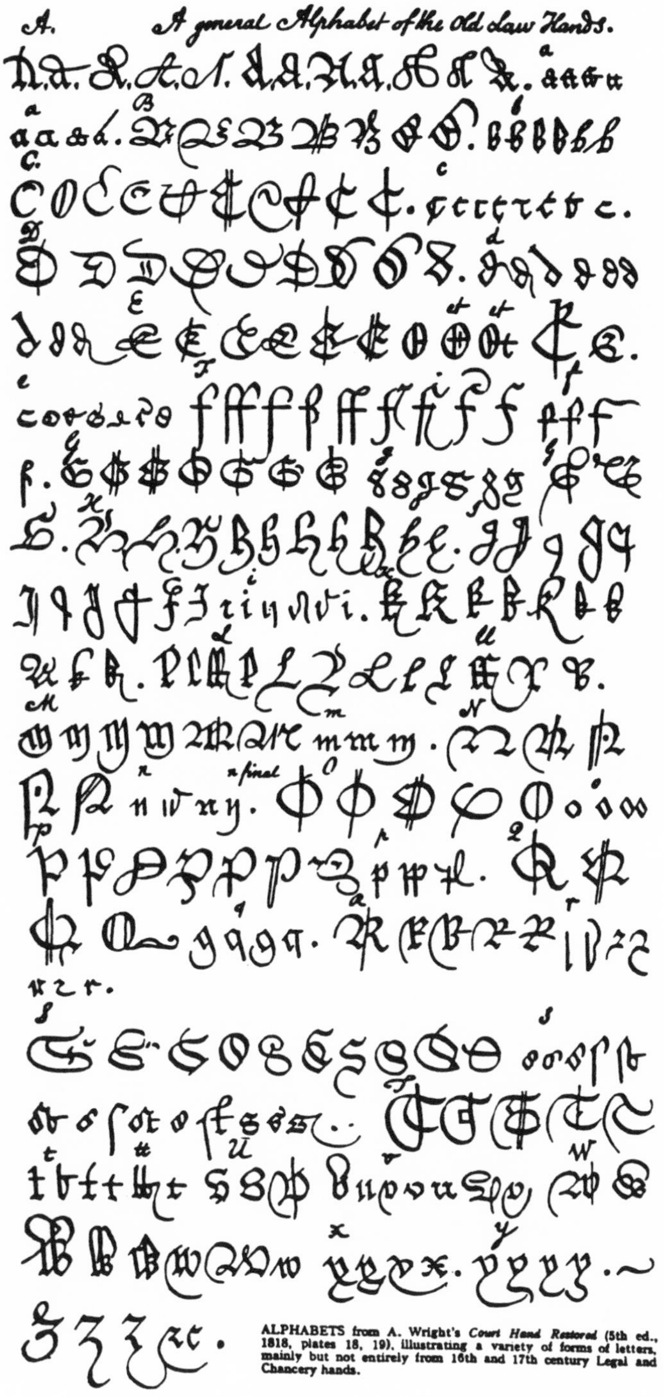

ALPHABETS from A. Wright's *Court Hand Restored* (5th ed., 1818, plates 18, 19), illustrating a variety of forms of letters, mainly but not entirely from 16th and 17th century Legal and Chancery hands.

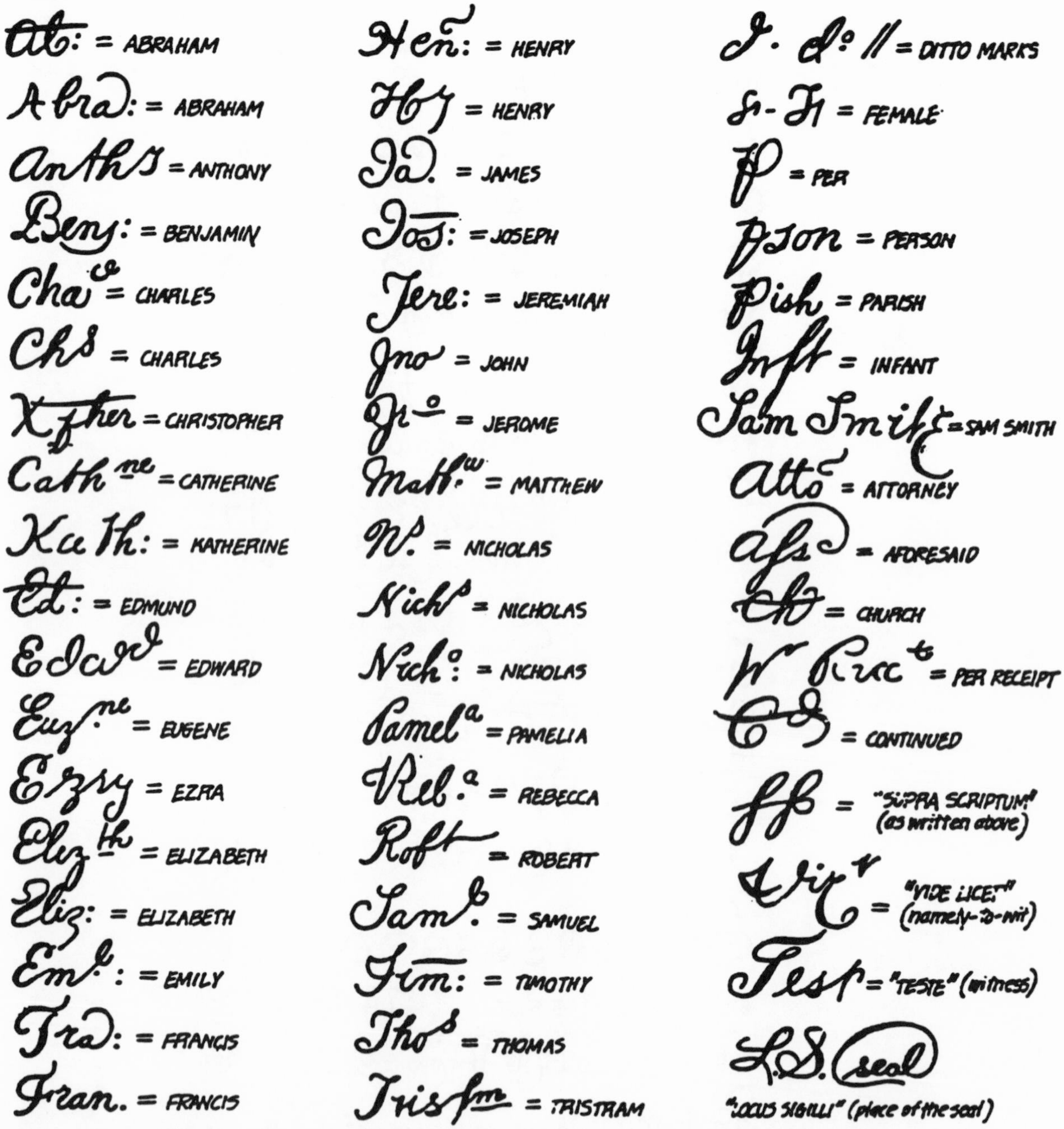

Kansas Review, Kansas Council of Genealogical Societies, Topeka, Kansas, vol. 11, no. 3 (1986); and *CSGA Newsletter*, California State Genealogical Alliance, vol. 12, no. 2 (Feb. 1994), p. 34.

Chapter 8
Accreditation and Certification

"The genealogist must be accurate. Accuracy is a prime essential for the professional."

—Donald Lines Jacobus

There are similar aspects of the accreditation examination of the International Commission for the Accreditation of Professional Genealogists (ICAPGen), formerly offered by the Family History Library in Salt Lake City, and the certification examination of the Board for Certification of Genealogists in Washington, D.C. Both examinations require the ability to transcribe or abstract documents for the areas of research interest. Both examinations require a comprehensive knowledge of genealogical sources for the area, and both examining organizations require applicants to agree to a code of ethics. This guidebook should assist applicants in preparing for the paleography portions of the accreditation and certification examinations.

Both are rigorous examinations and require the applicant to abstract or transcribe specific documents (depending on the geographical area); this part of the examination is designed to test the ability to read a genealogical document. Documents may include probate records, land records, court records, church records, and so forth.

Accreditation

Applicants for accreditation are given a series of written and oral examinations which test the individual's competence to perform genealogical research in a geographical area of specialization (for example the New England states, England, Scotland, Norway, Denmark, Germany, etc.). The accreditation program is international in scope and requires a working knowledge of a foreign language for some areas, such as French Canada, Scandinavia, and Continental Europe. Upon reaching 90 percent or better on the written portion of the test and passing an oral examination, the individual is acknowledged as an Accredited Genealogist (for that particular geographical region). If you are interested in learning more about accreditation, contact:

International Commission for the Accreditation of Professional Genealogists
P.O. Box 1144
Salt Lake City, UT 84110-1144

Karen Clifford has written a useful guidebook, *Becoming an Accredited Genealogist*, that explains how to prepare for the accreditation examination.[32] In addition, articles published in the *Association of Professional Genealogists Quarterly* frequently discuss the accreditation program. Two examples are Ruth McMahon, "The Path Toward Accredited Genealogist" (September 1996) and Kory L. Meyerink, "The Accreditation Program of the Family History Library" (March 1992).

Information regarding the accreditation program may be obtained by email:
info@infouga.org

Certification

"For many years there was a growing demand by libraries, archival institutions, and societies for a register of competent genealogists and genealogical record searchers. To meet this demand the Board for Certification of Genealogists [BCG] was incorporated in Washington, D.C. in June 1964 for the purpose of formulating standards of genealogical research and the establishment of a register of persons who are deemed to be qualified for this type of work. The Board's Trustees include distinguished genealogists, historians, and archivists from all parts of the United States."[33]

Applicants for certification are required to submit—for evaluation—a portfolio of materials that demonstrate their level of expertise and competence in many aspects of research and evidence analysis. The exact material required depends upon the category of certification that is sought. For all categories, applicants must be able to read the handwriting of various documents; make accurate transcriptions and abstracts containing all relevant details; discuss the genealogical value of the records; and devise a research plan for each, listing steps for further research.

BCG offers several areas of certification, such as Certified Genealogist^SM^ (CG), Certified Genealogical Record Specialist^SM^ (CGRS), Certified American Lineage Specialist^SM^ (CALS), among

---

[32]Karen Clifford, *Becoming an Accredited Genealogist*. Salt Lake City: Ancestry, 1998.

[33]Milton Rubincam, in Jacobus, *Genealogy as Pastime and Profession*, 2nd ed., p. 120.

others, which require the ability to read and interpret early handwriting.[34] For further information and for more details regarding each category of certification contact:

Board for Certification of Genealogists
P.O. Box 14291
Washington, DC 20044

BCG has a web site which describes BCG and certification, categories of certification, educational preparation, their code of ethics, co-sponsored institutes, and related topics:
www.bcgcertification.org

Helen Leary wrote an article published in the *National Genealogical Society Quarterly*, "Certification of Genealogists: A Consumer Report," which discusses the functions of BCG and describes the different certification categories.[35] Also significant and an update to some of the information in Leary's article is the article by Elizabeth Mills and Paul Smart, "Research Ethics: Genealogical Accreditation and Certification."[36] Articles published in various issues of *Association of Professional Genealogists Quarterly* frequently include information regarding certification and the Board for Certification of Genealogists, such as William M. Litchman's article, "Applying for Certification? It's Worth It!"[37]

Individuals who wish to become certified in any category would do well to carefully study BCG's publications, including its newsletter *OnBoard*. This newsletter is available by subscription and is complimentary to preliminary certification applicants and dues-paying certified associates.

---

[34]Service marks are marks of the Board for Certification of Genealogists that identify its programs of genealogical competency evaluation.

[35]Helen F. M. Leary, "Certification of Genealogists: A Consumer Report," *National Genealogical Society Quarterly* 79 (March 1991), pp. 5-18.

[36]Elizabeth Shown Mills and Paul Smart, "Research Ethics: Genealogical Accreditation and Certification," *Ancestry* 15 (March/April 1997), pp. 14-19.

[37]William M. Litchman, "Applying for Certification? It's Worth It!, *Association of Professional Genealogists Quarterly* 11 (September 1996), pp. 78-79.

Appendixes

Appendix A
Using Archives and Record Repositories

> "The greater the obstacle, the more glory we have in overcoming it."
>
> —Jean Molière

Using Archives

Today, original documents found in archives are generally kept in acid-free folders and boxes and are usually arranged by numbered record groups, such as RG1, RG10, and so forth. Records in most archives are arranged by the archival principle of provenance (where records are attributed to the agency or individual who created or maintained them). Records are usually arranged in the way they were filed when in use, with the exception of photographs which may have been removed from a collection and placed in a separate photograph collection.

Researchers should determine if inventories, finding aids, guides to manuscript collections, and card or computer catalogs are available. Many online public catalogs may be accessed through the Internet. These research tools will identify and describe the collection and make it easier to locate documents of interest.

It is important that researchers handle original records carefully, not damage documents in any way, and keep the records in the order in which they were filed in the archival folders or boxes. Pages must be turned carefully. Some archives and historical societies require that readers wear white gloves in order to protect the documents. Most archives require researchers to use a pencil. Be very careful not to make marks on documents if you use a pen or a pencil. Most archives will allow the use of a typewriter or lap-top computer for note taking. Briefcases, notebooks, and research folders are seldom permitted in archives and historical societies. If you use original documents, you should lay them on a flat surface when studying them, or use special manuscript reading stands provided for this purpose.

Determine if the record repository has an Internet web site or e-mail address. A listing of major Internet search engines and web sites is included in Chapter 8. Determine if inventories or finding aids are available. A massive number of manuscripts are available on microfilm and microfiche in archives and libraries, and some of this material may be available through interlibrary loan.

Record Repositories

The largest storehouse of government records in the United States is the National Archives and Records Administration in Washington, D.C. Together with their own regional archives, they house approximately 1.9 million cubic feet of archival holdings (excluding holdings in the Presidential Libraries).[38]

Three essential guides to records in the National Archives are *Guide to Genealogical Research in the National Archives*,[39] *Guide to Federal Records in the National Archives of the United States*,[40] and *The Center: A Guide to Genealogical Research in the National Capital Area*.[41]

The regional archives of the National Archives Regional Records Services Facilities, located throughout the United States, house original records and microfilm copies of records from the National Archives. Although partially out of date, a valuable reference guide describing the holdings

---

[38]Address: National Archives and Records Administration, Washington, DC 20408. National Archives e-mail inquiries may be addressed to: inquire@nara.gov.

[39]National Archives and Records Administration, *Guide to Genealogical Research in the National Archives*, rev. ed. (Washington, D.C.: National Archives and Records Administration, 1985). This is the major guidebook for describing genealogical records at the National Archives.

[40]National Archives and Records Administration, *Guide to Federal Records in the National Archives of the United States*, compiled by Robert B. Matchette, et al., 3 vols. (Washington, D.C.: National Archives and Records Administration, 1995). This valuable three-volume reference work describes federal archival records housed at the National Archives. Volume 3 is the index to this guide. This guide is also available online in its entirety. See http://www.nara.gov.

[41]Christina K. Schaefer, *The Center: A Guide to Genealogical Research in the National Capital Area* (Baltimore: Genealogical Publishing Co., 1996). This well-illustrated book describes genealogical holdings in the Washington, DC area. Previous editions of this valuable reference guide were published under the title *Lest We Forget: A Guide to Genealogical Research in the Nation's Capital*.

of National Archives regional archives is *The Archives: A Guide to the National Archives Field Branches*.[42] A listing of regional archives is available from the National Archives web site:

http://www.nara.gov

Every state has a state archives, state historical society, state library, or similar repository where original state and local records are maintained. On a local level, original records are kept in county courthouses, regional record centers (such as Ohio and Illinois), city and local archives, town halls (in New England), or township halls (in Ohio, for example).

Many United States records of interest to genealogists, such as census schedules, wills, tax rolls, and land, military, and court records, have been microfilmed by the Genealogical Society of Utah (GSU), by federal, state, or local agencies, or by historical societies. The largest collection of microfilmed genealogical records in the world is found in the Family History Library™ in Salt Lake City.[43]

---

[42]Loretto Dennis Szucs and Sandra Hargreaves Luebking, *The Archives: A Guide to the National Archives Field Branches* (Salt Lake City: Ancestry Publishing, 1988).

[43]Family History Library, 35 North West Temple Street, Salt Lake City, UT 84150. Address e-mail inquiries to: fhl@byu.edu. Internet: http://www.lds.org

Appendix B
The Internet and Compact Discs

> "Like all technology, the World Wide Web is not perfect, nor will you be able to do all of your genealogical research with the click of a mouse."
>
> —Myra Vanderpool Gormley

Copies of original records are being made available with increasing frequency on the Internet and on compact discs (CD-ROMs). In addition, many agencies provide photocopies of original records, either by mail or by FAX.

The Internet

A useful Internet web site, *Deciphering Old Handwriting*, provides tips on how to read early American handwriting and serves as an online tutorial for those beginning their study of American paleography:

http://www.firstct.com/fv/oldhand.html

More and more local genealogical records are now available on the Internet. As one example, copies of original Hillsborough County, Florida, marriage licenses, marriage license record books, and their respective indexes for the period 1846 to 1988 may be searched and printed from the following Internet site:

http://www.lib.usf.edu/spccoll/marriage.html

Early American documents may also be seen at the Library of Congress web site:

http://lcweb.loc.gov/homepage

Reading Early American Handwriting

and the National Archives and Records Administration web site:

http://www.nara.gov

Both the National Archives and Library of Congress web sites will continue to add more records as time goes on. Links are available on their web pages.

Compact Discs

Copies of early American documents (page images), such as wills, town records, and correspondence, are also being made available on compact discs. One fine example is the periodical entitled *The Mayflower Descendant*, which also includes some New England vital records. It is available on compact disc from Search & ReSearch Publishing Corporation.[44]

Scanned images of U.S. census records may be seen on compact discs. An example of the 1850 census is *Census Microfilm Records: Virginia, 1850*, which contains scanned images of microfilmed census records.[45]

Whenever possible, search the original sources. Indexes, such as those found on the Internet or on compact discs, are not an original source.

---

[44]Search & ReSearch Publishing Corp., P. O. Box 436, 12265 West 34th Place, Wheat Ridge, CO 80034–0436. Every word is indexed and searchable on this compact disc.

[45]Broderbund Software, P. O. Box 6125, Novato, CA 94948–6125. Their web site is: http://www.familytreemaker.com. Broderbund publishes *Family Tree Maker Magazine*.

Internet Search Tools

This section identifies search engines and Internet sites (URLs) to help you identify personal names, compiled genealogies, locality sources, record repositories, indexes to records, publications, online public library catalogs, as well as copies of American records or record extracts available on the Internet. Type the name of the library or locality of interest in the search engines. Be sure to check county and locality sites on the U.S. Gen Web home page. Most of the tools support the use of boolean operators and truncation. All of the Internet web sites listed here begin with: **http://**

All-In-One Search Page
www.albany.net/allinone

Alta Vista
www.altavista.digital.com

Argus Clearinghouse
www.clearinghouse.net

C/NET Search.Com
www.search.com

Deja News
www.dejanews.com

DOG PILE
www.dogpile.com

Excite
www.excite.com

Family Tree Maker
Internet Family Finder
www.familytreemaker.com/
iffintro.html

Galaxy
www.einet.net/galaxy.html

HotBot
www.hotbot.com

I Found It! Genealogy Search Engine
www.gensource.com/ifoundit/index.htm

Inference Find
www.inference.com/ifind

Infoseek
www.infoseek.com

JUMPCITY
www.jumpcity.com/cgi-bin/search?passed

Lycos
www.lycos.com

Netscape Net Search
home.netscape.com/home/internet-search.html

NOCCC Web Search Assistant
www.noccc.ORG/search/index.html

Open Text Index
search.opentext.com

Ready Reference Collection
www.ipl.org/ref/RR

Savvy Search
www.cs.colostate.edu/~dreiling/smartform.html

Webcrawler
webcrawler.com

Yahoo!
www.yahoo.com

Internet Web Sites

Allen County Public Library
www.acpl.lib.in.us

Ancestry Home Town/Reference Library
www.ancestry.com

Association for the Preservation of Virginia Antiquities
www.apva.org

Association of Professional Genealogists
www.apgen.org/~apg

A Barrel of Genealogy Links
cpcug.org/user/jlacombe/mark.html

Board for Certification of Genealogists
www.genealogy.org/~bcg

Cyndi's List of Genealogical Sites on the Internet
www.oz.net/~cyndihow/sites.htm

Everton's Genealogy Site
www.everton.com

Family History Centers
www.genhomepage.com/FHC

Family History Library
fhl@byu.edu
www.lds.org

Family Tree Maker Online
www.familytreemaker.com

Federation of Genealogical Societies
www.fgs.org

Genealogical Publishing Company
www.genealogical.com

Genealogy Helplist United States
www.concentric.net/~mikerice/hl/usa/index.shtml

The Genealogy Home Page
www.genhomepage.com

Genealogy Links for Historians
www.ucr.edu/h-gig/hist-preservation/genea.html

Genealogy Online
genealogy.emcee.com

Genealogy Resources
fhss.byu.edu/history/genealogy/index.html

Genealogy Resources on the Internet
www.tc.umn.edu/~pmg/genealogy.html

Genealogy Resources on the World Wide Web
www.execpc.com/~dcollins/resource.html

Genealogy Services Online
ourworld.compuserve.com/homepages/roots/homepage.htm

Genealogy ToolBox
genealogy.tbox.com

Genealogy WWW Pages
www.tic.com/gen.html

Introduction to Genealogy on the Web
pages.prodigy.com/UT/fhl

Journal of Online Genealogy
www.online.genealogy.com

Librarians' Index to the Internet
sunsite.berkeley.edu/InternetIndex

Libraries and Information Databases
www.carl.org/carlweb

Libraries on the Web
sunsite.berkeley.edu/Libweb

Library of Congress
lcinfo@loc.gov
www.loc.gov (or, lcweb.loc.gov)
telnet://locis.loc.gov

Link-O-Mania Genealogy Lots-A-Links
link-o-mania.com/lotsofl.htm

LYCOS PeopleFind
www.lycos.com/pplfndr.html

Massachusetts Historical Society
masshist.org

National Archives and Records Administration
inquire@nara.gov
www.nara.gov

National Genealogical Society
www.genealogy.org/~ngs

New England Historic Genealogical Society
nehgs@nehgs.org
www.nehgs.org

North American Genealogy Resources
www.genhomepage.com/northamerican.html

Online Genealogical Database Index
www.gentree.com

Rand Genealogy Club
www.rand.org/personal/Genea

Roots-L Home Page
www.rootsweb.com/roots-l

Roots-L Resources: United States
www.rootsweb.com/roots-l/usa.html

RootsWeb Genealogical Data Cooperative
www.rootsweb.com

State Libraries Web Listing
www.state.wi.us/0/agencies/dpi/www/statelib.html

U.S.G.S. National Mapping Information
mapping.usgs.gov

U.S. GenWeb Project
www.usgenweb.org

Western Reserve Historical Society
www.wrhs.org

What's Really New in WWW Genealogy Pages
www.genhomepage.com/really_new.html

Yahoo's Listing of Genealogy Sites
www.yahoo.com/arts/Humanities/History/Genealogy

Bibliography

In addition to titles relating to reading early American handwriting, this bibliography also includes British and other titles dealing with the subject of paleography, reading manuscripts, using archives, methodology, and other aspects associated with reading old handwriting.

Alcock, N.W. *Old Title Deeds: A Guide for Local and Family Historians*. Chichester, Sussex, England: Phillimore, 1986.

American Council on Education. *The Story of Writing*. Washington, D.C., 1932.

American Society of Genealogists. *Genealogical Research: Methods and Sources*. 2 vols. Rev. ed. Vol. 1 edited by Milton Rubincam; vol. 2 edited by Kenn Stryker-Rodda. Washington, D.C.: The Society, 1980-83.
Although partially outdated, this is a standard American genealogical textbook. See especially volume 1, chapter 3, "Interpreting Genealogical Records."

Anderson, Donald M. *The Art of Written Forms*. New York: Holt, Rinehart and Winston, 1969.

Anglo-Saxon Manuscripts, Basic Readings. Edited by Mary P. Richards. Garland Reference Library of the Humanities, vol. 1434. New York: Garland Publishing, 1994.

Axelrod, Todd M. *Collecting Historical Documents: A Guide to Owning History*. Rev. ed. Neptune City, N.J.: T.F.H. Publications, 1986.

Bailey, Kent P. and Ransom B. True. *A Guide to Seventeenth-Century Virginia Court Handwriting*. Richmond, Va.: Association for the Preservation of Virginia Antiquities, 1980.
An important discussion of handwriting found in seventeenth-century Virginia court records. Well illustrated.

Barrett, John and David Iredale. *Discovering Old Handwriting*. Princes Risborough, Buckinghamshire, England: Shire Publications Ltd., 1995.

Bately, Janet, Michelle P. Brown, and Jane Roberts, eds. *A Palaeographer's View: The Selected Writings of Julian Brown*. London: Harvey Miller Publishers, 1993.
This work is especially valuable for its illustrations, glossary, and the bibliography.

Baxter, James Houston and Charles Johnson. *Medieval Latin Word-List from British and Irish Sources*. 1934. Reprint. London: Oxford University Press, 1947.

Beal, Peter and Jeremy Griffiths, eds. *English Manuscript Studies, 1100-1700*. Oxford, England: Basil Blackwell Ltd., 1989.
A study of English medieval and Renaissance manuscripts. Illustrated.

Beeson, Charles Henry. *A Primer of Medieval Latin*. Chicago: Scott, Foresman, 1925.

Bennett, Archibald F. *A Guide for Genealogical Research*. Salt Lake City: Genealogical Society of the Church of Jesus Christ of Latter-day Saints, 1951.
See especially Appendix II, "Key to Early Styles of Handwriting."

Bentz, Edna M. *If I Can, You Can Decipher Germanic Records*. 3rd ed. San Diego, Calif.: The author, 1985.
Useful for a study of German alphabets and terminology found in German records.

Bischoff, Bernhard. *Latin Palaeography: Antiquity and the Middle Ages*. 1990. Reprint. Cambridge: Cambridge University Press, 1993.
A scholarly study of Latin and Latin paleography.

Bishop, Terence Alan Martyn. *English Caroline Minuscule*. Oxford, England: Clarendon Press, 1971.

Black, Henry Campbell. *Black's Law Dictionary*. Rev. ed. St. Paul, Minn.: West Publishing Co., 1991.
The standard authoritative dictionary for identifying and understanding legal terms. An

essential reference for American genealogists.

Bolton, Charles Knowles. "Colonial Handwriting." *The Essex Antiquarian* 1 (Nov. 1897): 175-76.
A brief discussion of handwriting styles, with examples. Reprinted in E. Kay Kirkham, *How to Read the Handwriting and Records of Early America*, rev. ed. (Salt Lake City: Deseret Book Co., 1965).

Boyle, Leonard E. *Medieval Latin Palaeography: A Bibliographical Introduction*. Toronto: University of Toronto Press, 1984.
Serves as a reference source for Latin paleography.

Braswell, Laurel Nichols. *Western Manuscripts from Classical Antiquity to the Renaissance: A Handbook*. New York: Garland Publishing, 1981.

Briggs, Elizabeth. *A Family Historian's Guide to Illness, Disease, and Death Certificates*. Winnipeg, Manitoba: Westgarth, 1993.

______. *Handbook for Reading & Interpreting Old Documents, with Examples from the Hudson's Bay Company Archives*. Winnipeg, Manitoba: Manitoba Genealogical Society, 1992.
A valuable paleography reference guide to reading British documents.

British Library. Dept. of Manuscripts. *Catalogue of Dated and Datable Manuscripts, ca. 700-1600, in the Department of Manuscripts, the British Library*. 2 vols. London: British Library, 1979.

British Literary Manuscripts. 2 vols. New York: Pierpont Morgan Library, 1981.
Volume 1 covers the years 800 to 1800; volume 2, years 1800 to 1914.

Brook, G. L. *An Introduction to Old English*. 1955. Reprint. Manchester, England: University of Manchester Press, 1966.

Brown, Julian. *What is Palaeography?* Online. Available: http://www.mlab.uiah.fi/simultaneous/Text/Paleography.html

Brown, Michelle P. *A Guide to Western Historical Scripts from Antiquity to 1600.* Toronto: University of Toronto Press, 1990; London: British Library, 1990.
Traces the evolution of scripts in the West. Illustrated.

______. *Anglo-Saxon Manuscripts*. London: British Library, 1991.

Brown, Thomas Julian. *A Palaeographer's View: The Selected Writings of Julian Brown.* London: Harvey Miller Publishers, 1993.

Buck, W.S.B., comp. *Examples of Handwriting, 1550-1650.* 1965. Reprint. London and Chichester, England: Phillimore, 1973; London: Society of Genealogists, 1996.
An alphabet of single letters, Christian names alphabetically arranged, abbreviations, numbers, and dates. A useful reference source for genealogists.

Bushman, Richard L. *The Refinement of America: Persons, Houses, Cities*. New York: Vintage Books, 1993.
Includes a discussion of the history of handwriting and colonial handwriting in America.

Byrne, Muriel St. Clare. "Elizabethan Handwriting for Beginners." *Review of English Studies* 1 (April 1925): 198-209.

The Cambridge Gazetteer of the United States and Canada: A Dictionary of Places. Edited by Archie Hobson. Cambridge, England: Cambridge University Press, 1995.

Cappelli, Adriano. *The Elements of Abbreviation in Medieval Latin Paleography.* Lawrence, Kansas: University of Kansas Libraries, 1982.

Cartlidge, Anna M. "How to Read the Old Records." *Maryland Genealogical Society Bulletin* 15 (1974): 63-67.

Chaplais, Pierre. *English Royal Documents, King John-Henry VI, 1199-1461*. Oxford: Oxford University Press, 1971.

Cheney, Christopher Robert, ed. *Handbook of Dates for Students of English History*. 1945. Reprint. London: Offices of the Royal Historical Society, 1961.
A valuable reference source for studying dates and dating.

Colange, Leo de. *The National Gazetteer: A Geographical Dictionary of the United States*. Cincinnati: J. C. Yorston & Co., 1884.

Colbert, Roy. "Reading Old Handwriting." *Reflector* (Amarillo Genealogical Society).
Article title varies. Reprinted in *Bluegrass Roots* (Kentucky Genealogical Society), *The Longhunter* (Southern Kentucky Genealogical Society) 7 (Summer 1984): 84-87; *Tree-shaker* (Permian Basin Genealogical Society) 32 (April 1994): 5-8; *Links and Bridges* 10 (April 1996): 6-7, 7-8; and *The Pastfinder* (Genealogical Association of Southwestern Michigan) 14 (Spring 1985).

Colwell, Stella. *Tracing Your Family History*. London: Hodder & Stoughton, 1997.
A useful guide to British family history sources.

Cook, Michael L. *Genealogical Dictionary with Alphabetical Nationwide County Index Included*. Evansville, Ind.: Cook Publications, 1979.
A dictionary of many terms and abbreviations of interest to genealogists. Includes an alphabetical list of counties in the U.S.

Cope, Emma Elizabeth (Thoyts). *How to Read Old Documents*. 1893. Reprint. Christchurch, England: Dolphin Press, 1972.
A useful introduction to British paleography and reading old documents.

______. *How to Decipher and Study Old Documents: Being a Guide to the Reading of Ancient Manuscripts*. 2nd ed. 1903. Reprint. Detroit: Gale Research Co., 1974.

______. *The Key to the Family Deed Chest: How to Decipher and Study Old Documents*. 2nd ed. 1903. Reprint. Detroit: Gale Research Co., 1974.
Tips for reading old handwriting; illustrated.

Crandall, Ralph J. *Shaking Your Family Tree: A Basic Guide to Tracing Your Family's Genealogy*. Dublin, N.H.: Yankee Publishing, 1986.
This authoritative work is especially useful for a discussion of New England records and includes examples of records. Nicely illustrated.

Crowe, Elizabeth Powell. *Genealogy Online: Researching Your Roots*. New York: McGraw-Hill, 1998.
A nicely illustrated reference source for genealogists searching the Internet.

Daniels, Maygene. "The Ingenious Pen: American Writing Implements from the Eighteenth Century to the Twentieth." *The American Archivist* 43 (Summer 1980): 312-24.
A history of American handwriting implements, including a discussion of the quill pen and other writing instruments in early America.

Dawson, Giles Edwin and Laetitia Kennedy-Skipton. *Elizabethan Handwriting, 1500-1650: A Guide to the Reading of Documents and Manuscripts.* 1968. Reprint. Chichester, Sussex, England: Phillimore, 1981.
A well-illustrated text, with copies of documents and transcriptions. See especially Chapter 3, "Historical Developments," and Chapter 4, "The Mechanics of Writing."

Day, Lewis F. *Penmanship of the 16th, 17th, and 18th Centuries*. London: B.T. Batsford, n.d.
Useful illustrations of handwriting, but does not include transcriptions.

Denholm-Young, Noel. *Handwriting in England and Wales.* 2nd ed. Cardiff, Wales: University of Wales Press, 1964.
A valuable guide for students of British paleography. Includes a history of handwriting. Nicely illustrated, but does not include transcriptions.

Derbyshire County Council. *How to Read Early Handwriting and Understand Roman Numerals: A Beginner's Guide*. Derby, England: Derbyshire County Council, 1995.

Diringer, David. *The Alphabet*. 2 vols. 3rd ed. London: Hutchinson, 1968.

Drake, Paul. *What Did They Mean by That?: A Dictionary of Historical Terms for Genealogists.* Bowie, Md.: Heritage Books, 1994.
A dictionary of historical and genealogical terms. Includes sample documents.

Eichholz, Alice, ed. *Ancestry's Red Book: American State, County & Town Sources.* Rev. ed. Salt Lake City: Ancestry, 1992.
This well-organized guidebook is useful for locating U.S. county information, along with valuable genealogical details and maps.

Emery, Donald William. *Variant Spellings in Modern American Dictionaries.* Rev. ed. Urbana, Ill.: National Council of Teachers of English, 1973.

Emmison, Frederick George. *How to Read Local Archives, 1550-1700.* London: The Historical Association, 1967.
Examples of early English documents from local English archives, with transcriptions.

______. *Introduction to Archives.* 1964. Reprint. Chichester, Sussex, England: Phillimore, 1978.

English Manuscript Studies, 1100-1700. New York: B. Blackwell, 1988; Oxford, England: Basil Blackwell, 1989-.

Evans, Barbara Jean. *A to Zax: A Comprehensive Dictionary for Genealogists & Historians.* 3rd ed. Alexandria, Va.: Hearthside Press, 1995.
A valuable reference source and dictionary of terms and abbreviations of interest to genealogists, historians, librarians, and others. Concludes with a list of Dutch given names and common nicknames.

Examples of Letters of the 17th Century Found in Parish Registers. Online. Available: http://www.rootsweb.com/~genepool/oldalpha.htm

Fairbank, Alfred J. *A Book of Scripts.* Rev. ed. Hardmondsworth: Penguin, 1968.

______ and Berthold Wolpe. *Renaissance Handwriting: An Anthology of Italic Scripts.* Cleveland:

World Publishing Co., 1960; London: Faber and Faber, 1960.

Fanning's Illustrated Gazetteer of the United States. 1855. Reprint. Bowie, Md.: Heritage Books, 1990.
A popular gazetteer of American place names.

FitzHugh, Terrick V.H. *The Dictionary of Genealogy*. 4th edition revised by Susan Lumas. London: A&C Black (Publishers) Ltd., 1994.
See especially "Handwriting," "Secretary Hand," and the illustrations.

Franklin, Peter. *Some Medieval Records for Family Historians*. Birmingham, England: Federation of Family History Societies, 1994.

Fredregill, Ernest J. *1000 Years: A Julian/Gregorian Perpetual Calendar, A.D. 1100 to A.D. 2099*. New York: Exposition Press, 1970.

Fry, Roger Eliot and E.A. Lowe. *English Handwriting, with Thirty-four Facsimile Plates and Artistic and Paleographical Criticisms*. Oxford, England: Clarendon Press, 1926-27.

Gandy, Michael. *Basic Approach to Latin for Family Historians*. Birmingham, England: Federation of Family History Societies (Publications) Ltd., 1995.

Gannett, Henry. *The Origin of Certain Place Names in the United States*. 2nd ed. 1905. Reprint. Baltimore: Genealogical Publishing Co., 1973.

Gardner, David E. and Frank Smith. *Genealogical Research in England and Wales*, vol. 3. Rev. ed. Salt Lake City: Bookcraft, 1966.
A valuable discussion of reading Old English handwriting and Latin. Useful for reading exercises and a study of alphabets. Discusses research methodology and procedures.

Garman, Leo H. "Genealogists and the Gregorian Calendar." *NEXUS* [New England Historic Genealogical Society] 6 (April 1989): 61-62.

Geiger, Linda A. Woodward. "Techniques for Transcribing and Abstracting Documents: A Refresher Course." *Association of Professional Genealogists Quarterly* 10 (Sept. 1995): 87-88.
Presents tips on abstracting and transcribing wills and deeds.

Gibbens, Lilian. *An Introduction to Church Registers*. Birmingham, England: Federation of Family History Societies, 1994.

Goldberg, Jonathan. *Writing Matter: From the Hands of the English Renaissance*. Stanford, Calif.: Stanford University Press, 1990.

Good, Noah G. "How to Read German Script." *Mennonite Family History* 1 (Oct. 1982): 5-7.
This article is helpful for reading early German records in colonial Pennsylvania.

Gooder, Eileen A. *Latin for Local History: An Introduction.* 2nd ed. London: Longman Group Ltd., 1978.
A basic Latin text of interest to genealogists and historians. Includes a valuable word list and an introduction to Latin paleography.

Goulden, R. J. *English Royal Signatures.* London: Her Majesty's Stationery Office, 1973.
Examples of the handwriting of English kings and queens.

Greenwood, Val D. *The Researcher's Guide to American Genealogy*. 2nd ed. Baltimore: Genealogical Publishing Co., 1990.
See especially chapters 2, 13, 14, and 18. Includes a discussion of handwriting, abbreviations, naming practices, and the calendar change.

Greg, Walter Wilson. *English Literary Autographs, 1550-1959.* 1932. Reprint. Kraus Reprint, 1968.

Grieve, Hilda Elizabeth Poole. *Examples of English Handwriting, 1150-1750, with Transcripts and Translations.* 1954. Reprint. Essex, England: Essex Education Committee, 1995.
Includes a secretary hand alphabet, facsimiles of documents, transcriptions, and a

bibliography. Examples are from Essex parish records and other records. Part 1 includes Essex parish records, and part 2 has examples from other Essex archives.

______. *More Examples of English Handwriting from Essex Parish Records of the 13th to the 18th Century, with Transcripts and Translations.* Publication no. 9. Chelmsford, England: Essex County Council, 1950.

______. *Some Examples of English Handwriting from Essex Official, Ecclesiastical, Estate and Family Archives of the 12th-17th Century.* Chelmsford, England: Essex Record Office Publications, 1949.

Hall, Hubert. *Studies in English Official Historical Documents*. 1908. Reprint. New York: Burt Franklin, 1969.
An introduction to the study of official sources and English historical documents.

Hamilton, Charles. *The Book of Autographs*. New York: Simon and Schuster, 1978.
A collection of autographs and handwriting of Americans and world leaders.

The Handy Book for Genealogists. 8th ed. Logan, Utah: Everton Publishers, 1991.
A useful reference source for locating U.S. county and other genealogical information. Includes useful maps.

Hardy, William John. *The Handwriting of the Kings and Queens of England*. London: Religious Tract Society, 1893.

Harris, Maurine and Glen Harris, comps. *Ancestry's Concise Genealogical Dictionary.* Salt Lake City: Ancestry Publishing, 1989.
Although not comprehensive, this is a valuable dictionary of interest to genealogists and other researchers. Includes a list of useful abbreviations.

Harris, Virgil McClure. *Ancient, Curious and Famous Wills*. London: Stanley Paul & Co., 1912.

Harrison, Darline and Richard Harrison. "Paleography: Handwriting, 1800s." *Trails to Churchill*

County (Churchill County Historical and Genealogical Society) 6 (Fall 1988): 11-13.

Haselden, R.B. *Scientific Aids for the Study of Manuscripts*. Oxford, England: Oxford University Press for the Bibliographical Society, 1935.

Hayward, John. *A Gazetteer of the United States of America*. Hartford: Case, Tiffany and Co., 1853.

Heal, Ambrose. *The English Writing-Masters and Their Copy-Books, 1570-1800: A Biographical Dictionary and a Bibliography*. 1931. Reprint. Hildesheim, 1962.

Hector, Leonard Charles. *The Handwriting of English Documents.* 2nd ed. 1966. Reprint. Dorking, Surrey, England: Kohler and Coombes Ltd., 1980.
Illustrations from old English documents, with transcriptions, historical background, and a bibliography. This is one of the standard British paleography texts. See especially Chapter 6, "English Handwriting Since 1500."

Helmbold, F. Wilbur. *Tracing Your Ancestry: A Step-by-Step Guide to Researching Your Family History*. Birmingham, Ala.: Oxmoor House, 1976.

Hill, Ronald A. "Interpreting the Symbols and Abbreviations in 16th and 17th Century English Documents." *On to Richmond: Four Centuries of Family History; Federation of Genealogical Societies and Virginia Genealogical Society,* 12-15 Oct. 1994; Richmond, Va., pp. 162-65, T-61. (Repeat Performance, 2911 Crabapple Lane, Hobart, IN 46342)

______. "Interpreting the Symbols and Abbreviations in 16th and 17th Century English Documents." *Genealogical Journal* 21 (1993): 1-13.
A valuable overview of English paleography and abbreviations.

How to Read English Documents. Salt Lake City: Family History World, n.d.

Howells, Cyndi. *Netting Your Ancestors: Genealogical Research on the Internet*. Baltimore: Genealogical Publishing Co., 1997.
A useful guide to the Internet for genealogists, written by one of the experts on this subject.

Hunter, Dean J. "Handwriting Workshop–Reading British Documents." *From Sea to Shining Sea; Federation of Genealogical Societies and Seattle Genealogical Society*, 20-23 Sept. 1995; Seattle, Wash., T-60. (Repeat Performance, 2911 Crabapple Lane, Hobart, IN 46342)

Iredale, David. *Enjoying Archives: What They Are, Where to Find Them, How to Use Them*. Chichester, Sussex, England: Phillimore, 1985.
See especially Chapter 12, "Palaeography and Diplomatic."

Irvine, Martin. *Paleography and Codicology: Introductory Bibliography*. Online. Available: http://www.georgetown.edu/labyrinth/subjects/mss/paleobib.html

Ison, Alf. *A Secretary Hand ABC Book*. 1982. Reprint. Reading, England: Berkshire Books, 1994.
An illustrated and basic approach to reading secretary hand. This small booklet plainly shows how to read secretary hand.

Jackson, Donald. *The Story of Writing*. New York: Taplinger Publishing Co., 1981.
The history and origins of writing; nicely illustrated.

Jacobus, Donald Lines. *Genealogy as Pastime and Profession*. 2nd ed. Baltimore: Genealogical Publishing Co., 1968.
Helpful advice for American genealogists. See especially Chapter 18, "Dates and the Calendar."

Jean, Georges. *Writing: The Story of Alphabets and Scripts*. New York: Harry N. Abrams, 1992.

Jenkins, John. *The Art of Writing*. Boston: Isaiah Thomas and Ebenezer T. Andrews, 1791.

Jenkinson, Hilary. "Elizabethan Handwritings: A Preliminary Sketch." *The Library*, 4th series, vol. 3, no. 1 (1 June 1922): 1-52.

______. *The Later Court Hands in England from the Fifteenth to the Seventeenth Century*. 2 vols. Cambridge, England: Cambridge University Press, 1927; New York: Frederick Ungar Publishing, 1969.

A scholarly survey of English paleography, with useful illustrations, transcriptions, and alphabets. Illustrations taken from public records. Helpful transcripts.

______. "Notes on the Study of English Punctuation of the Sixteenth Century." *The Review of English Studies* 2 (April 1926): 152-58.

______. *Palaeography and the Practical Study of Court Hand.* Cambridge, England: Cambridge University Press, 1915.

______. "The Teaching and Practice of Handwriting in England." *History* 11 (July 1926): 130-38, 211-18.

______. "The Use of Arabic and Roman Numerals in English Archives." *The Antiquaries Journal* 6 (1926).

Johnson, Arta F. *A Guide to the Spelling and Pronunciation of German Names.* (Columbus, Ohio): A.F. Johnson, 1981.

______. *How to Read German Church Records Without Knowing Much German* (Columbus, Ohio): A.F. Johnson, 1980.

Johnson, Charles and Hilary Jenkinson. *English Court Hand, A.D. 1066 to 1500, Illustrated Chiefly from Public Records*. 2 vols. 1915. Reprint. New York: F. Ungar Publishing Co., 1967.
Evolution of court hand, abbreviations, facsimiles, and transcripts.

Johnston, Edward. *Writing & Illuminating & Lettering.* New York: Pitman, 1948.

Judge, Cyril Bathurst. *Specimens of Sixteenth-Century English Handwriting Taken from Contemporary Public and Private Records*. Cambridge, Mass.: Harvard University Press, 1935.
Facsimiles and alphabets.

Kemp, Thomas Jay. *Virtual Roots: A Guide to Genealogy and Local History on the World Wide*

Web. Wilmington, Del.: Scholarly Resources, 1997.
Useful for identifying genealogical and historical sites on the Internet.

Kennedy, Benjamin Hall. *The Shorter Latin Primer*. Revised by J.W. Bartram. London: Longman Group Ltd., 1931.

Ker, Neil Ripley. *Books, Collectors, and Libraries*. Edited by Andrew G. Watson. London: Ronceverte, 1985.

______. *English Manuscripts in the Century After the Norman Conquest*. Oxford: Clarendon Press, 1960.

Kirkham, E. Kay. *The Handwriting of American Records for a Period of 300 Years.* Logan, Utah: Everton Publishers, 1973.
A general introduction to reading early American handwriting. Appendixes include foreign alphabets, a document written by Roger Williams, and a glossary of words, terms, phrases, and legal terminology. This work is especially useful for beginners.

______. *How to Read the Handwriting and Records of Early America.* Rev. ed. Salt Lake City: Deseret Book Co., 1965.
A revised edition of this title was reprinted by Everton Publishers in 1973.

______. *Simplified Genealogy for Americans*. Salt Lake City: Deseret Book Co., 1968.
See especially Chapter 15, "Old Handwriting and Records."

Knight, Stan. *Historical Scripts: A Handbook for Calligraphers*. London: Adam & Charles Black (Publishers) Ltd., 1984; New York: Taplinger Publishing Co., 1986.
Glossary of terms, example documents with transcriptions, and a useful bibliography.

Lackey, Richard S. *Cite Your Sources: A Manual for Documenting Family Histories and Genealogical Records*. New Orleans: Polyanthos, 1980.
This is a standard genealogical reference source that gives guidelines for citing sources. See also Elizabeth Shown Mills, *Evidence! Citation & Analysis for the Family Historian.*

Lamont-Brown, Raymond. "Genealogy and Paleography: Deciphering Old Documents." *Ancestry Newsletter* 10 (January 1991): 3-7.

______. "Genealogy and Paleography: Deciphering Old Documents." *Prospector* (Antelope Valley Genealogical Society) 14 (May 1992): 27-29. Reprint.

Land Indentures Collection, 1613-1881. N.p., n.d. Copy at Harold B. Lee Library, Special Collections, Brigham Young University, Provo, Utah.
Original English land indentures covering the time period 1613-1881.

Langston, Pamela M. "Deciphering Old Documents." *Blackhawk Genealogical Society Quarterly* 15 (Fall 1988): 9-13.

Larson, Frances Dunfee. *The Genealogist's Dictionary*. Bellevue, Wash.: The author, 1986.
A selected list of terms and abbreviations found in genealogical and historical research. Although this work is incomplete, it is still a useful reference.

Late-Medieval Religious Texts and Their Transmission. Edited by A.J. Minnis. Cambridge, England: D.S. Brewer, 1994.

Latham, Ronald Edward. *Revised Medieval Latin Word-List from British and Irish Sources.* London: Oxford University Press, 1965.

Linder, Bill R. *How to Trace Your Family History*. New York: Everest House, 1978.
See especially Chapter 18, "The Early Handwriting," and Chapter 19, "Abstracting Information from Documents."

Little, Thomas Vance. *Legal Terms for the Genealogist.* Nashville, Tenn.: Southern Resources Unlimited, 1980.
A selected list of legal and court terms found in genealogical and historical research.

Lowe, E. A. "The Handwriting of the Middle Ages." In *The Legacy of the Middle Ages.* Edited by Charles George Crump and E.F. Jacob. Oxford, England: Clarendon Press, 1926.

______. *English Uncial.* Oxford, England: Clarendon Press, 1960.

McCutcheon, Marc. *The Writer's Guide to Everyday Life in the 1800s.* Cincinnati: Writer's Digest Books, 1993.
Useful for those studying or writing about the nineteenth century.

McKerrow, Ronald Brunless. *The Capital Letters in Elizabethan Handwriting.* London: Sidgwick & Jackson, ca. 1927. Reprinted from *The Review of English Studies*, vol. 3, no. 9 (Jan. 1927): 28-36.

McLaughlin, Eve. *Further Steps in Family History.* 1990. Reprint. Newbury, Berkshire, England: Countryside Books, 1995.
See Chapter 2, "Reading Old Handwriting." This work is nicely illustrated.

______. *Reading Old Handwriting.* 3rd ed. Aylesbury, England: The author, 1995 (earlier editions published by Federation of Family History Societies).
This small booklet includes many handwriting illustrations.

______. *Simple Latin for Family Historians.* 5th ed. Aylesbury, England: Varneys Press, 1994.
Useful for beginning genealogists studying Latin.

Madan, Falconer. "Mediaeval British Handwriting." In *Mediaeval England,* a new edition of Barnard's *Companion to English History.* Edited by H.W.C. Davis. Oxford, England, 1924, pp. 451-69.

Maness, Ruth Ellen. "This Record is Fraktured!! Or The Chicken Walked Here!! Learning to Read the Gothic Script: Principles and Procedures." *From Sea to Shining Sea; Federation of Genealogical Societies and Seattle Genealogical Society*, 20-23 Sept. 1995; Seattle, Wash., T-61. (Repeat Performance, 2911 Crabapple Lane, Hobart, IN 46342)

Manuscripts, Paleography, Codicology. Online. Available: http://www.georgetown.edu/labyrinth/subjects/mss/mss.html

Markwell, F.C. and Pauline Saul. *Facsimiles of Documents of Use to Family Historians*. [Birmingham, England]: Federation of Family History Societies, 1987.
Examples of documents used in British family history research.

Marshall, Richard Lucas. *The Historical Criticism of Documents*. London: Society for Promoting Christian Knowledge, 1920.

Martin, Charles Trice, comp. *The Record Interpreter: A Collection of Abbreviations, Latin Words and Names Used in English Historical Manuscripts and Records*. 2nd ed. 1910. Reprint. Dorking, Surrey, England: Kohler & Coombes, 1976; Chichester, Sussex, England: Phillimore, 1982.
A valuable reference and glossary of Latin words, abbreviations, and Latin name forms.

Meyerink, Kory and Jayare Roberts. "Handwriting Workshop: Early American Handwriting." *From Sea to Shining Sea; Federation of Genealogical Societies and Seattle Genealogical Society*, 20-23 Sept. 1995; Seattle, Wash., T-62. (Repeat Performance, 2911 Crabapple Lane, Hobart, IN 46342)

Miller, Fredric. *Arranging and Describing Archives and Manuscripts*. Chicago: Society of American Archivists, 1990.

Mills, Elizabeth Shown. *Evidence! Citation & Analysis for the Family Historian*. Baltimore: Genealogical Publishing Co., 1997.
An excellent reference guide to source citations for genealogists.

______. "Skillbuilding: Producing Quality Research Notes." *OnBoard* [Board for Certification of Genealogists Newsletter] 3 (January 1997): 8.

______. "Skillbuilding: Transcribing Source Materials." *OnBoard* [Board for Certification of Genealogists Newsletter] 2 (January 1996): 8.
Valuable instructions for correctly transcribing old documents.

Mitchell, C.A. *Documents and Their Scientific Examination*. 2nd ed. n.p., 1935.

Moorman, Charles. *Editing the Middle English Manuscript*. Jackson, Miss.: University Press of Mississippi, 1975.

Morison, Stanley. *American Copybooks: An Outline of Their History from Colonial to Modern Times*. Philadelphia, 1951.

______. "The Development of Hand-Writing: An Outline." In Ambrose Heal, *The English Writing-Masters*, pp. ix-xxi, xxv-xxxiii.
The history of handwriting since the Renaissance.

Morse, Jedediah. *The American Gazetteer.* New York: Arvo Press, 1971.
A useful gazetteer of American place names and locality references.

Morris, Janet. *A Latin Glossary for Family and Local Historians*. 1989. Reprint. Birmingham, England: Federation of Family History Societies (Publications) Ltd., 1995.
Although this booklet is not a comprehensive dictionary, it includes many Latin words found in records of interest to genealogists.

Moulton, H.R. *Palaeography, Genealogy and Topography: Historical Documents, Ancient Charters, Leases, Court Rolls, Pedigrees, Marriage Settlements, Fine Seals, Commissions, Papal Bulls, Hand-Drawn Maps, and Autographs*. Surrey, England: H.R. Moulton, [1930]; London: Geo. Aug. Mate & Son.

Munby, Lionel Maxwell. *Reading Tudor and Stuart Handwriting*. Chichester, Sussex, England: British Association for Local History, 1988.
A popular, but brief, study of early English handwriting.

______. *Secretary Hand: A Beginner's Introduction.* Cromford, Derbyshire, England: British Association for Local History, 1984.
A small booklet showing the secretary hand alphabet. Valuable illustrations.

Munger, Donna Bingham. *Pennsylvania Land Records: A History and Guide for Research.* Wilmington, Del.: Scholarly Resources, 1991.

See especially examples of early Pennsylvania land records.

Murray, Sabina J. *Deciphering Old Handwriting*. Online. Available: http://www.firstct.com/fv/oldhand.html
A useful Internet genealogy site and general introduction to reading early American handwriting. Especially valuable for beginning researchers. Illustrated.

Myrick, Shelby, Jr., comp. *Glossary of Legal Terminology: An Aid to Genealogists.* Technical Leaflet No. 55. Nashville, Tenn.: American Association for State and Local History, 1970.
A short glossary of legal terms found in early American records. This reference is of interest to genealogists and historians.

Nash, Ray. *American Penmanship, 1800-1850.* Worcester, Mass.: American Antiquarian Society, 1969.

______. *American Writing Masters and Copybooks: History and Bibliography through Colonial Times*. Boston: Colonial Society of Massachusetts, 1959.

______. *Some Early American Writing Books and Masters.* Hanover, N.H.: The author, 1942.

National Archives and Records Administration. *Guide to Federal Records in the National Archives of the United States*. Compiled by Robert B. Matchette, et al. 3 vols. Washington, D.C.: National Archives and Records Administration, 1995.
Describes federal records in the National Archives and Records Administration as of 1994. Arranged by National Archives Record Groups. These volumes are nicely indexed. They are also available online from the National Archives web site: http://www.nara.gov

______. *Guide to Genealogical Research in the National Archives*. Rev. ed. Washington, D.C.: National Archives and Records Administration, 1985.
A well-illustrated and excellent guide to genealogical and historical records housed at the National Archives and its regional archives. Many of the records are on microfilm.

______. *Teaching with Documents: Using Primary Sources from the National Archives.*

Washington, D.C.: National Archives and Records Administration and National Council for the Social Studies, 1989.
Valuable for a study of documents housed at the National Archives, Washington, D.C.

The New Palaeographical Society. *Facsimiles of Ancient Manuscripts*. Edited by E.A. Bond, E.M. Thompson, G.F. Warner, and J.P. Gilson. London. 1st series, 1903-12; 2nd series, 1913-32; indexes, 1914, 1932.

Newton, Kenneth Charles. "Reading Medieval Local Records." *The Amateur Historian*, vol. 3, no. 2, pp. 81-93. Reprint. *The Amateur Historian* 7 (1966): 88-91.
Documents selected are from the Essex Record Office.

______. *Medieval Local Records: A Reading Aid.* London: The Historical Association, 1986.

Nickell, Joe. *Pen, Ink & Evidence: A Study of Writing and Writing Materials for the Penman, Collector, and Document Detective*. Lexington, Ky.: University Press of Kentucky, 1990.
A highly useful reference for genealogists and historians.

Osley, A.S., ed. *Calligraphy and Palaeography: Essays Presented to Alfred Fairbank on His 70th Birthday.* New York: October House, 1966.

Ostwald, L.T. "Resolving Discrepancies in Genealogical Dates." *CO-Pal-Am Newsletter* 9 (Dec. 1992): 3-4.

The Oxford English Dictionary. 2nd ed. 20 vols. Oxford, England: Clarendon Press, 1989.
Known as OED, this enormous dictionary is especially valuable in identifying abbreviations, occupations, and terms found in older American and British documents. A second edition of this title is available on compact disc (Oxford, England: Oxford University Press, 1992). See also *Encyclopedia Britannica*, 11th ed. (1910). Available in many libraries.

Oxford Latin Dictionary. Edited by P.G.W. Glare. 1982. Reprint. Oxford: Oxford University Press, 1996.
A comprehensive Latin dictionary and reference source; available in many libraries.

Palaeography: Examples of Historical Documents, Ancient Charters and Deeds, Seals, Autographs, etc. Surrey, England: n.p., n.d.

"Palaeography." In *The New Cambridge Bibliography of English Literature*. Edited by George Watson. Cambridge, England: Cambridge University Press, 1974, columns 209-220.

"Paleography." In *The Encyclopedia Americana*, vol. 21, p. 296 (Danbury, Conn.: Grolier, 1996).

"Paleography." In *The New Encyclopaedia Britannica*, 15th ed., vol. 9, pp. 78-79; vol. 20, pp. 609-11. Chicago: Encyclopaedia Britannica, 1997.

Parkes, Malcolm Beckwith. *English Cursive Book Hands, 1250-1500*. 1969. Reprint. London: Scolar Press, 1979; Berkeley, Calif.: University of California Press, 1980.
Valuable handwriting examples and transcriptions for the time period 1250-1500.

______. *Scribes, Scripts, and Readers*. London: Hambledon Press, 1991.

______. *Pause and Effect: An Introduction to the History of Punctuation in the West.* Berkeley, Calif.: University of California Press, 1993.

Petti, Anthony G. *English Literary Hands from Chaucer to Dryden.* Cambridge, Mass.: Harvard University Press, 1977.
A scholarly study of early English handwriting. Describes the handwriting of literary texts in England from the late fourteenth century to the end of the seventeenth century. It includes a comprehensive set of examples and facsimiles with transcriptions.

Powicke, Frederick Maurice and E.B. Fryde, eds. *Handbook of British Chronology*. 2nd ed. London: Offices of the Royal Historical Society, 1961.

Preservation of Historical Records. Washington, D.C.: National Academy Press, 1986.
Discusses preservation techniques at the National Archives.

Preston, Jean F. and Laetitia Yeandle. *English Handwriting, 1400-1650: An Introductory Manual.*

Binghamton, N.Y.: Center for Medieval and Early Renaissance Studies, State University of New York at Binghamton, 1992.
A scholarly and well-produced manual with clear illustrations; includes bibliographies.

Purvis, John Stanley. *Notarial Signs from the York Archiepiscopal Records.* London: St. Anthony's Press, 1957.

Quaritch, Bernard. *Palaeography: Notes Upon the History of Writing*. London: privately printed, 1899.

"Report on Editing Historical Documents." In *Bulletin of the Institute of Historical Research*, vol. 1. London, 1923. Reprint, London: Wm. Dawson & Sons Ltd., 1964.

Richardson, John. *The Local Historian's Encyclopedia.* 2nd ed. New Barnet, Herts, England: Historical Publications Ltd., 1986.
See especially the "Palaeography" section.

Robinson, Andrew. *The Story of Writing*. New York: Thames and Hudson, 1995.

Robinson, Fred Colson. *The Editing of Old English.* Oxford, England: Blackwell, 1994.

Rose, Christine and Kay Germain Ingalls. *The Complete Idiot's Guide to Genealogy*. New York: Alpha Books, Macmillan Company, 1997.

Rubincam, Milton. *Pitfalls in Genealogical Research.* Salt Lake City: Ancestry Publishing, 1987.
See especially Chapter 5, "The 1752 Calendar Change."

Runestone Press. Geography Department. *Scrawl! Writing in Ancient Times*. Minneapolis: Runestone Press, 1994.
A history of writing, writing instruments, materials, and printing.

Rycraft, Ann, comp. *English Mediaeval Handwriting*. 2nd ed. York, England: University of York, Borthwick Institute of Historical Research, 1973.

______, comp. *Sixteenth and Seventeenth Century Handwriting: Series 1.* 3rd ed. St. Anthony's Press, 1972 (York, England: Borthwick Institute of Historical Research, vol. 1).

______, comp. *Sixteenth and Seventeenth Century Handwriting: Series 2.* 3rd ed. St. Anthony's Press, 1972 (York, England: Borthwick Institute of Historical Research, vol. 2).

______, comp. *Sixteenth and Seventeenth Century Wills, Inventories and Other Probate Documents.* University of York, 1973.

Saunders, William. *Ancient Handwritings: An Introductory Manual for Intending Students of Palaeography and Diplomatic.* Walton-on-Thames, England: Chas.A. Bernau, 1909.
An introductory text with handwriting illustrations.

Schaefer, Christina K. *The Center: A Guide to Genealogical Research in the National Capital Area.* Baltimore: Genealogical Publishing Co., 1996.
Describes the genealogical holdings of the National Archives, Library of Congress, DAR Library, and other repositories in the Washington, D.C., area.

Schulz, Herbert C. "The Teaching of Handwriting in Tudor and Stuart Times." *The Huntington Library Quarterly* 6 (August 1943): 381-425.

Scott, Henry Thomas. *A Guide to the Collector of Historical Documents, Literary Manuscripts, and Autograph Letters, etc.* London: S.J. Davey, 1891.

Scottish Records Association. *Scottish Handwriting, 1500-1700: A Self-help Pack.* Edinburgh: Scottish Record Office, 1994.

Scripta: The History of Handwriting. Online. Available:
http://www.ets.bris.ac/uk/tosolini/scripta
An experimental project that aims at an easier approach to the study of paleography.

Sealock, Richard Burl, Margaret M. Sealock, and Margaret S. Powell. *Bibliography of Place-Name Literature: United States and Canada.* 3rd ed. Chicago: American Library Association, 1982.

Seid, Timothy W. *Interpreting Ancient Manuscripts*. Online. Available: http://www.stg.brown.edu/projects/mss/overview.html

Shea, Jonathan D. and William F. Hoffman. *Following the Paper Trail: A Multilingual Translation Guide*. New Milford, Conn.: Language & Lineage Press, 1991.

Simpson, Elizabeth, comp. *Latin Word-List for Family Historians*. Solihull, West Midlands, England: Federation of Family History Societies, 1985.

Simpson, Grant Gray. *Scottish Handwriting, 1150-1650: An Introduction to the Reading of Documents.* 1973. Reprint. Aberdeen, Scotland: Aberdeen University Press, 1977.
This is the major guide to reading Old Scottish handwriting.

Skeat, Walter William. *Twelve Facsimiles of Old English Manuscripts, with Transcriptions and An Introduction*. Oxford, England: Clarendon Press, 1892.
Copies of twelve Old English documents, with transcriptions.

Smith, Charles. *The American Gazetteer, or Geographical Companion.* New York: Charles Smith, 1797.

Smith, Kenneth Lee. *Genealogical Dates: A User-Friendly Guide*. Camden, Maine: Picton Press, 1994.
A major reference source for identifying dates. This work is an expanded version of the author's *A Practical Guide to Dating Systems for Genealogists* (1983).

______. *German Church Books: Beyond the Basics*. Camden, Maine: Picton Press, 1989.

Sperry, Kip. "Reading Early American Handwriting." *Traveling Historic Trails; National Genealogical Society and Middle Tennessee Genealogical Society*, 8-11 May 1996; Nashville, Tenn., F-85. (Repeat Performance, 2911 Crabapple Lane, Hobart, IN 46342)

Stewart, George R. *American Place-Names: A Concise and Selective Dictionary for the Continental United States of America*. New York: Oxford University Press, 1970.

Stieg, Lewis. "An Introduction to Palaeography for Librarians." Ph.D. diss., University of Chicago, 1935. Microfilm, University of Chicago Library, Department of Photoduplication.

Storrer, Norman J. *A Genealogical and Demographic Handbook of German Handwriting, 17th-19th Centuries*. Pleasant Grove, Utah: The author, 1977.
Useful in studying early German handwriting found in American records.

Strassburger, Ralph Beaver. *Pennsylvania German Pioneers: A Publication of the Original Lists of Arrivals in the Port of Philadelphia from 1727 to 1808.* Edited by William John Hinke. 3 vols. Norristown, Pa.: Pennsylvania German Society, 1934.
See especially volume 2, facsimile signatures. Useful for studying early signatures.

Stryker-Rodda, Harriet. *Colonial Handwriting Problems.* World Conference on Records and Genealogical Seminar, Area I-37. Salt Lake City: Genealogical Society, 1969.
An overview to reading American handwriting, with letter forms and selected examples from various documents.

______. "Understanding Colonial Handwriting." *New Jersey History* 98 (Spring-Summer 1980): 81-96. Reprint. Newark, N.J.: New Jersey Historical Society, 1980.

______. *Understanding Colonial Handwriting.* Rev. ed. Baltimore: Genealogical Publishing Co., 1986.
This small booklet is a practical overview for reading colonial American handwriting. Includes some examples of colonial letter forms and script.

Stuart, Denis. *Latin for Local and Family Historians: A Beginner's Guide*. Chichester, Sussex, England: Phillimore, 1995.
A valuable guide to basic Latin grammar. Includes exercises with answers.

______. *Manorial Records: An Introduction to Their Transcription and Translation*. Chichester, Sussex, England: Phillimore, 1992.

Szucs, Loretto Dennis and Sandra Hargreaves Luebking. *The Archives: A Guide to the National*

Archives Field Branches. Salt Lake City: Ancestry Publishing, 1988.
Describes genealogical holdings of National Archives regional archives. Illustrated.

______, eds. *The Source: A Guidebook of American Genealogy.* Rev. ed. Salt Lake City: Ancestry, 1997.
One of the standard American genealogical reference sources.

Tannenbaum, Samuel Aaron. *The Handwriting of the Renaissance.* 1930. Reprint. New York: Frederick Ungar Publishing Co., 1967.

Temple. Elzbieta. *Anglo-Saxon Manuscripts, 900-1066.* London: Harvey Miller, 1976.

Thompson, Sir Edward Maunde. *A Handbook of Greek and Latin Palaeography.* Chicago: Argonaut, 1966.

______. *An Introduction to Greek and Latin Palaeography.* 1912. Reprint. New York: B. Franklin, 1966.

______. "The History of English Handwriting, A.D., 700-1400." *Transactions of the Bibliographical Society* 5 (1898-1901): 109-42, 213-53.

Thompson, Samuel Harrison. *Latin Bookhands of the Later Middle Ages, 1100-1500.* London: Cambridge University Press, 1969.

Thornton, Tamara Plakins. *Handwriting in America: A Cultural History.* New Haven, Conn.: Yale University Press, 1996.
A discussion of American handwriting styles from the colonial to modern period, although this is not a paleography manual. This is a scholarly work.

Thoyts, E. E. *or* Emma Elizabeth. *See* Cope, Emma Elizabeth (Thoyts)

Tillott, P.M. "Transcribing Parish Registers." *The Amateur Historian* 7 (1967): 138-45.

Tschichold, Jan. *An Illustrated History of Writing and Lettering.* London: A. Zwemmer, 1946. An introduction and history of writing; illustrated.

Ullman, Berthold Louis. *Ancient Writing and Its Influence*. 1932. Reprint. Cambridge, Mass.: M.I.T. Press, 1969 (with a new introduction by Julian Brown).

United States. National Archives and Records Administration. *See* National Archives and Records Administration.

University of Chicago Press. *The Chicago Manual of Style.* 14th ed. Chicago: University of Chicago Press, 1993.

University of London. Library. *The Palaeography Collection.* 2 vols. Boston: G.K. Hall & Co., 1968. Volume 1, Author Catalogue; volume 2, Subject Catalogue.

Webb, Clifford. *Dates and Calendars for the Genealogist*. London: Society of Genealogists, 1994.

Westward Expansion, 1842-1912: Teachers Guide. Boca Raton, Fl.: National Archives and Records Administration and Social Issues Resources Series, n.d.
See for copies of documents from the National Archives, with selected transcriptions.

Whalley, Joyce Irene. *English Handwriting, 1540-1853*. London: Her Majesty's Stationery Office, 1969.

______. *The Pen's Excellence: A Pictorial History of Western Calligraphy.* New York: Taplinger Publishing Co., 1982.

______. *The Student's Guide to Western Calligraphy: An Illustrated Survey*. Boulder, Colo.: Shambhala Publications, 1984.

______. *Writing Implements and Accessories*. Detroit: Gale Research Co., 1975.

Whipple, Blaine. "Genealogical Dates." *Roots Users Group Newsletter*, Portland, Oregon 3 (Nov.-Dec. 1992): 211-13.

Wheelock, Frederic M. *Latin: An Introductory Course Based on Ancient Authors*. 2nd ed. New York: Barnes & Noble, 1960.

Wolpe, Berthold L., ed. *A Newe Booke of Copies, 1574*. London, Oxford University Press, 1962. See especially the secretary hand examples in this book.

Woodard, Nell Sachse. "Strokes from a Quill Pen." *The Genealogical Helper* (Sept.-Oct. 1982): 7-17.

"Words, Words." *Quill Pen* 32 (February 1990): 12.

Wright, Andrew. *Court Hand Restored, or the Student's Assistant in Reading Old Deeds, Charters, Records, etc.* 8th ed. 1867. Reprint. Ashland, Oregon: Gareth L. Mark, 1989.
An illustrated introduction to court hand, with transcriptions. Includes a glossary of Latin words. Other editions were published and are also useful.

Wright, Cyril Ernest. *English Vernacular Hands from the Twelfth to the Fifteenth Centuries.* Oxford, England: Oxford University Press, 1960.

Wright, Raymond S. III. "Latin for Genealogists." *A Place to Explore; National Genealogical Society and San Diego Genealogical Society*, 3-6 May 1995; San Diego, Calif., pp. 193-96. (Repeat Performance, 2911 Crabapple Lane, Hobart, IN 46342)

______. *The Genealogist's Handbook: Modern Methods for Researching Family History.* Chicago: American Library Association, 1995.
Includes many examples of early American records and descriptions of records.

Yeandle, Laetitia. "The Evolution of Handwriting in the English-Speaking Colonies of America." *The American Archivist* 43 (Summer 1980): 294-311.
This well-illustrated article discusses the evolution of handwriting in colonial America.

Documents and Transcriptions

Clariſsa

Suſsana

Maſs

Miſsiſsippi

Tenneſsee

Roſs

Auguſt

Miſsouri

Wd

Examples of the old style, long *s*, found in American documents from the seventeenth century to the middle eighteenth century. Note also the *l* in Clarissa, the ending *a* in Sussana, the rounded ending *s* in Mass, the ending *ee* in Tennessee (which looks like a *u*), the ending *s* in Ross, the ending *t* in August, and the ending *s* in Ch^{s}.

Clarissa

Sussana

Mass [Massachusetts]

Mississippi

Tennessee

Ross

August

Missouri

Ch^{s} [Charles]

Adapted from E. Kay Kirkham, *The Handwriting of American Records for a Period of 300 Years* (Logan, Utah: Everton Publishers, 1973), p. 42. Courtesy Everton Publishers.

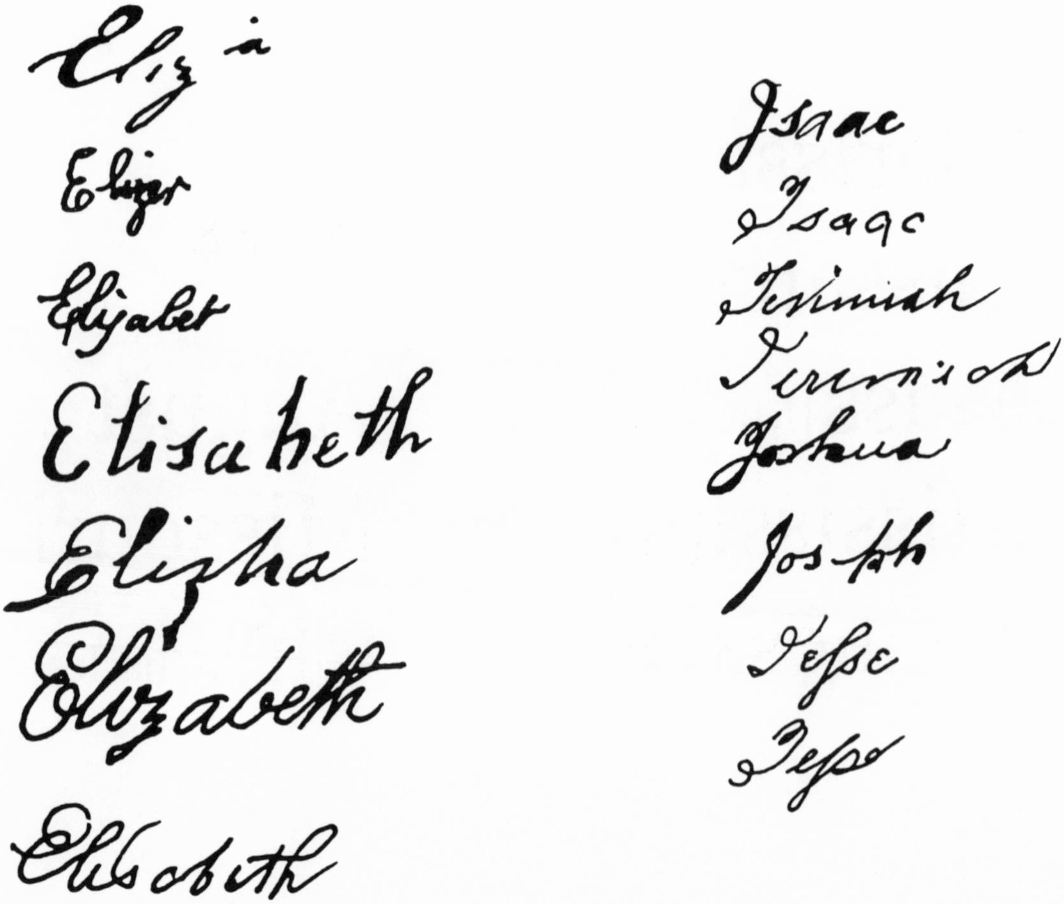
Elisabeth
Elizabeth
Isaac
Joshua
Jesse

Eliz[a]

Eliza [Elizet] [Elizabeth]

Elisabet [Elizabet]

Elisabeth

Elizha [Elizabeth]

Elizabeth

Elisabeth

Isaac

Isaac

Jerimiah

Jeremiah

Joshua

Jos[e]ph

Jesse

Jesse

Harriet Stryker-Rodda, *Understanding Colonial Handwriting*, rev. ed. (Baltimore: Genealogical Publishing Co., 1986), pp. 24, 26. Courtesy Genealogical Publishing Company.

-Abigail. Spolding

Peggy Mitchel

-Elizabath Kimpfield

-Abigail Mors

Anoxa Fletcher

-Hannah Boardman

-Milenda Senter

-Elmina Varnum

-Gemima Glover

-Polley Fellows

-Polley Barnes

-Sarah Fletcher

-James Varnum

Nathan Fletcher

Edward Senter

Joshua Fletcher

Abigail Spalding
Peggy Mitchel
Elizabath Kimpfield
[Rimpfield]
Abigail Mors
Anora Sleeper
Hannah Boardman
Milenda Senter
Elmira Varnum
Gemima [Jemima] Glover
Polley Fellows
Polley Barned [Banned]
Sarah Fletcher

James Varnum
Nathan Fletcher
Edward Senter
Joshua Fletcher

Bridgewater, New Hampshire, Congregational Church Records, 1817. Original records at New Hampshire Historical Society, Concord, N.H. Copy in possession of Kip Sperry. For an extensive index of New Hampshire residents, see William Copeley, *Index to Genealogies in New Hampshire Town Histories* (Concord, N.H.: New Hampshire Historical Society, n.d.). Notice in the above document that the capital "K" and capital "R" look very similar. Notice also that the small "n" and "r" look very much alike.

Months

January Jan^{e} Jan:
February Febry feb:
March March march
Aprill Aprill Ap^{ll}:
Maye May may
June June June
July July July
August Augt Aug:
September Sept^{e} Sept
October Octob^{r} Octobr
November Novemb^{r} Nov^{e}
December December decemb^{r}

Months

January	Jan[r]	Jan:
ffebruary	ffebry	ffeb:
March	March	march
Aprill	Aprill	Ap[ll]:
Maye	May	may
June	June	June
July	July	July
August	Aug[t]	Aug:
September	Sept[r]	Sept
October	Octob[r]	Octobr
Nouembr	Novemb[r]	Nov.[r]
December	Decembr_	decem[b]

Kent P. Bailey and Ransom B. True, *A Guide to Seventeenth-Century Virginia Court Handwriting* (Richmond, Va.: Association for the Preservation of Virginia Antiquities, 1980), p. 26. Courtesy Association for the Preservation of Virginia Antiquities.

Randolph, Portage Co. Ohio
Jan 13. 1874

Dr. F. V. Hayden
Washington. D.C.

Dear Sir.

I have just read, with more than common interest, your review of The Hayden Expedition as published in the N. Y. Tribune of Jan. 6th.

In speaking of the Publications of the Survey you say. "The annual reports are usually printed in large editions, & distributed freely among the people." I desire very much to possess a copy of these reports. Be so good as to inform me how I may be enabled to obtain them.

Yours truly

H. L. Smalley

Randolph, Portage Co. Ohio

Jan 13. 1874

Dr. F.V. Hayden

Washington. D.C.

Dear Sir.

I have Just read, with more than commen interest, your review of the Hayden Expedition as published in the N. Y. Tribune of Jan. 6."

In speaking of the Publications of the Survey you say, "The annual reports are usually printed in large editions, & distributed freely among the people." I desire very much to possess a copy of these reports. Be so good as to inform me how I may be enabled to obtain them.

Yours truly

H. D. Smalley

Letter from H.D. Smalley to Ferdinand Hayden, 13 Jan. 1874. National Archives and Records Administration (RG 57). See also *Westward Expansion, 1842-1912* (Boca Raton, Fl.: Social Issues Resources Series).

Family Register.

Eliza Parmele Hubbell. Born at Buffalo Nov. 1st 1866
254 Pearl St. above Chippewa St Baptised. January 17th 1867
by Rev Dr. Pitkin

Edward Parmele Hubbell Born at Buffalo N.Y.
February 7th 1869 - Baptised May 9th Sunday. 1869. by
Rev Dr. Witherspoon -

William Spring Hubbell Born at Toledo Ohio
September 10th 1871 - Sunday morning 4 OClock.
Baptised January 7th 1872. Sunday. by
Rev Dr. Mulchahey -

Jannie Waterbury Hubbell Born at Toledo Ohio
September 6th. 1874. Saturday. Half past 2 O'Clock in
the morning. 685 Erie St. between Locust & Lagrange.
Baptised 27th January. 27th 1873 by Rev Dr Mulchahey -

Family Register.

Eliza Parmele Hubbell Born at Buffalo Nov. 1st 1866
254 Pearl St. above Chippewa St. Baptised. January 17th 1867
by Rev. Dr. Pitkin

Edward Parmele Hubbell Born at Buffalo N.Y.
February 7th 1869– Baptised May 9th Sunday. 1869 by
Rev. Dr. Witherspoon –

William Spring Hubbell Born at Toledo Ohio
September 10th 1871 – Sunday Morning 4 O Clock
Baptised January 7th 1872. Sunday by
Rev. Dr. Mulchahey –

Fannie Waterbury Hubbell Born at Toledo Ohio
September 6th 1874. Saturday. Half past 2 O'clock in
the Morning. 685 Erie St. between Locust & Lagrange
Baptised 27th January 27th 1875 by Rev. Dr. Mulchahey

Copy of Hubbell family register in possession of Kip Sperry.

Balt Nov 7th
~~63~~

L Thomas Adgt Gen

Dear Sir

You will please
inform of the wheareabouts of my
three Sons Not having ~~heard~~
from them for a long time and
Since reported killed any
information Concerning them
Will be most thankfully received
by ~~his~~ thair poor old Father
they are Named Peter Cook
Joseph Cook Joshua Cook
Company E 30th Regt U S C T

~~Or~~ please adress Peter
Cook 558 West Baltimore Street

Balt Md

Balt [Baltimore] Nov 7th [1864]

L Thomas Adgt Gen [Adjutant General]

Dear Sir

You will please

inform [me] of the whearebouts of My
three Sons not haveing head [heard]
from them for a long time and
Since repotted [reported] killed any
information concerning them
Will be most thankfully recievd [received]
by their poor old Father
they are Named Peter Cook
Joseph Cook [&] Joshua Cook
Compay [Company] E 30th Regt [Regiment] U S C T [United States
Colored Troups]

please adrees [address] Peter
Cook 558 West Baltimore Street

Balt Md [Baltimore, Maryland]

Civil War letter to Adjutant General Thomas, RG94, Civil War correspondence, National Archives. and Records Administration.

Camp of the 28 Regiment N.C.S.
Wilmington New Hanover Co
December the 18th A.D. 1861

Dear Mother I recived a letter from you on the fourteenth Inst which pleased me very mutch to hear that you were all well and doing well I recived a letter from Cousin Martin Whitaker on the 6 of December stating you had been down to see Grand-mother which I understood in his letter I am in common health at this time you stated in your letter you had some wood and fire halled Jesse Stanly will let you have his oxen this winter to hall with I do not want my oxen to to be worked any at all I got $33,00 Dollars that is what I drew and I sent $30,00 of it home by Thos Anthony I have not heard whither or not you got I want you to write soon and not fail Sarah I want my oxen to be well wintered if you think you have not food enough you had better a bout it before Spring because every thing is going to be very high do not let any person have any salt I will want it before you get any more as cheap as that Mother I can send you plenty of paper if you cannot get there Mother I send you some Tobacco to chew this is very good tobacco Sheriff Dobson is at home if you want to send any thing to me you can send it by him we have any amount of Sweet potatoes here I have some that I brought from home to eat a christmas also some sweet cakes Mrs Cillen sent me John Coe has a discharge and has come home Sarah I will send you $10,00 odd dollars in about three weeks if nothing happens write if you have paid Uncle Silas and Mrs Marbo it or not you must write as soon as you get this letter and not fail write whither you have heard from Liind (mot) and Calvin and Nancy and Mark or not I am going to write them all in a few days if nothing happens you aught to write to Calvin and Nancy by all means I have nothing of mutch importance to write at present

Camp of the 28 Regiment N.C.V.s [North Carolina Volunteers]
Wilmington, New Hanover Co
December the 1st A.D. 1861

Dear Mother I received a letter from you on the fourteenth Inst. [instant] which pleased me very mutch to hear that you were all well and doing well I received a letter from Cousin Martin Whitaker on the 6d of December Stating you had been down to see Grand=mother which I understood in his letter. I am in common health at this time you Stated in your letter you had some wood and pine holled [hauled]. Jesse Stanly will let you have his oxen this winter to holl [haul] with I do not want my oxen to to be worked any at all, I got $33,00 Dollars that is what I drew and I Sent $30,00 of it home by Thos Anthony I have not heared [heard] whither or not you got I want you to write soon and not fail Sarah I want my oxen to be well wintered if you think you have not food enough you had better [be] about it before spring becouse [because] every thing is going to be very high do not let any person have any Salt, I will want it before you get any more as cheap as that Mother I can Send you plenty of paper if you cannot get there Mother I sent you some Tobacco to chew this is very good tobacco. Smith Dobson is at home so if you want to send any thing to me you can Send it by him we have any amount of Sweet potatoes here I have some that I brought from home to eat a [at] christmas also some sweet cakes Mrs. Gillem Sent me John Crae has a discharge and has come home Sarah I will Send you $20,00 odd dollars in about three weeks if nothing happens write if you have paid Uncle Silas and Mrs. Rartis . . . .
you must write as Soon as you get Hiz letter and not fail write whither you have heard from Sion (and) and Calvin and Nancy and Mark or not I am going to write them all in a few days if nothing happens you ought to write to Calvin and Nancy by all means I have nothing of mutch importance to write at present

The Surry County Book: Recollections of the Life, History & Culture of Old Surry County in Northwestern North Carolina, 2nd ed. (Elkin, N.C.: Surry County American Revolution Bicentennial Commission, 1978), p. 74. Courtesy Surry County Historical Society.

WARRANTY DEED—FULL COVENANT. Printed and Sold by BENTON & ANDREWS, Rochester, N. Y.

This Indenture, Made this Thirty first day of March in the year of our Lord one thousand eight hundred and sixty Four BETWEEN Elisebeth North of the Town of Lansing County of Tompkins and State of New york

of the first part, and Vanrensler Doty of the Town of Ithaca County of Tompkins and State of New york

of the second part,

Witnesseth, That the said party of the first part, in consideration of the sum of One Thousand Dollars

to her duly paid, hav sold, and **By These Presents** do grant and convey to the said party of the second part, His heirs and assigns, **All that Tract or Parcel of Land** situate in the Villiage of Ithaca and distinguished as part of lot Number eight of said villiage Bounded on the north by Bufalo Streat on the East by land owned by the said ~~Bais~~ Elisebeth North on the south by lot number Nine owned by Alexander King and on the west by Aurora Streat being in breadth North and south Sixty Six feet and extending east from the said Aurora Streat Sixty one feet Reserveing the wright & use of the well which is on the line for the use of the property adjoining on the East in common with the occupant of the above granted premises

This Indenture, *Made this* Thirty first *day of* March *in the year of our Lord one thousand eight hundred and sixty* Four BETWEEN Elisebeth North of the Town of Lansing County of Tompkins and State of New York...

of the first part, and Vanransler Doty of the Town of Ithaca County of Tompkins and State of New York

....

....*of the second part,*

Witnesseth, *That the said party of the first part, in consideration of the sum of* One Thousand Dollars ....

....

....*to* her *duly paid, has sold, and*

By These Presents *do.........grant and convey to the said party of the second part,*

His *heirs and assigns,* **All that Tract or Parcel of Land** *situate in the* Villiage *of* Ithaca and distinguished as part of lot Number eight of said Villiage Bounded on the north by Buffalo Streat on the East by land owned by the said Mrs Elisebeth North on the South by lot number nine owned by Alexander King and on the west by Aurora Streat being in breadth north and south Sixty Six feet and extending east from the said Aurora Streat Sixty one feet Reserveing the wright & use of the well which is on the line for the use of property adjoining on the east in common with the occupant of the above granted premises

Original 1860 warranty deed in possession of Kip Sperry.

Surry county } Rules and regulations for a school
N. Carolina } for a school

Rule the 1st but one male to go out at a time and the others to stay in the house untill they return.

Rule the 2nd but two females to go out at a time and the others to stay in the house untill they return

Rule the 3rd
no immorral games nor plays what ever

Rule the 4th
no cursing nor swearing nawking nor calling names but call each one by there proper name

Rule the 5th
the schollars must say yes sir & no sir or yes madam & no madam as the nature of the case may be

Rule the 6th
no climbing no wrestling nor throwing rocks at school nor in going to & from school

Rule the 7th
the schollars must not delay there time going to & from school

Rule the 8th
the schollars if meeting with any person going to & from school shal speak potitely to them, but if said person or persons should say any thing that is immorral the schollars shal pass on and not indulge them selves in that which is immorral

Rule the 9th no talking and laughing in time of books

Rules the 10 all males over the age of eightee and all females over the age of twelve years for not obeying these rules shal be expell'd

Surry County — Rules and regulations for a school
N. Carolina — for a school

Rule the 1st but one male to go out at a
time and the others to stay in the [school] house untill
they return.

Rule the 2nd but two females to go out at a time
and the others to stay in the house untill they return.

Rule the 3rd
No immorral games nor plays what ever

Rule the 4th
No cursing nor swearing, mawking nor calling names
but call each one by there [their] proper name

Rule the 5th
The schollars must say yes sir & no sir or
yes madam & no madam as the nature of
the case may be

Rule the 6th
No climbing, no Wrestling nor Throwing rocks
at school nor in going to & from school

Rule the 7th
The schollars must not delay There [their] time going
to & from school

Rule the 8th
The schollars if meeting with any person
going to & from school shal speak politely
to them, but if said person or persons should
say any thing that is immorral the schollars
shal pass on and not indulge them selves
in that which is immorral

Rule the 9th no Talking and laughing in
time of books

Rule the 10 all males over the age of eightee[n]
and all females over the age of twelve years
for not obeying these rules shal be expell'd

The Surry County Book: Recollections of the Life, History & Culture of Old Surry County in Northwestern North Carolina, 2nd ed. (Elkin, N.C.: Surry County American Revolution Bicentennial Commission, 1978), p. 96 [year 1858]. Courtesy Surry County Historical Society.

Treasury Department,
Third Auditors Office,
May 22, 1854.

Sir:

I have received your letter of the 9th inst, enclosing letters of Administration to Mrs Hannah Kallmyer, upon the Estate of her husband Charles Kallmyer, dec'd, late Quartermaster Sergeant of the 1st Regiment of U. S. Artillery, who died at Pensacola Harbor, Florida, in September last.

In reply, I have to inform you that the letters of Administration has been referred, together with your letter enclosing ~~it~~ them, to the Second Auditor for his action thereon, to whose office it is presumed they properly belong.

Respectfully,
Your Obt servt,
F. Burt
Auditor.

Maj Jno Munroe,
Fort Brooke,
Fla.

Treasury Department,
Third Auditors Office,
May 22, 1854.

Sir:

I have received your letter of the 9th inst., enclosing letters of Administration to Mrs Hannah Kallmyer upon the Estate of her husband Charles Kallmyer, decd., late Quartermaster Sergeant of the 1st Regiment of U. S. Artillery, who died at Pensacola Harbor, Florida, in September last.

In reply, I have to inform you that the letters of Administration has been referred, together with your letter enclosing them. to the Second Auditor for his action thereon, to whose office it is presumed they properly belong.

Respectfully,
Your Obt [obedient] servant
F. Burt
Auditor.

Maj Jno Munroe,
Fort Brooke,
Fla.

United States, Adjutant General's Office, Letters Sent, Registers of Letters Received, and Letters Received by HQ Troops in Florida (National Archives microfilm M1084, roll 3, frame 792). FHL film 1, 695, 527.

COPY of Report and List of the Passengers taken on board the Brig Acadian of Boston whereof Thos S Wood is Master, burthen 157 tons, and 95ths of a ton, bound from the Port of Halifax for Boston

140

NAMES.	AGE.	SEX.	Occupation, Trade, or Profession.	Country to which they severally belong.	Country of which they intend to become inhabitants.	Remarks relative to any who may have died or left the vessel during the voyage.
Mrs Susan McLane	30	Female		Nova Scotia	Nova Scotia	
Miss Isabella McTemlett	18	"		New Foundland	·	
" Louisa A Temlett	10			"	·	
Mr B C Beehm	36	Male	Merchant	Nova Scotia		
Wm Mowat	25	"	Carpenter	Scotland	Canada	
Revd Peter Ross	38			U States	U States	
Cath McIntosh	20	Female		Nova Scotia	"	
Mary Herne	40	"	Servant	"	"	
Mary Herne	19	"		·	·	
Cath Welsh	21	"	Dress Maker	·	"	
Mary Ann Fuzzle	17	"	"		·	
Ellen Flinn	32	"	"	Ireland	·	
Mary Mackie	53	"	Servant	·	·	
Sarah McGlinch	45	"		·	·	
Mary McGlinch	13	"		·	·	
Bridget McGlinch	7	"		·	·	
Ann McGlinch	10	"		·	·	
Anny Brogin	20	"	Servant	·	·	
Catharine Dolin	24	"		·	·	
Mary Dolin	14 Mo	"		·	·	
Patk Murphy	30	Male	Trader	·	·	
John Buckly	30	"	Mechanic	"	"	
Danl McLeod	40	"	Farmer	"	·	
Edward O'Conor	40	"	Lawyer	·	·	
Michael Elward	32	"	Labourer	·	·	

COPY of Report and List of the Passengers taken on board the Brig Acadian – of Boston whereof Thos F Wood – is Master, burthen 157 – tons, and 95ths of a ton, bound from the Port of Halifax – for Boston.

NAMES	AGE	SEX	Occupations, Trade or Profession.	Country to which they severally belong.	Country of which they intend to become inhabitants	Remarks relative to any who may have died or left the vessel during the voyage.
Mrs Susan McLane	30	female		Nova Scotia	Nova Scotia	
Miss Isabella M Tremlett	18	"		New Foundland	"	
" Louisa A Tremlett	10	"		"	"	
Mr B C Brehm	36	Male	Merchant	Nova Scotia	"	
Wm Mowat	25	"	Carpenter	Scotland	Canada	
Revd Peter Ross	38	"		U. States	U. States	
Cath McIntosh	20	female		Nova Scotia	"	
Mary Herne	40	"	Servant	"	"	
Mary Herne	19	"		"	"	
Cath Welsh	21	"	Dress Maker	"	"	
Mary Ann Fuzzle	17	"	"	"	"	
Ellen Flinn [Flinny]	32	"	"	Ireland	"	
Mary Mackie	53	"	Servant	"	"	
Sarah McGlinch	45	"		"	"	
Mary McGlinch	13	"		"	"	
Bridget McGlinch	7	"		"	"	
Ann McGlinch	10	"		"	"	
Ann Brogin	20	"	Servant	"	"	
Catharine Dolin	24	"		"	"	
Mary Dolin	14 Mo	"		"	"	
Pat Murphy	30	Male	Trader	"	"	
John Buckly	30	"	Mechanic	"	"	
Danl McLeod	40	"	farmer	"	"	
Edward O'Coner	40	"	Lawyer	"	"	
Michael Elward	32	"	Labourer	"	"	
					"	

Ship's Manifest, Boston, Massachusetts, 1847. National Archives and Records Administration. See also National Archives and Records Administration, *Teaching With Documents: Using Primary Sources from the National Archives* (Washington, D.C., 1989).

At a meeting of the citizens of Wallamette valley, Oregon, convened at the instance of Doctor White Agent of Indian Affairs, for the purpose of communicating certain information from ~~from~~ the Government of the U.S. relative to this country, the following buisness was transacted —

The object of the meeting being stated by Doct White the convention proceeded to organise by choosing ~~choosing~~ their officers —

On motion, Doctor I. L. Babcock was unanimously chosen Chairman —

On motion, Geo. W. LeBreton was unanimously elected Secretary —

Doct. White then presented the credentials of his appointment to the office of Sub. Agt. of Indian affs. for the Territory West of the Rocky Mountains, and was most cheerfully received by the assembly —

At a meeting of the citizens of Wallamette Valley, Oregon, convened at the instance of Doctor White Agent of Indian Affairs, for the purpose of communicating certain information from ~~from~~ the Government of the U.S. relative to this country, the following buisness was transacted

The object of the meeting being stated by Doct [Dr.] White the convention proceeded to organize by choosing ~~choosing~~ their officers

On motion, Doctor J. L. Babcock was unanimausly chosen Chairman

On motion, Geo. [George] W. LeBreton was unanimously elected secretary

Doct. White then presented the credentials of his appointment to the office of Sub. Agt. [Agent] of Indian affs. [Affairs] for the Territory West of the Rocky Mountains, and was most cheerfully received by the assembly

Petition from residents of Wallamette [Willamette] Valley, Oregon Territory, to the Bureau of Indian Affairs, Oct. 1842, National Archives and Records Administration (RG 75). See also *Westward Expansion, 1842-1912* (Boca Raton, Fl.: Social Issues Resources Series).

BAPTISMS

Parents Names	Child's Name	Time of Baptism
Thomas Goodwillie & Alison Goodwillie	David Henderson	May 25th 1834 by Dr David Goodwillie
Elijah McLaren & Wife	Alexander	June 7th 1835
John Somers Sr & Wife	Melinda	" 14th "
Robt Gilfillan & Wife	John Bachop	" 21st "
Nathaniel Roy & Wife	Joseph	" 24th "
Jennet Walson	Marion	" 26th "
Jas Coulter & Wife	Robt Blaine	" 27 "
Mrs Somers (Danville)		29
Peter Kennedy & Wife		" " "
John Lang & Wife		" " "
James Lang & Wife	Nancy	July 19 "
Susan McNarre		" " "
Wm Warden Jr & Wife	Abigail Jane	" 26 "
Robt [redacted]on & Wife	Jane	August 23 "
Claud Gilfillan	Thomas	"

BAPTISMS.

Parents Names	Child's Name	Time of Baptism
Thomas Goodwillie &) Alison Goodwillie)	David Henderson	(May 25th 1834 by (Rev. David Goodwillie
Elijah McLaren & Wife	Alexander	June 7th 1835
John Somers 1st & Wife	Melinda	" 14th "
Robt. Gilfillan & Wife	John Bachop	" 21st "
Nathaniel Roy & Wife	Joseph	" 24th "
Jennet Walson	Marion	" 26th "
Jas. Coultes & Wife	Robt Blane	" 27 "
Mrs. Somers (Danville)		" 29 "
Peter Kennedy & Wife		" " "
John Lang & Wife		" " "
James Lang & Wife	Nancy	July 19 "
Susan McNarre		" " "
Wm Warden Jr & Wife	Abigail Jane	" 26 "
Robt Gilkerson & Wife	Jane	August 23 "
Claud Gilfillan	Thomas	" " "

Barnet, Caledonia Co., Vermont, Session Records, Associate Church, Baptisms, vol. 2.
FHL film 914, 061 (2nd item).

State of Georgia }
County of Franklin } Ss.

On this ninth day of October in the year Eighteen Hundred and thirty two personally appeared before the Superior Court for the County and State aforesaid now sitting William Aaron a resident of Capt Freemans district in the County and State aforesaid aged Seventy nine or Eighty years who being first duly sworn according to Law doth on his oath make the following declaration in order to obtain the benefit of the Act of Congress passed June 7 1832

That he entisted in the Army of the United States in the year 1777 in January or February under Lieutenant Cluff Shelton and Capt Jas. Franklin and served in the 10th Virginia Regiment of the Virginia Line The regiment was commanded by Col. Stevens. He enlisted in Amherst County Virginia & was marched and joined Head quarters at Bonbrook New Jersey & from there was marched over the mountain - and was there taken with the Measles & was sent to a hospital at Mendon in New Jersey he thinks, or Penn - when he recovered he joined Head quarters at Germantown Pennsylvania, was taken with a relapse & was again put in the White Horse Hospital near Philadelphia from there he was carried to Peel Hall in the neighborhood of Philadelphia, From there he was removed to Burlington N. Jersey on the Bullet guard, from there was removed to Princeton from there he was removed to Valley Forge Head quarters Penn. where he received a furlough by order of Genl Muhlenburg for leave of absence until his health was perfectly recovered if not sooner called for was afterwards called for & reported himself to Genl Muhlenburg at Rocky [illegible] [illegible] his three years service for which he had [illegible] expired, he however underwent an examination

State of Georgia)
County of Franklin) Ss.

On this [the] ninth day of October
in the year Eighteen Hundred and thirty two per-
=sonally appeared before the Superior Court for the
County and State aforesaid now setting [sitting] William
Aaron a resident of Capt Freemans district
in the County and state aforesaid aged Seventy
nine or Eighty years who being first duly sworn
according to Law doth on his oath make the
following declaration in order to obtain the benefit
of this [the] Act of Congress passed June 7 1832
That he enlisted in the Army of the United States
in the year 1777 in January or February under
Lieutenant Cluff Shelton and Capt Jas. [Jos.] Franklin
and served in the 10th Virginia Regiment of the
Virginia Line The regiment was commanded by
Col. Stevens, He enlisted in Amherst County
Virginia & was marched and joined Head quarters
at Bowbrook New Jersey & from thence [there] was
marched over the mountain - and was there
taken with the Measles & was sent to a hospital
at Mendon in New Jersey he thinks, or Penna [Pennsylvania] when he
recovered he joined Head quarters at Germantown
Pennsylvania, was taken with a relapse & was
again put in the White House Hospital near
Philadelphia from thence he was carried to
Peck [Pech] Hall in the neighborhood of Philadelphia,
From thence he was removed to Burlington N. Jersey
on the Bullet guard, from there was removed
to Princeton, from there he was removed to
Valley Forge Head quarter Penna [Pennsylvania] where
he received a furlough by order of Genl Muh=
lenberg for leave of absence until his health
was Perfectly recovered if not sooner called for
was afterwards called for & reported himself to
Genl Muhlenberg at Rocky Ridge, but his
three years service for which he enlisted had
expired he however underwent an examination

Revolutionary War Pension File, National Archives and Records Administration.
FHL film 970, 001.

by the Inspector & was condemned as unfit for service and was discharged by Genl Muhlenberg. He further states that it was reported when he returned to Camp that his Captain (Franklin) had been cashiered, and he found Lieutenant Shelton in Command of the Company

He hereby relinquishes every claim whatever to a pension or annuity except the present & declares that his name is not on the Pension roll of any agency in any state within his knowledge or belief

Sworn to and subscribed in open Court the day & year first above written } William Aaron

Test. Jab. Morris Clk

And the said Court do hereby declare their opinion do hereby declare their opinion That the above named applicant was a Revolutionary Soldier and served as he states.

Chas Doughtery, J.S.C.W.C.

I James Morris Clerk of the Superior Court for the County and State first aforesaid Do hereby certify that the foregoing contains the original proceedings of the said Court in the matter of the application of William Aaron for a pension.

In testimony whereof I have hereunto set my hand & seal of office this Eleventh day of October 1832

James Morris Clk

by th [the] Inspector & was condemned as unfit for service and was discharged by Genl Muhlenberg. He further states that it was reported when he returned to Camp that his Captain (Franklin) had been captured, and he found Lieutenant Shelton in Command of the Company
He hereby relinquishes every claim whatever to a pension or annuity except the present & declares that his name is not on the Pension roll of any agency in any state within his knowledge or belief
Sworn to and subscribed in open Court the day & year first above written
Tst. [Test] Jas. Morris Clk

William Aaro[n]

And the said Court do hereby declare their opinion do hereby declare their opinion that the above named applicant was a Revolutionary Soldier and served as he states.

Cha[s] Dougherty J.S.C.W.C.

I James Morris Clerk of the Superior Court for the County and State first aforesaid Do hereby certify that the foregoing contains the original proceedings of the said Court in the matter of the application of William Aaron for a pension. In testimony whereof I have hereunto set my hand & seal of office this Eleventh day of October 1832

James Morris Clk

Revolutionary War Pension File, National Archives and Records Administration.
FHL film 970, 001.

Baptized One adult, Mrs Mary Lorimer and one infant, Thomas Conner, son of Joseph and Nancy

Removed— June 9th 1828
Margaret Lonefrank— By dismissio
William McDonald July 22d 1828 By death—
March 30th 1829.
John Walters senr. By death

Thus far examined & approved
Zanesville April 8th 1829
John Hunt Mod.

[page] 10

Baptized One adult Mrs. Mary Loremer [Loremere] and one infant, Thomas Conner, son of Joseph and Nancy

Removed — June 9th 1828

Margaret Sone [Margaret's son] frank — By dismission

— — — —

July 23d 1828

William McDanald [McDonald] — By death

March 30, 1829

John Walters [Senr] By death

Thus far examined & approved

Zanesville April 8th: 1829

John Hurst Modr [Moderator]

Pleasant Hill Presbyterian Church, Session Records, New Concord, Muskingum Co., Ohio. FHL film 912, 247 (2nd item), p. 10.

State of North Carolina } In persuance to an order
Surry County } to us Directed we William
Slaid a Justice of the peace Charles Tolifaro
William Early and Mordacai Flemings have this
day proceded to lay off one Years allowance
to Lucy Golding widow of William Golding Ded
in the Maner following to wit we give to her
all the Bacon she has in posesion and five choice
hogs out of the number Belonging to the estate
all the corn she has in posesion and an allowance
of $22- 50 Cents in Cash to Buy an additional
supply of corn we give to her too choice cows
and Calfs out of the Number Belonging to the
Estate 2 Bushels of Salt we give her an
allowance of $5 to Bye Sugar and Coffee
and Spirits we also give her one Bed furniture
Cotton wheel and pair Cotton Cards and one
flax wheel We give her one plate one knife
and fork and give her an allowance of $2
in Cash to pay a Midwifes fee

Wm Slaid (Seal)
C Tolifaro (Seal)
Wm Early (Seal)
M Flemings (Seal)

State of North Carolina) In persuance to an order
Surry County) to us Directed we William
Slaid a Justice of the peace Charles Tolifaro
William Easly and Mordaca Flemings have this
day proceeded to lay off one Years allowance
to Lucy Golding widow of William Golding Ded [deceased]
in the Maner following to wit we give to her
all the Bacon she has in possesion and five choice
hogs out of the number Belonging to the estate
all the corn she has in possession and an allowance
of $22 – 50 Cents in Cash to Buy an additional
Supply of corn we give to her too [two] choice cows
and Calves out of the Number Belonging to the
Estate 2 Bushels of Salt we give her an
allowance of $5 to Bye Shugar and Coffee
and Sperits [Spirits] we also give her one Bed furniture
Cotton wheel and pair Cotton Cards and one
flax wheel We give her one plate one knife
and fork and give her an allowance of $2
in cash to pay a Mid wifes fee

W^{m} [William] Slaid [seal]
C. Tolifaro [seal]
Wm Easly [seal]
M. [Mordaca] Flemings [seal]

Surry County, North Carolina, Widow's allotment, May term 1826, North Carolina State Archives, Surry County Original Estate Papers, William Golding, 1826 (C.R.092.508.28). Courtesy North Carolina State Archives, Raleigh, N.C.

Marriages.

In 1821.

Dec 27. Mr. John Pierce Houghton to Miss Relief Goold both of Harvard.

In 1822.

January 2nd Mr. Simeon Wetherbee of Boxborough to Miss. Persis Whitney of Harvard.

May 16th. Mr. Abel Sawtell of Groton to Miss. Susanna French Bardeen of Harvard. —

July 7th. Mr. Otis Jefferson of Uxbridge to Miss. Eliza D. Conant of Harvard.

September 16th Mr. Joseph Brown of Petersham to Miss. Mary Reed of Harbard.

October 6th. Mr Hosea Fessenden of Concord. New-Hamshire, to Miss. Nancy Chaffin of Harvard.

May 21st. 1823. Mr. John Chaffin of Concord, N.H. and Miss Rebacca Pollard of Harvard.

Oct 13th. 1823. The Rev. James Howe of Pepperell to Miss Harriet Mason of Harvard. —

Nov. 9th. 1823. Mr. Josiah Bigelow of Leominster to Miss Ession Patterson of Harvard.

March 30th, 1824. Mr. Thomas P. Reed to Miss Hannah B. Farnsworth — both of Harvard.

May 16 1824. Mr. Walter H. Davis of Worcester to Miss Roxana Adams of Harvard.

July 22nd—1824. Capt. William Smith of Lexington to Miss Mary R. Green of Harvard.

---

73 Marriages.

In 1821.

Dec. 27. Mr. John Pierce Houghton to Miss Relief Gould both of Harvard.

In 1822.

January 2nd, Mr. Simeon Wetherbee of Boxborough [Boxboro, Middlesex Co.] to Miss. Persis Whitney of Harvard.

May 16th. Mr. Abel Sawtell of Groton [Middlesex Co.] to Miss. Susanna French Bardeen of Harvard. —

July 7th. Mr. Otis Jefferson of Uxbridge [Worcester Co.] to Miss. Eliza D. Conant of Harvard.

September 16th Mr. Joseph Brown of Petersham [Worcester Co.] to Miss. Mary Reed of Harvard.

[1822] October 6th. Mr. Hosea Fessenden of Concord New-Hampshire to Miss. Nancy Chaffin of Harvard.

May 21st. 1823. Mr. John Chaffin of Concord N.H. and Miss Rebecca Pollard of Harvard.

1823

Oct 13th. The Rev. James Howe of Pepperell [Middlesex Co.] to Miss. Harriet Nason of Harvard.

Nov. 9th 1823. Mr. Josiah Bigelow of Leominster [Worcester Co.] to Miss Exian [Exion] Patterson of Harvard.

March 30th. 1824. Mr. Thomas P. Reed to Miss Hannah B. Farnsworth - both of Harvard.

May 16. 1824. Mr. Walter H. Davis of Worcester to Miss. Roxana Adams of Harvard.

July 22nd - 1824. Capt. William Smith of Lexington to Miss Mary C. Green of Harvard

---

First Congregational Church records, Harvard, Worcester Co., Massachusetts, p. 73. FHL film 859, 189.

Know all men by these presents that I Hannibal Farwell of Vassalborough and County of Kennebec Yeoman in consideration of five dollars paid to me in hand by my mother Ruth Farwell of Vassalborough aforesaid, the receipt whereof I do hereby acknowledge do hereby give, grant bargain sell and convey all my right and interest in the following described lots of land situated in Harlem, Vassalborough, Sidney and Augusta viz. half of all the land I own on Seven mile brook half of a lot situated at the head of Spectacle pond so called in Vassalboro, half of the Jones lot at the foot of the said pond in Augusta, half of lot No 64 in Harlem on the fifth range of lots and all my right and interest to lot No 50 in Augusta known by the name of the Goodwin lot — To have and to hold all that above granted property to her the said Ruth her heirs and assigns forever, so that neither I the said Hannibal nor my heirs nor any other person or persons shall have any claim upon the same from by or under me or them or in stead of me or them — In witness whereof I have hereunto set my hand and seal this fifteenth day of June in the year of our Lord one thousand eight hundred and twenty one.

Signed sealed and delivered in presence of us — Daniel Stone, Samuel Redington

Hanl. Farwell (Seal)

Kennebec ss. June 15. 1821 Then personally appeared the above named Hannibal Farwell and acknowledged the above written by him signed to be his free act and deed before me,

Samuel Redington Justice of Peace

Kennebec ss Recd. June 22. 1822 and entered & compared with the original by

John Hovey Regr.

Know all men by these presents that I Hannabel Farwell of Vassalborough and County of Kennebec [Maine] Yeoman in consideration of of five dollars paid to one in hand by my mother Ruth Farwell of Vassalborough aforesaid, the receipt whereof I do hereby acknowledge do hereby give, grant bargain sell and convey, all my right and interest in the following described lots of land situated in Harlein [Harlan], Vassalborough Sidney and Augusta Elis [Ellis] half of all the land I own on seven mile brook half of a lot situated at the head of Spectacle pond so called in Vasselboro. half of the Jones lot at the foot of the said pond in Augusta, half of lot No. 64 in Harlein on the fifth range of lots and all my right and interest - to lot No 50 in Augusta Known by the name of the Goodwin lot — To have and to hold all the above granted property to her the said Ruth her heirs and assigns forever. So that neither I the said Hannabell nor any heirs nor any other person or persons shall have any claim upon the same from by or under me or them or in stead of me or them — In witness whereof I have hereunto set my hand and seal this fifteenth day of June in the year of our Lord one thousand eight hundred and twenty one.

Signed Sealed and delivered in presence of Hanl. Farwell Seal
us Daniel Stone, Samuel Redington

Kennebec S^{s}. June 15. 1821 Then personally appeared the above named Hannabel Farwell and acknowledged the above written by him signed to be his free act and deed before me.

Samuel Redington Justice of the Peace

Kennebec S^{s} Rec^{d}. June 22. 1822 and entered & Compared with the original by John Hovey Regr^{e}

Deed, Kennebec Co., Maine, vol. 40, p. 401. FHL film 011,090 (2nd item).

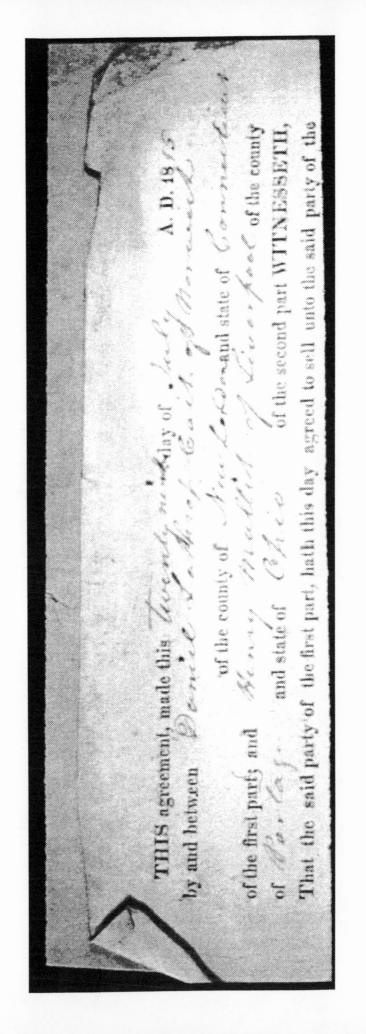

THIS agreement, made this *twenty ninth* day of *July* A. D. 18*15*
by and between *Daniel Lathrop Coit of Norwich*
of the county of *New London* and state of *Connecticut*
of the first part; and *Henry Mullet of Liverpool* of the county
of *Portage* and state of *Ohio* of the second part **WITNESSETH**,
That the said party of the first part, hath this day agreed to sell unto the said party of the

THIS agreement, made this twenty ninth day of July A. D. 1815
by and between Daniel Lathrop Coit of Norwich
of the county of New London and state of Connecticut
of the first part; and Henry Mallit of Liverpool of the county
of Portage and state of Ohio of the second part WITNESSETH,

That the said party of the first part, hath this day agreed to sell unto the said party of the

Daniel L. Coit Papers, 1815-1822, Mss 1314, in Western Reserve Historical Society, Cleveland, Ohio. Courtesy Western Reserve Historical Society.

346

Record of the births of Mr Nathaniel Bevrages Children entered March y 11th 1812

Thomas Beverage born October y 5th half past six in the Evening 1810

Susanna H Beverage born March y 10th twelve Clock in the Morning 1812

Harriet Beverage born May 14th 1816.

John Beverage born July 29th 1818

[page] 346

Record of the births of Mr Nathaniel Beverage's
Children entered March ye 11th 1812

Thomas Beverage born October ye 5th half past six in the Evening 1810
Susanna K. Beverage born March ye 10th twelve ^{o}Clock in the Morning 1812
Harriet Beverage born May 14th 1816.
John Beverage born July 29th 1818

Vinalhaven, Knox Co., Maine Town Records, p. 346. FHL film 012, 274.

In the Name of God, Amen.

I Samuel Tillett of the state of North Carolina, Currituck county, being in an afflicted state of health and weak in body, but of sound mind memory, thanks be given to Almighty God, calling to mind the mortality of my body, and knowing that is appointed for all men once to die, do make and ordain this my last Will and Testament Viz. principally and first of all I commend my soul into the hands of Almighty God that gave it, and my body I commend unto the earth to be buried in decent christian burial at discretion of my executors hereafter to be named, and touching such worldy estate wherewith it hath pleased God to bless me with in this life. I give, devise and dispose of the same in the following manner and form.

Item. I lend to my beloved wife Lovey Tillett (whose maiden name was Lovey Russell, afterwards the lawfull wife of Jesse Etheridge, and married to me after his decease, by which reason I title her now Lovey Tillett my wife) the use of the mannor plantation whereon I now live, with the dwelling house and all other out houses belonging to said plantation during her widowhood. Item. I give and bequeath to my son Thomas Tillett, one hundred and thirty acres of land, to the northward of my land adjoining William Etheridges, to him and his heirs forever. I give and bequeath to my daughter Sally Tillett one hundred and thirty acres to the southward of my land, to her and her heirs forever: Also I give to said daughter one negro, named Luis, to her and heirs forever. I give and bequeath to son Jesse Tillett one hundred and thirty acres in the middle between my son Thomas and Sally Tillett's land, to him and his heirs forever. Item, my Will is, that my vessel be sold to pay my debts. Item. All the rest of my property not given away, to be equally divided among my wife as before mentioned, and my three children, Thomas, Sally and Jesse Tillett. Item. I do nominate and appoint my brother Thomas Tillett, whole and sole executor of this my last Will and Testament ratifying and confirming this and no other to be my last Will and Testament. In witness whereof I have hereunto set

In the name of God, Amen,

I Samuel Tillett of the State of North Carolina, Currituck county, being in an afflicted State of health and weak in body, but of sound mind memory, thanks be given to Almighty God, calling to mind the Mortality of my body, and knowing that is appointed for all men once to die, do make and ordain this my last will and Testament Viz. principally and first of all I command my soul into the hands of Almigh =ty God, that gave it, and my body I commend unto the earth to be buried in decent christian burial at discretian of my executors hereafter to be named, and touching such worldy estate wherewith it hath pleased God to bless me with in this life. I give, devise and dispose of the same in the following manner and form.

Item. I lend to my beloved wife Lovey Tillett (whose maiden name was Lovey Russell, afterwards the lawful wife of Jessee Ethridge, and married to me after his decease, by which reason I title her now Lovey Tillett my wife) the use of the mannor plantatian whereon I now live, with the dwelling house and all other out houses belonging to said plantation during her widowhood. Item. I give and bequeath to my son Thomas Tillett, one hundred and thirty acres of land, to the northward of my land adjoining William Ethridges, to him and his heirs forever. I give and bequeath to my daughter Sally Tillett one hundred and thirty acres to the southward of my land, to her and her heirs forever: Als. I give to said daughter one negro, named Luis, to her and heirs forever. I Give and bequeath to [my] son Jessee Tillett one hundred and thirty acres in the middle between my son Thomas and Sally Tillett's land, to him and his heirs forever. Item, my Will is that my vessel be sold to pay my debts. Item. All the rest of my property not given away, to be equally divided among my wife as before mentioned, and my three children. Thomas, Sally and Jessee Tillett.

Item. I do nominate and appoint my brother Thomas Tillett whole and sole executor of this my last Will and Testament satisfying and canfirming [confirming] this and no other to be my last Will and Testament. In Witness whereof I have hereunto set

Will of Samuel Tillett, County Court of Pleas and Quarter Sessions, 20 Jan. 1812, Currituck Co., North Carolina, vol. 3, p. 13. FHL film 018,753.

This Indenture made this 5th day of June in the year of our Lord eighteen hundred and Eleven between Thomas John and Annie his wife in Adams County and state of Ohio of the one part and Owen John of the County and state aforesaid of the other part. That the said Thomas John and Annie his wife for and in consideration of the sum of Fifty dollars lawful money of the United States to them in hand paid by the said Owen John before the ensealing and delivering hereof the receipt whereof they doth hereby acknowledge and hereof acquit and forever discharge the said Owen John his heirs executors and administrators by these presents by these presents hath granted bargained sold aliened and enfeoffed released and confirmed and by these presents do grant bargain sell alien enfeoff release and confirm unto the said Owen John his heirs and assigns forever a certain inlot in the town of Hillsboro known and designated on the plat of said town by number one hundred and fifty-five together with all and singular the ways and woods, waters, watercourses rights liberties privileges hereditaments and appurtenances whatsoever thereunto belonging or anywise appertaining and the reversions and remainders rents issues and profits thereof and also all the estate right title and interest, property claim and demand of them the said Thomas John and Annie his wife of in and to the same, to have and to hold the lots hereby conveyed with all and singular the premises and every part and parcel thereof with every of the appurtenances unto the Owen John his heirs and assigns forever to the only proper use of and behoof of him the said Owen John his heirs and assigns. And the said Thomas John and Nancy his wife doth covenant and agree to with the said Owen John his heirs and assigns by these presents that the above described lots thereby granted is free from all former grants bargains or sales whatsoever, and the same against them the said Thomas John and Annie his wife and against all and every other person or persons whatsoever lawfully claiming or to claim by from or under them shall and will warrant and forever defend the. In witness whereof the said Thomas John and Annie his wife has hereunto set their hands and seals the year and day first above written.

Signed sealed and delivered in presence of us

Thomas John (seal)

Annie John (seal)

This Indenture made this 5th day of June in the year of our Lord eighteen hundred and Eleven between Thomas John and Annie his wife in Adams County and state of Ohio of the one part and Owen John of the County and state aforesaid of the other part.   That the said Thomas John and Annie his wife for and in consideration of the sum of Fifty dollars lawful money of the United States to them in hand paid by the said Owen John before the ensealing and delivering hereof the receipt whereof they doth hereby acknowledge and hereof acquit and forever discharge the said Owen John his heirs executors and administrators by these presents by these presents hath granted bargained sold aliened and enfeoffed released and confirmed and by these presents do grant bargain sell alien enfeoff release and confirm unto the said Owen John his heirs and assigns forever a certain inlot in the town of Hillsboro Known and designated on the plat of said town by number one hundred and fifty-five together with all and singular the ways and woods, waters, watercourses rights liberties priviliges hereditaments and appurtenances whatsoever thereunto belonging or iny [any] wise appertaining and the reversions and remainders rents issues and profts thereof and also all the estate right title and interest, property claim and demand of them the said Thomas John and Annie his wife of in and to the same, to have and to hold the lots hereby conveyed with all and singular the premises and every part and parcel thereof with every of the appurtenances unto the Owen John his heirs and assigns forever to the only proper use of and behoof [behalf] of him the said Owen John his heirs and assigns.   And the said Thomas John and Nancy his wife doth covenant and agree to, with the said Owen John his heirs and assigns by these presents that the above described lots hereby granted is free from all former grants bargains or sales whatsoever, and the same against them the said Thomas John and Annie his wife and against all and every other person or persons whatsoever lawfully claiming or to claim by from or under them shall and will warrant and forever defend...   In witness whereof the said Thomas John and Annie his wife has hereunto set their hands and seals the year and day first above written.
Signed sealed and delivered in presence of us

Thomas John { seal }
her
Annie X John { seal }
mark

Deeds, Highland County, Ohio, vol. 1, p. 42. FHL film 912, 247.

A List of free Male inhabitants from the Age of twenty One Years and upwards taken by the Sheriff in the County of Knoxo in the Year — 1807

Persons Names	Number
Charles A Boils	1
Josiah Price	2
Joel Collins	3
Abraham Haff	4
James price	5
William price	6
Samuel Johnston	7
John Neely	8
John McConnel	9
Mathew Neely	10
Daniel Hazleton	11
William Berry	12
Jonathan Purcell	13
Thomas Sturman	14
Humphrey Sturman	15
James McClanahan	16
Levi Engle	17
John Engle Sen	18
Richard Engle	19

A List of free Male inha
bitants from the Age of
twenty One years and up
wards taken by the Sheriff
in the County of Knox
in the year – 1807

Persons Names	Number
Charles A Boils	1
Josiah Price	2
Joel Collins	3
Abraham Haff	4
James Price	5
William Price	6
Samuel Johnston	7
John Neely	8
John McConnel	9
Mathew Neely	10
Daniel Hazleton	11
William Berry	12
Jonathan Purcell	13
Thomas Sturman	14
Humphrey Sturman	15
James McClanahan	16
Levi Engle	17
John Engle Sen	18
Richard Engle	19

Rebah M. Fraustein, ed., *Census of Indiana Territory for 1807* (Indianapolis: Indiana Historical Society, 1980; reprint 1990), p. 1. Courtesy Indiana Historical Society.

John Smith	9
William Brazzleton	180
Daniel McCluer	1
William purcell Sen	2
Edward purcell Jun	3
John McCluer Jun	4
John purcell Jun	5
Jonathan purcell Esq	6
Robert Bratten	7
Josiah Carrico	8
Charles polke Sen	9
Charles polke Jun	190
William Bruce	1
James Neal	2
William Smith	3
John Murphey	4
Isaac Chancellor	5
Adam Goodlette	6
John Woodcock	7
William Wood	8
William Tayler	9
David Price	200
Smith Hansbury	1
Charles Carrico	2
John Widner	3
Jacob Widner	4
Joseph Ransford	5

William Watson	6
David Watson Sen	7
David Watson Jun	8
John F Thompson	9
James Thompson	210
Thomas Sturman	1
Gabiel Bunch	2
David Cole	3
Jesse Anderson	4
William Hariss	5
James Jones	6
Abraham Jones	7
Arthur Jones	8
Joel Jones	9
Isaac Elledge	220
James Jennings	1
James Evans	2
William Waldrup	3
Joseph Shaw	4
James Shaw	5
Enock Davis	6
James Dunkin	7
John Foulger Sen	8
Jesse Mounts	9
William Hogue	230
Zachariah Price	1
John McKee	2

John Smith	9	William Watson	6
William Brazleton	180	David Watson Sen	7
Daniel McCluer	1	David Watson Jun	8
William Purcell Sen	2	John F Thompson	9
Edward Purcell Jun	3	James Thompson	210
John McCluer Jun	4	Thomas Sturman	1
John Purcell Jun	5	Gabriel Bunch	2
Jonathan Purcell Esq[r]	6	David Cole	3
Robert Bratten	7	Jessee Anderson	4
Josiah Carrico	8	William Hariss	5
Charles Polke Senr	9	James Jones	6
Charles Polke Jun	190	Abraham Jones	7
William Bruce	1	Arthur Jones	8
James Neal	2	Joel Jones	9
William Smith	3	Isaac Elledge	220
John Murphey	4	James Gennings	1
Isaac Chancellor	5	James Evans	2
Adam Goodlette	6	William Waldrys	3
John Woodcock	7	Joseph Shaw	4
William Wood	8	James Shaw	5
William Tayler	9	Enock Davis	6
David Price	200	James Dunkin	7
Smith Hansbury	1	John Foulger Sen	8
Charles Carrico	2	Jessee Mounts	9
John Widner	3	William Hogue	230
Jacob Widner	4	Zachariah Price	1
Joseph Ransford	5	John McKee	2

Rebah M. Fraustein, ed., *Census of Indiana Territory for 1807* (Indianapolis: Indiana Historical Society, 1980; reprint 1990), p. 5. Courtesy Indiana Historical Society.

Poll of an Election held at Kaskaskia in the County of Randolph to elect a Representative to the Assembly of the Indiana Territory,

2nd February 1807. —

Candidate George Fisher Esqr. —	votes.	Candidate Robert Robinson Esqr.	votes
James McNabb	1	James Fulton	1
William Chaffin	2	William Wilson	1
Henry Noble	3	William Lemon	1
Gilbert Noble	1	Miles Hotchkiss	1
Joseph Archambeau	1	Michel Danis	1
Jean Guitard	1	Joseph Pagé	1
Diego Roderigues	1	Robert Reynolds	1
Joseph Devignois	1	Ephraim Bilderbach	1
John Worley	1	John Bilderbach	1
Antoine LaChapelle	1	William McRoberts	1
Michael Smith	1	William Roberts	1
Alexis Dozau	1		
René Goder	1		
Samuel Jaquaway	1		
Henry Bienvenu	1		
Baptiste Gendron	1		
John Menard	1		
Henry Levens	1		
Baptiste Seguin	1		
Baptiste Chamberland	1		
Louis Chamberland	1		
David Fulton	1		
Jean Baptiste Barbeau	1		
Michel Bienvenu	1		
Antoine Bienvenu	1		
Nicholas Canada	1		
François Menard	1		
Antoine Louviere	1		
Joseph LaMarro	1		
Charles Bouter Danis	1		
Jean Baptiste Goder	1		11
	31		

Poll of an Election held at Kaskaskia in the County
of Randolph to elect a Representative to the Assem=
=bly of the Indiana Territory,

2nd February 1807. —

Candidate George Fisher Esqr.	votes.	Candidate Robert Robinson Esqr.	votes
James McNabb- - - - - - - -	1	James Fulton - - - - - - - -	1
William Chaffin - - - - - - -	1	William Wilson - - - - - -	1
Henry Noble - - - - - - - - - -	1	William Lemon - - - - - -	1
Gilbert Noble - - - - - - - - -	1	Miles Hotchkiss - - - - - -	1
Joseph Archambeau - - - - -	1	Michel Danis - - - - - - - -	1
Jean Guitard - - - - - - - - - -	1	Joseph Pagé - - - - - - - - -	1
Diego Roderigues - - - - - -	1	Robert Reynolds - - - - - -	1
Joseph Devignois - - - - - -	1	Ephraim Bilderbach - - -	1
John Worley - - - - - - - - - -	1	John Bilderbach - - - - - -	1
Antoine La Chapelle - - - -	1	William McRoberts - - -	1
Michael Smith - - - - - - - -	1	William Roberts - - - - - -	1
Alexis Dozain [Dozau] - - -	1		
Rene Goder [Godet] - - - - -	1		
Samuel Jaquaway - - - - - -	1		
Henry Bienvenu - - - - - - -	1		
Baptisto [Baptiste] Gendoon [Gendron]- -	1		
John Menard - - - - - - - - - -	1		
Henry Levins [Levens] - - -	1		
Baptiste [Baptisto] Seguin [Lequin] - - - -	1		
Baptiste [Baptisto] Chamberland - - - - - -	1		
Louis Chamerland - - - - - -	1		
David Fulton - - - - - - - - -	1		
Jean Baptiste [Baptisto] Barbau - - - - - - - - - -	1		
Michel Bienvenu - - - - - - -	1		
Antoine Bienvenu - - - - - -	1		
Nicholas Canada [Canade]-	1		
François Menard - - - - - - -	1		
Antoine Louviere - - - - - -	1		
Joseph LaMarre - - - - - - -	1		
Charlo [Charle] Bouten Danis - - - - - - - - - - -	1		
Jean Baptiste Goden [Goder] - - - - - - - - -	1		
	31		11

Rebah M. Fraustein, ed., *Census of Indiana Territory for 1807* (Indianapolis: Indiana Historical Society, 1980; reprint 1990), p. 43. Courtesy Indiana Historical Society.

Sophia Daughter of William Edwards and Betsy 63
his Wife was born at Poland June ye 18th 1801 -
Louraina Theresa Daughter of Wm Edwards & betsey
his Wife - was born at Poland July 16th 1804
George, William, Frederick Edwards was born
at Poland February 4th 1807
Harriet a daughter of William Edwards and
Betsy his Wife was born June 8th 1809
Lydia Jane Edwards born March 3d 1812
Charity Edwards born October 10th 1814
Julia Ann Edwards born March 25th 1817
William a Son to William Edwards and
Betsey his wife was born January 31st 1820

[page] 163

Sophia Daughter of Wiliam Edwards and Betey [Betsey]
his Wife was born at poland [Maine] June ye 18th 1801

Lourana Theresa daughter of Wm Edwards & betsey
his Wife was born @ poland July 16th 1804

George, William, Frederick Edwards was born
at poland February 4th 1807

Harriet a daughter of William Edwards and
Betey his wife was born June 8th 1809

Lydia Jane Eedwards born March 3rd 1812

Fanny Edwards born October 18th 1814

Julia Ann Edwards born March 25th 1817

William a son to William Edwards and
Betsey his wife was born January 31st 1820

Poland, Androscoggin Co., Maine, Town Records, Births, p. 163. FHL film 011, 739 (8th item).

Records of Marriages

for the Year 1799

July 4th — Andrew Arnold to Deborah Marshall
10 dls (5 (2

July 20th — Robert Reid to Sarah Ann Charlton
10 dls

December 29th — Andrew Stewart to Mary Keef.
5 dls

1800

January 16th Martin
Elizabeth Martin
10 dls

Feby. 13 — Capt. William Gibson to Jane Philips
5 dls

Feby. 15 — Capt. John E. Swords to Ann Cathne. Dunn
30 dls

~~James Caldwell to Susan~~

March 15. Bartholemew Graves to Mary Burk

July — James Caldwell to Susan
20 dls

Records of Marriages

for the Year - 1799

July 4th Andrew Arnold to Deborah Marshall

July 20th Robert Kid to Sarah Ann Charlton

December 29th Andrew Stewart to Mary Keef

1800

January 16th Martin
Elizabeth Martin

Feby 13 Capt William Gibson to Jane Philips

Feb 15 Capt Capt John E. Swords to Ann Cath.ne Dunn

March 15 Bartholemew Graves to Mary Burk

July - - James Caldwell to Susan

Marriages, Presbyterian Church, Philadelphia, Pennsylvania. Copy in possession of Kip Sperry.

Meeting Broake up by prayre — amen

March the 25th the Church Met and after prayr and Exertation dore opened for fellowship Reced by Letter Nancy Meritt and Mary Meritt Sunday quarterly Meeting

April the 23d the Church Met after prayr and Exertation the Church found in peace proceed to point out the Names of the Comettee

Larkin Clevland	William Martin
William Gates	William Swift
John Carter	Benjaman Barton
William Clevland	Nicklis Darnal
John McNeil	John Barton
James Jackson	Robt Walker

The Church Reced a Complant against Brother Moses denman and Brother Walker Brother Chery to Cite Brother denman to Next meeting

Meeting Broake up by prayre [prayer] amen

March the 25th the Church Met

and after prayer and Exertation adore [a door] opened for fellowship Recvd [Received] by Letter Nancy Meritt and Mary Meritt Sunday quartely [quarterly] Meeting ov[er?]

April The 23^{d} the Church Met

after prayer and Exertation the Church found in pea...[peace?] proceed to point out the Names of the Cometee [committee]

Larkin Clevland	William Martan
William Gates	William Swift
John Carter	Benjamin Barton
William Clevland	Nicklis Darnal
John McNeil	John Barton
James Jackson	Robt Walter [Walters]

The Church Recvd [received] a Complant [complaint] against Brother Moses denman [Lenman; Serman] and Brother Mathe... [Mathews/Mattie?]

Brother Chery to Cite Brother denman [Lenman; Serman] to Nextt [Next] meeting

Shoal Creek Baptist Church (also known as Chauga Baptist Church), Beaverdam Baptist Association, Oconee County, South Carolina, Church Records, 1796-1853, p. 9. FHL film 022, 812, second page of minutes.

Know all Men by these presents that I James
Thompson of Libanon in the County of Windham
and State of Connecticut for the Consideration
of thirty pounds Lawful money Recd to my full
Satisfaction of Joel Loomis of sd Libanon do for
my Self my Heirs and assigns Sell alienate Con
vey and Confirm unto him his Heirs and assigns
one Certain piece of land in sd Libanon and is bounded
as follows Beginning at a Stake and Stones which
is on the north Side of Nathan Loomis Land
then Running Northerly by Sylvester Manleys
land to Hop River to a Stake and Stones on the
Bank of Said River thence by Hop River to Silas
Brusters land then Southerly by Said Brusters land
and By the land of Samuel Thompsons to a Stake
and Stones which is on the north Side of Nathan
Loomis land then by Said Loomis land westerly
to the first Mentioned Bounds Containing
Eighteen acres more or less to have ~~and to have~~
and to hold with the Privileges & appurtenances there
... ... Indefeasable Estate

Know all Men by these presents that I James
Thompson of Lebanon in the County of Windham
and State of Connecticut for the Consideration
of thirty pounds Lawful money Recivd [received] to my full
Satisfaction of Joel Loomis of S[d] [said] Lebanon did for
my Self my Heirs and assigns Sell alionate [alienate] con
vey and Confirm unto him his Heirs and assigns
one Certain piece of land in S[d] Lebanon and is bounded
as follows Beginning att a Stake and Stones which
is on the north Side of Nathan Loomis Land
then Running Northerly by Sylvester Manleys
Land to Hop River to a Stake and Stones on the
Bank of Said River thence by Hop River to Silas
Brusters land then Southerly by Said Brusters land
and By the land of Samuel Thompson to a Stake
and Stones which is on the north Side of Nathan
Loomis land then by Said Loomis land westerly
to the first Mentioned Bounds Containing
Eighteen acres more or less to have
and to hold with the Privileges & appurtenances there

...able Estate

Original Windham County, Connecticut, deed dated 1799, in possession of Kip Sperry.

And the said Glover defendant comes and defends against the s,d Blanchard plaintiff at a Court to be holden before Just Stephen Chase Jus peace to be holden on Monday the 30 day of August at his Dwelling House and pleads abatement of writ agreeable to Statute made and provided in case where the summons is not endors'd by the officer serving the same

Jon Stiles for Eber Glover

And the s,d Foss defendant comes and defends against the s,d Blanchard Pl at a Court to be holden before Stephen Chase Jus peace at his Dwelling House and pleads abatement of writ agreeable to statute made and provided in case Summons is not endorsed by the officer serving the same

Jon Stiles for Eber Glover

And the said Glover ^~~defendent~~ comes and defends against the s,d [said] Blanchard ^~~plaintiff~~ at a Court to be holden before ~~Just~~ Stephen Chase Jus [Justice] peace to be holden on Monday the 30 days of August at his dwelling House and pleads abatement of writ agreeable to Statute made and proided [provided] in case where the summons is not endorsd by the officer serving the same

Jon Ayers for Eber [Ebenezer] Glover

And the s,d [said] Foss ~~defendant~~ comes and defends against the s.d [said] Blanchard pl [plaintiff] at a Court to be ^holdun [holden] before Stephen Chase Jus [Justice] peace at his dwelling House and pleads Abatement of writ agreeable to statute made and proveded in Case Summons is not endorsed by the officer serving the Same

Jon Ayers for Eber [Ebenezer] Glover

Original New England court record in possession of Kip Sperry.

Febr 21th 1794 These Certefie that the Propperty of this Execution Belongs to Elias miller & that He Has Got His Pay By the Constabels Viz: Alson Hoskins Giveing Sd miller an order on Cpt oliver Hanchet for the money, and as Sd miller Put the note in to my hands to Be Sewed & as it lingered in the Colection & Sd miller Found Grate fault with me I took up the order that Hoskins Gave Sd miller on Hanchet & Paid Sd miller my Self —————— & I Gave up Sd orders that Sd Hoskins Gave to Sd miller on Sd Hanchet & Sd Hoskins Gave me an other there for on Sd Hanchet on which I Got the Pay —— Test Joseph Forward

Febr 21th 1794 These Certefie that the Proppperty of
this Execution Belongs to Elias miller & that He
Has Got His Pay By the cunstabels [constables]. Viz: Alson Hoskins
Giveing S^{d} [said] miller an order on Cpt [Captain] oliver Hanchet for
the money, and as S^{d} [said] miller Put the note in to my hands
to Be Served & as it lingered in the colection & S^{d} [said] miller
Found Grate fault with me - I took up the order that
Hoskins Gave S^{d} [said] miller on Hanchet & Paid S^{d} miller
my Self ———————— & I Gave up S^{d} order
that S^{d} Horskins [Hoskins] Gave to S^{d} miller on S^{d} Hanchet & S^{d}
Hoskins Gave me an other there for on S^{d} Hanchet
on which I Got the Pay ——— Test. [Attest] Joseph Forward

Original document in possession of Kip Sperry.

Lancaster May 19th 1793—

Dear Nephew,

the very distressing Events which We have been expecting for Weeks past has now taken place — Jeffry — our dear Son Jeffry expired about one of the Clock P.M. Yesterday, — his Funeral is to be on Wednesday next at 3 o'Clock P.M — We wish to have You and as many of his Class mates as can & Who have a Friendship for him, to attend on the melancholly occasion — You will be so good as to give them seasonable Information &c —

Mr. Thayer, I suppose has written to Halbert, and has consented to stay & attend the Funl. and will I suppose deliver a Discourse in the Meetinghouse &c &c —

I am yours with affection
Israel Atherton

Mr. Charles H. Atherton

Lancaster May 19th. 1793

Dear Nephew,

the very distressing Events
which We have been expecting for Weeks past
has now taken place — Jeffry — our dear
Son Jeffry expired about one of the Clock P.M.
Yesterday! — his Funeral is to be
on Wednesday next at 3 ^{o}'Clock P.M.
We wish to have You and as many of his
Class mates as can & Who have a Friendship
for him, to attend on the melancholly occasion

You will be so good as to give them
seasonable Information &c
Mr. Thayer, I suppose has written to Halbert
and has consented to stay & attend the Fun^{l} [Funeral]
and will I suppose deliver a Discourse in
the Meetinghouse &c &c

I am yours with affection

Israel Atherton

M^{r}. Charles H. Atherton

Original 1793 letter in possession of Kip Sperry.

Canandaigua May 29th 1796

Friends and Brothers of the Six Nations at Buffalo Creek I am the head Man from the East and now with my Brethren am going on to the West to Settle Lands on the South side of Lake Erie I and my Brethren who have purchased ~~Land~~ those Lands, and those with me are your Friends and are willing to embrace an opportunity to explain to you our right both Government & native and to remove doubts if any in your Minds And also to convince you that We mean to treat you as Friends and Brothers and act honestly & honorably with you and meet each other as Friends & Brothers and shall not go any farther then what the President & Government of the United States approve. I have come a great distance am now waiting at great expense and wish an Answer from you and tell me when I shall meet you at Buffalo Creek and talk with you I beg of you to hasten and be as quick as possible

I am your Friend & Brother

Moses Cleaveland

To Sachems & Chiefs of the Six Nations

Facsimile of Moses Cleaveland's Speech to the Six Nations, May 29th, 1796, from the Original in The Western Reserve Historical Society.

Canandaigua [Ontario County, New York] May 29th 1796

Friends and Brothers of the Six Nations at Buffalo
Creek I am the head Man from the East and
now with my Brethren am going on to the West
to Settle Lands on the South side of Lake Erie
I and my Brethren who have purchased these
Lands and those with me are your Friends and
and are willing to embrasse [embrace] an opportunaty to
to explain to you and right both Governments &
native and to remove doubts if any in your
Minds And also to convince you that We
mean to teat [treat] you as Friends and Brothers and
Act honestly & honourabley with you and meet
each others as Friends & Brothers and shall not go
any farther then what the President & Government
of the United States approve I have come a great
distance am now waiting at great expense and
wish an Answer from you and tell me when
I shall mett [meet] you at Buffalo Creek and talk with
you I beg of you to hasten and be as quick as
possible I am Your Friend & Brother

Moses Cleaveland

La [To] Sachems &
Cheifs of the Six Nations

Facsimile of Moses Cleaveland's speech to the Six Nations, 29 May 1796. Original in the Western Reserve Historical Society, Cleveland, Ohio. Courtesy Western Reserve Historical Society.

Rockingham ss William Parker Esq one of
the Justices of the Peace for said County
To Nicholas Rollins Esq Benjamin Clark Yeoman
both of Stratham in said County & James Smith
of Newmarket in said County Esq Greeting
Whereas there is a Controversy subsisting between
Daniel Hoit Gent & Tobias Cutler Yeoman both
of Stratham aforesaid — for the Settlement whereof
they have this day appeared before me by their
Attorney & entered into a Rule to refer the same
to you or any two of you You are therefore
to hear the said Parties on the premises & to make
report to me of your determination thereon under
your or any two of your hands as soon as may
be — which Report being received & Judgment
entered thereon is to be final & conclusive between
the said parties & Execution is to issue thereon
provided the damages do not exceed ten pounds
Nicholas Rollins Esq is appointed Chairman
Dated at Exeter aforesaid the fifteenth Day of
October A D 1796

Wm Parker

Rockingham Ss [supra scriptum] William Parker Esqr one of
the Justices of the Peace forsaid County
To Nicholas Rollins Esq Benjamin Clark Yeoman
both of Stratham insaid County & James Smith
of Newmarket in said County Esqr Greeting
Whereas there is a Controversy subsisting between
Daniel Hoit Gent & Tobias Cutler Yeoman both
of Stratham aforeaid [aforesaid] — for the Settlement whereof
they have this day appeared before me by their
Attorney & entered into a rule to refer the Same
to you or any two of you   You are therefore
to hear the said Parties on the premises & to make
report to me of your determination thereon under
your or any two of your hands as soon as may
be - which report being received & Judgment
entered thereon is to be final & conclusive between
the Said parties & Execution is to issue thereon
provided the damages do not exceed ten pounds
Nicholas Rollins Esqr is appointed Chairman
Dated at Exeter aforesaid the fifteenth Day of
October AD 1796

Wm Parker

Original New Hampshire settlement document in possession of Kip Sperry.

Otis, Son of William Caswell & Hannah his
Wife was Born Middleborough May ye 12, 1784,
Nancy, Daughter of William Caswell & Hannah his
Wife was Born Taunton June ye 10, 1787,
Hannah, Daughter of William Caswell & Hannah his
Wife was Born Poland September ye 10, 1793,

Otis Son of William Caswell & Hannah his Wife was Born Middeleborough May y[e] 12, 1784,

Nancy Daughter of William Caswell & Hannah his Wife was Born Taunton June y[e] 10, 1787,

Hannah Daughter of William Caswell & Hannah his Wife was born Poland [Maine] September y[e] 18, 1793,

Poland, Androscoggin Co., Maine Town Records, p. 52. FHL film 011, 739 (8th item).

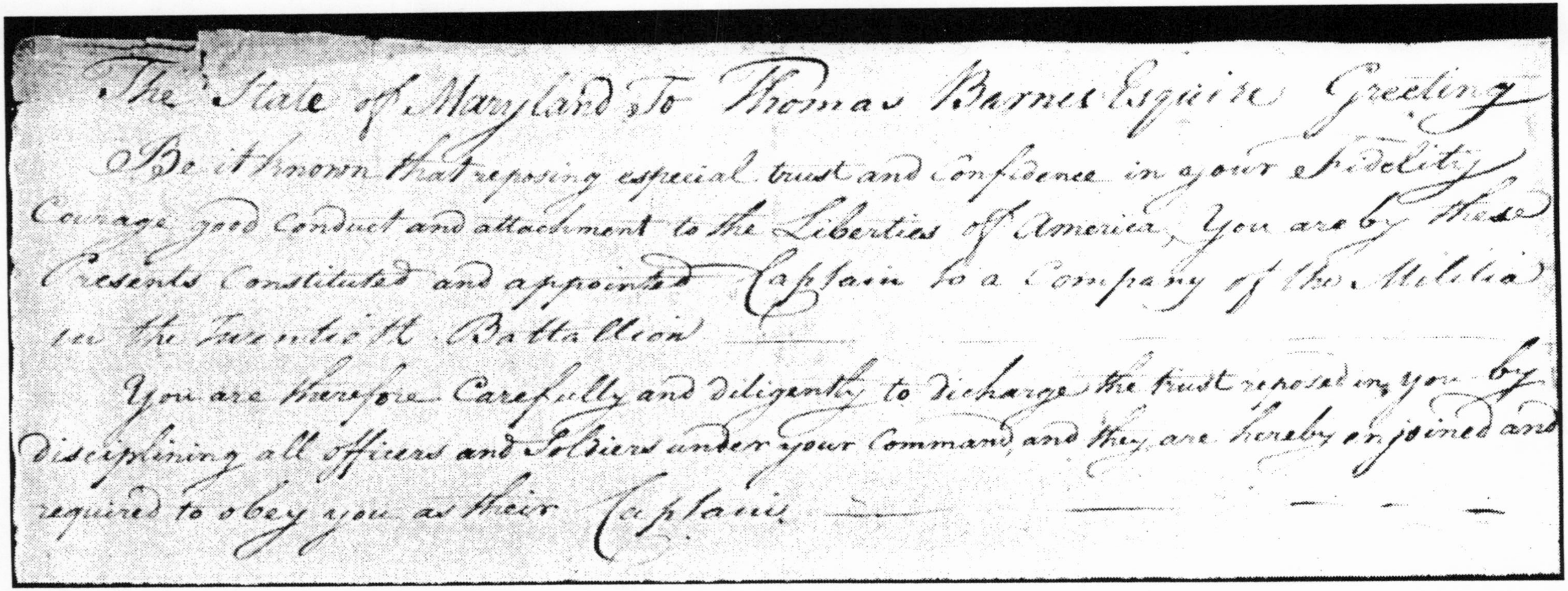

The State of Maryland To Thomas Barnes Esquire Greeting

Be it known that reposing especial trust and Confidence in your Fidelity Courage good Conduct and attachment to the Liberties of America You are by these Presents Constituted and appointed Captain to a Company of the Militia in the Twentieth Battallion

You are therefore Carefully and diligently to discharge the trust reposed in you by disciplining all officers and Soldiers under your Command, and they are hereby enjoined and required to obey you as their Captain

The State of Maryland To Thomas Barnes Esquire   Greeting

Be it known that reposing especial trust and Confidence in your Fidelity Courage good conduct and attachment to the Liberties of America, You are by these Presents Constituted and appointed   Captain to a Company of the Militia in the Twentieth Battallion

You are therefore Carefully and diligently to dicharge the trust reposed in you by disciplining all officers and Soldiers under your Command, and they are hereby enjoined and required to obey you as their Captain.

Petition, Maryland, 1777. National Archives and Records Administration.

A Muster Roll of the Field Staff and the other commissioned Officers in the third New York Battalion in the Service of the United States commanded by Colonel Peter Gansevoort.

When appointed		Officers Names	Rank	Remarks
1776 Nov.	21.	Peter Gansevoort	Colonel	
D.	D.	Marinus Willett	Lieu. Coll.	On Furlough Sept. 26th for 4 weeks
D.	D.	Robert Cochran	Major	D. — — Sept. by Lieut. Coll. Willett
D.	D.	George Sytez	Adjutant	
D.	D.	Thomas Williams 2nd	Q. M.	
D.	D.	Jeremiah Van Rensselaer	Paym.	
D.	D.	Hunlock Woodruff	Surgeon	
D.	D.	John Elliott Jun.	Mate	
D.	D.	John Mason	Chaplain	[illegible] of a Resolution of Congress allowing only one Chaplain to a Brigade
		1st Compy.		
D.	D.	Elias Van Benschoten	Captain	on furlough by Coll. Gansevoort Sept. 26th for 4 weeks
D.	D.	Henry Diffendorph	1st Lieut.	
D.	D.	Thomas Ostran[illegible]	[illegible]	
D.	D.	Peter Mage[illegible]	Ensign	Sick at Schenectady
		2d Compy.		
D.	D.	Thomas [illegible]	[illegible]	
D.	D.	William Tapp[illegible]	[illegible]	
D.	D.	Benjamin Bogardus	2d Lieut.	On Command at Oricks
D.	D.	John Spoor	Ensign	Taken Prisoner July 3d 1777.
		3d Compy.		
D.	D.	Cornelius T. Jansen	Captain	
D.	D.	Henry Vanderheyden	1st Lieut.	
D.	D.	Moses Jermans	2d Lieut.	on furlough by Coll. Gansevoort Oct. 1. for 4 weeks
D.	D.	Josiah Bagley	Ensign	
		4th Company		
D.	D.	Abraham Swartwout	Captain	on furlough by Coll. Gansevoort Sept. 26th for 4 weeks
D.	D.	Philip Conine	1st Lieut.	
D.	D.	Gilbert R. Livingston	2d Lieut.	gone to Genl. Gates to resign by Permission of Lieut. Coll. Willett
D.	D.	Samuel Lewis	Ensign	
		5th Compy.		
D.	D.	Aaron Aorson	Captain	
D.	D.	John Ball	1st Lieut.	
D.	D.	Garrit Staats	2d Lieut.	
D.	D.	Ubert Ament	Ensign	on furlough by Coll. Gansevoort Sept. 26th for 2 weeks

Example document from the National Archives and Records Administration. This document shows when appointed (date), officers' names, rank, and remarks.

Notice the ink spot in the middle of the page covering up personal names and other important details. Note also the ink bleed-through from handwriting on the reverse side of the document.

A Muster Roll of the Field Staff and the other commissioned officers in the Third
New York Battalion in the Service of the United States commanded by Colonel Peter Gansevoort.

Notice that Colonel Peter Gansevoort is the first officer listed.

Revolutionary War muster roll, 1776, New York. National Archives and Records Administration.

the Com^ee of the whole Congress to whom was referred the resolution and ~~resp~~ the Declaration respecting independence. — 17

Resolved That these united colonies are and of right ought to be free and independant states; that they are absolved from all allegiance to the british crown and that all political connection between them and the state of great Britain is and ought to be totally dissolved

The Com^{ee} of the whole Congress to whom was referred the resolution and the Declaration respecting independence. 17

Resolved That these united colonies are and of right ought to be free and independant states; that they are absolved from all allegiance to the british crown and that all political connection between them and the state of great Britain is and ought to be totally dissolved

Richard Henry Lee's resolution of independence adopted by the Continental Congress, 2 July 1776. National Archives and Records Administration, RG 360.

(64)

year	Mo	Day	A Record of Baptisms in ye ~~Chh~~ in Ashfield
1775	Dec	31	Sarah, Daughter of Jonathan & Sarah Lillie.
1776	Feb	18,	Ebenezer, Son of Jonathan and Thankful Taylor.
	Mar.	19	Anna, Elijah & Elisha } Children of Levi & Chloe Steel. At their own House, the youngest Sick.
	May.	12	Dillingham, Rebekah & Susanna } Children of Isaac & Keziah Clark.
	June	9	Alpheus Son of John and Lucy Briggs
	July	21	Lemuel, Son of Sam. & Elizabeth Trusfield
			Lucy, Daughter of Moses Jun. & Mary Tracy

year Mo Day (64)

A Record of Baptisms in ye Chh [Church] in Ashfield

1775 Dec 31 Sarah, Daughter of Jonathan & Sarah Lillie.

1776 Feb 18, Ebenezer, son of Jonathan and Thankful Taylor.

Anna)
Mar 19 Elijah &) Children of Levi & Chloe Steel.
Elisha) At their own House, the youngest Sick.

Dillingham)
May 12 Rebekah &) Children of Isaac & Keziah Clark
Susanna)

June 9 Alpheus son of John and Lucy Briggs

July 21 Lemuel, son of Saml. [Samuel] & Elisabeth Trusdel
_______ Lucy, Daughter of Moses (ju) & Mary Frary

Ashfield, Franklin Co., Massachusetts, Church Records, p. 64. FHL film 902, 902.

On the Seventh day of April 1773
were joined together in a Solemn &
legal manner in the presence of ~~Gen~~
a number of Creditable witnesses
Samuel Elliot & Susanah Hughs
both of Little Conastoga by me
John Carmichael

on the Seventh day of April 1773
were Joined together in a Solmn
[solemn] &
legal manner in the presence of
a number of Sponsable [responsible] Witnesses
Samuel Elliot & Susanah Hughs
both of little Conastoga by me
John Carmichael

Forks of Brandywine Presbyterian Church records, Chester Co., Pennsylvania, p. 53.
FHL film 503, 559.

Lords day May [illegible]
presence of the Congregation a Daughter of John Robeson
and his Wife by the Name of Ann also a Son
of Robert Carson Junior & his wife by the Name of
Robert
Lords day May 28 was baptised a Son of ~~John~~
William Smith & his Wife by the Name of John

June 29 being a day of humiliation and prayer
by the appointment of Synod ~~was ba~~
Robert Smith of Yockland Town Ship and his wife
had a Child Baptised by the Name of Robert
On the 3 Sabb: of July was Baptised in the presence
of the Congregation a Son of Samuel & Sarah Cuningham
by the Name of John
on the 4 Sabbath of July was baptised in the
presence of the Congregation a Son of George
Sloan and his Wife by the Name of Samuel
also a Daughter of ~~Will~~ Nathaniel Porter &
his Wife by the Name of Elisabeth &c
likewise a Daughter of Samuel Culbertson
Junior & his Wife by the Name of Elisabeth
the 1 Sabbath of August was baptised in the
House of God before the Congregation a Daughter
of John Gryms & his Wife by the Name of Mary
and likewise a Son of Peter Shields & his
wife by the Name of John

[page 204]

Lord's day May 14 1769 was baptised in the presence of the Congregation a Daugt[er] of John Robeson and his Wife by the Name of Ann also a Son of Robert Carson Junior & his wife by the Name of Robert

Lords day may 28 was baptised a son of ~~John Smith~~ William Smith & his Wife by the name of John

June 29 being a day of humiliation and prayer by the appointment of Synod ~~was bo~~ Robert Smith of Yockland Township and his wife had a Child Baptised by the Name of Robert

on the 3^{d} Sabb: of July was Baptised in the presence of the Congregation [a] Son of Samuel & Sarah Coning ham by the Name of John.

on the 4 Sabbath of July was baptised in the presence of the Congregation a Son of George Sloan and his Wife by the Name of Samuel also a Daughter of ~~Willi~~ Nattheniel Porter & his Wife by the Name of Elisabeth & likewise a Daughter of Samuel Culbertson Junior & his Wife by the Name of Elisabeth

the 1 Sabbath of august was baptised in the House of God before the Congregation a Daughter of John Gryms & his Wife by the Name of Mary and like wise a Son of peter Shields & his wife by the Name of John

Forks of Brandywine Presbyterian Church records, Chester Co., Pennsylvania, p. 204. FHL film 503, 559.

1000:

Lords day being the 26 of april 1761
and ye first Sabbath after my ordination
I baptized first one adult person
william temple, & children Sarah daughter
of paul mc Night and Margret daughter of
william ~~Byers~~ Byrs.

Tusday preached in the meeting House
Baptized Thomas the Son of Willm Temple

wednesday Baptized two Infants twins Samuel
& Joseph the Sons of Joseph Byrs — —

[page] 108:

Lords day being the 26 of april 1761
and ye first Sabbath after my ordination
I baptized first one adult person
william temple, & children Sarah daughter
of paul mcNight and Margret daughter of
william Byrs.

Tusday [Tuesday] preached in the meeting House
Baptized Thomas the Son of will^{m} Temple
Wednesday Baptized two Infants twins Samuel
& Joseph the Sons of Joseph Byrs

Forks of Brandywine Presbyterian Church records, Chester Co., Pennsylvania, Baptisms, p. 108. FHL film 503, 559 (item 2).

Ordered that John DuBois do hire hands to work on the Dock and Other Parts of the Town most in need, as far as the money in his hands will go —

Ordered that any person, who shall hereafter have Occasion for one of the Town Ladders to Sweep their Chimneys, shall first acquaint One of the Commissioners therewith, and shall return the same to the Court House in three hours after giving such Notice to said Commissioner under the Penalty of five Shillings Proclamation money for every such Offence — And that no Person shall presume to take any or either of the sd. Town Ladders for any other use whatsoever under the Penalty aforesaid

Corn. Harnett
Jno. DuBois
John Lyon
Moses Jn. DeRosset

Tuesday January the 7th 1755

The Freeholders met at the Court House to Choose Commissioners for the Ensuing Year, and agreed that Mr. Isaac Faries & James Arlow should take the Poll, when on Closing it there Appeared a Majority of Votes for Fredrick Gregg Esqr. Arthur Mabson John Maultsby Daniel Dunbibin & John Walker who thereupon were declared Duly Elected and are hereby returned as Such —

Isaac Faries C C

January the 8th 1755

Fredrick Gregg Esqr. Arthur Mabson John Maultsby Daniel Dunbibin & John Walker Qualified Before John DuBois According to Law

Jno. DuBois

Ordered that John DuBois do hire hands to work on the Dock and Other Parts of the Town most in need, as far as the money in his hands will go

Ordered that any person, who Shall hereafter have Occasion for one of the Town Ladders to Sweep their Chimneys, shall first acquaint One of the Commissioners therewith and shall return the same to the Court House in three hours after giving such Notice to said Commissioner under the Penalty of five shillings Proclamation money for every such offence And that no person shall presume to take any or either of the s[d] Town Ladders for any other use whatsoever under the Penalty aforesaid

Corn[s] Hamett
Jn[o] DuBois
John Lyon
Moses Jn[o] DeRosset

Tuesday January the 7th. 1755

The Freeholders met at the Court House to Choose Commissioners for the Ensuing year, and agreed that M[r]. Issac Faris & James Arlow shou'd take the Poll, when on Closeing it there appeared a majority of Votes for Frederick Gregg Esq[r]. Arthur Mabson John Maultsby Daniel Dunbibier & John Walker who thereupon were declared Duly Elected and are hereby returned as such

Isaac Faries CC

January the 8th. 1755

Frederick Gregg Esq[r]. Arthur Mabson John Maultsby Daniel Dunbibier & John Walker Qualified Before John DuBois. According to Law

Jn[o] DuBois

North Carolina State Archives, Municipal Records-Wilmington, Wilmington Town Book, 1743-1778. Courtesy North Carolina State Archives, Raleigh, N.C.

Oct: 3: 1745 Ebenezer Clark of
Ipswich and margery patch
of Wenham: — — —

oct 30 1745 Symond Burroughs
of Windsor and Lydia Porter
of Wenham — — —

Decem: 12 1715 William Payton
& hannah Trumbell both of wenham.

Decem 17 1745 Robert Dodge of
Beverly and Mary Tarbox
of Wenham — — —

The foregoing Certifications of
marriags are truly entered as
Delivered me to enter — —
Attest David Batchelder Town Clerk.

Octo: 3: 1745: Ebenezer Clerk of
Ipswich and margry [margery] patch
of Wenham:
Oct. 30 1745: Symond Burroughs
of Windsor and Lydia Porter
of Wenham
Decem: 12 1745 William Payton
& hannah Tremlett both of wenham
Decem 17 1745 Robart Dodge of
Beuerly [Beverly] and Mary Tar box [Tarbox]
of Wenham
The foregoing Certifications of
marriags are truly entered as
Delivered me to enter
Attest Dauid [David] Batcheller Town Clerk

Wenham, Essex Co., Massachusetts, Town Records, Marriages. FHL film 878, 669.

240

This Indenture Made this thirteenth Day of May in the Eight Year of the Reign of our Sove:rign Lord George the Second Annoq Domini one thousand Seven Hundred thirty and five Between Catherina Brett of the Fish Kill in the County of Dutchess in the Provence of New York in America of the one Part and Gysebert Peele of the Corporation of Kingstown in the County of Ulster in the Provence Aforesaid Yoeman of the other Part Wittnesseth that the said Catherina Brett for and in Consideration of the sum of Two Hundred and Ten Pounds Currant Lawfull Money of New York Aforesaid as also one Cow to her in hand paid by Gysebert Peele the Receipt whereof whereof Shee doth hereby Acknowlidge hath bar:gaind and sold and by these presents doth Bargain and Sell unto the said Gysebert Peele all that Certain Messuage Tract or Parcell of Land Scituating Lying and Being in the County of Dutchess Aforesaid and known to be part of that Land Called Menisink: Begining at the South East Corner of the Land Called Francois Possesion by a butten

[page] 248

This Indenture Made this thirteenth
Day of May in the Eight Year of the Reign of our Sove:
rign Lòrd George the Second Annoq Domini one thousand
Seven Hundred thirty and five Between Catherina
Brett of the Fish Kill in the County of Dutchess in the
Provence of New York in America of the one Part and Gyse-
bert Peele of the Corporation of Kingstown in the County of
Ulster in the Provence Aforesaid Yoeman of the other Part
Wittnesseth that the said Catherina Brett for and in
Consideration of the sum of Two Hundred and Ten Pounds
Currant Lawfull Money of New York Aforesaid as also one
Cow to her in hand paid by Gysebert Peele the Reciept
whereof whereof shee doth hereby Acknowledge hath bar
gaind and sold and by these presents doth Bargain and
Sell unto the said Gysebert Peele/all that Certain Messuage
Tract or Parcell of Land Scituating Lying and Being
in the County of Dutchess Aforesaid and known to be part
of that Land Called Menisinek: Begining at the South
East Corner of the Land Called Francoy's Possesion by a butter

Indenture, Dutchess County, New York, 1735, p. 248. FHL film 565, 011.

Received the fifteenth Day of March anno Domini: 1734 — by me Henry Smith of Medfield in the County of Suffolk within his majestyes Province of the massachusetts Bay in New England of John Pratt and Samuell wright of the said Province afore said = Executors of John Pratt of sd Medfield afore said late Deseaced the sum of Ten Pounds Current money Bills of Publick Credit — being a Legacye Given unto me the said Henry Smith by the said John Pratt in and by his last will and testament of which said sum of Ten Pounds and all other Debts Duties sum and sums of money and Demands what so Ever I the said Henry Smith Do acquitt and fully Discharge the said John Pratt and Samuel wright their heirs Executors Administrators and Every of them for Ever by these Presents — In wittness where of I have here unto sett my hand and seal this fifteenth Day of march anno Domini 1734 —

Signed Sealed and Delivered in the presence off —

Sarai Pratt
Jonathn Plimpton

Henry Smith

Received the fifteenth Day of March anno Domini: 1734
by me Henry Smith of Medfeld [Medfield] in the County of Suffolk
within his Majestyes Prouince [Province] of the Massachusetts Bay
in New England of John Pratt and Samuell wight of
the said Province above said = Executors of John Pratt
of s[d] Medfield aforesaid late Deseaced [deceased] the Sum of
Ten Pounds Current Money Bills of Publick Creditt
being a Legacye Given unto me the said Henry Smith
by the said John Pratt in and by his last will and
Testament of which said sum of Ten Pounds and
all other Debts Duties Sum and Sums of money and
Demands what soEver I the said Henry Smith Do
accquitt and fully Discharge the said John Pratt and
Samuel wight their heirs Executors Administrators
and Every of them for Ever by these Presents
In wittnes whereof I have here unto sett my hand and
seal this fifteenth Day of march anno Domini 1734

Signed sealed and
Delivered in the
presence off_

Sarai Pratt
Jonath[n] Plimpton

henry Smith

Henry Smith receipt, Wight Family Papers, 15 March 1734, Massachusetts Historical Society, Boston, MA. Courtesy Massachusetts Historical Society.

Joshua Rice
to
Z: Rice

To all Christian People to whom these Presents shall
come Greeting Know yee that I Joshua Rice of Marlborough in
the County of middlesex in his majesties Province of the massachusetts
Bay in New England yeoman for and in Consideration of that Parental
Love and affection which I have and do Bear ~~un~~ toward my son Zepha-
-niah Rice of Worcester in the County and Province aforesaid yeoman and
for the settlement of my said son and for his full Portion as a Child I have
Given Granted and Confirmed and by these Presents Do freely and absolute-
-ly Give Grant Convey and Confirm unto him my said son Zephaniah Rice
and to his Heirs and assigns forever as his and their full Portion out of my
Estate one Hundred and Twenty acres of Land Lying in Worcester in the
County aforesaid be the same more or Less Bounded Easterly Partly by the
Land of Josiah Maynard and Partly by my own Land Southerly Partly
by the County Road and Partly by a way Leading to Bever meadow
Westerly by the Land of Obadiah Ward and northerly by the Land of Danl
Ward with the Buildings thereon also a three ten acre Right in the
South East Part of the Town of Worcester afores^d To have & To Hold
the above Given and Confirmed Premisses with all their appurtenances
Priviledges and Commodities to the same Belonging or in any wise
appertaining to him the said Zephaniah Rice and to his Heirs and
assigns forever to his and their only proper use Benefit and Behoof
forever and that the said Zephaniah Rice his Heirs and assigns shall and
may from time to time and at all times forever hereafter by force
and virtue of these Presents Lawfully Peaceably and Quietly Have
Hold

Joshua Rice
To
Z: Rice

To all Christian People to whom these Presents shall come Greeting Know Ye that I Joshua Rice of Marlborough in the County of middlesex in his majesties Province of the Massachusetts Bay in New England yeoman ffor and in Consideration of that Parental Love and affection which I have and Do Bear toward My son Zephaniah Rice of Worcester in the County and Province aforesaid Yeoman and for the settlement of my said son and for his full Portion as a Child Have Given Granted and Confirmed and by these Presents Do freely and absolutely Give Grant Convey and Confirm unto him my said son Zephaniah Rice and to his Heirs and assigns forever as his and their full portion out of my Estate one Hundred and Twenty acres of Land Lying in Worcester in the County aforesaid Be the same more or Less Bounded Easterly Partly by the Land of Joseph Maynard and Partly by my own Land southerly Partly by the Country Road and Partly by a way Leading to Bever Meadow Westerly by ye Land of Obadiah Ward and northerly by the Land of Danl Ward with the Buildings thereon also a Three ten acre Right in the south Half Part of the Town of Worcester afores^{d} To have & To Hold the above Given and Confirmed Premisses with all their appurtenances Priviledges and Commodities to the same Belonging or in any wise appertaining to him the said Zephaniah Rice and to his Heirs and assigns forever to his and Theirs only proper use Benefit and Behoof forever and that the said Zephaniah Rice his Heirs and assigns shall and may from time to time and at all times forever hereafter by fore [force] and virtue of these Presents Lawfully Peaceably and Quietly Have Hold

Record book of the Registry of Deeds, Middlesex County, Massachusetts, vol. 31, p. 302. FHL film 554, 017.

New york June 17th 1724.

Then appeared before me William Burnet Esq. Captain General and Governour in Chief of the Province of New York &c. James [illegible] one of the within written Will of May Bickley and made Oath on the Holy Evangelists that he saw the Testator May Bickley Sign Seal Publish and Declare the within written Instrument to be his last Will and Testament and that at the time of

New York June 17th 1724.

Then appeared before me William Burnet Esqr. Captain General and Governour in Chief of the Province of New York James Adam one of the [Witnessis] the within written Will of May Bickley and made Oath on the Holy Evangelists that he saw the Testator May Bickley Sign Seal Publish and Declare the within written Instrument to be his last Will and Testament and that at the time

of

Will of May Bickley, Record of Wills Proved at Albany, New York, 17 June 1724 (AB9). FHL film 481,436.

William Burnet Esq.r Captain General and Governour in

Chief of the Provinces of New York New Jersey and Territories thereon Depending in America and Vice Admiral of the same

To All To Whom these presents shall come or may Concern Greeting Know Ye that at New York on the

Ninth Day of January the Last Will and Testament of Jacob Bonquet was proved Approved and Allowed of by me having while he lived

and at the time of his Death Goods Chattells and Credits in Diverse places within this Province by means whereof the full Disposition of all and

Singular the Goods Chattells and Credits of the said Deceased and the granting Administration of them Also the hearing of Account

Calculation or Reckoning and the final Discharge and Dismission from the same unto me Soly and not unto any other Inferior Judge

Manifestly known to belong And the Administration of all and Singular the Goods Chattells and Credits of the said Deceased and his

Will and Testament in any manner of ways concerning was Granted unto Margaret Bonquet the Executrix in the said Last Will and

Testament named Chiefly of well and truly Administring the same and of making a true and Perfect Inventory of all and Singular

the Goods Chattells and Credits of the said Deceased and Exhibiting the same into the Registry of the Prerogative Court in the

Secretary's Office at or before the Ninth Day of July next Ensuing and of Rendring a Just and true Account thereof when thereunto

Required In Testimony whereof I have Caused the Prerogative Seal to be hereunto Affixed at New York the Ninth

Day of January Anno Domini 1721/2

J Boone

William Burnet Esqr Captain General and Governor in Chief of the province of New York New Jersey and Territories thereon Depending in America and Vice Admirall of the same To All To. Whom these presents shall come or may Concern Greeting Know Yee that at New York Ninth Day of January the last Will and Testament of Jacob Bouquet was proved Approved and Allowed of by me having while and at the time of his Death Goods Chattells and Credits in Diverse places within this province by means whereof the full Disposition of all Singular the Goods Chattells and Credits of the said Deceased and the Granting Administration of them also the hearing of Accoun[ts] Calculation or Reckoning and the final Discharge and Dismission from the same unto me Soly and not unto any other Inferior Jus Manifestly known to belong and the Administration of all and Singular the Goods Chattells and Credits of the said Deceased and his Will and Testament in any manner of ways concerning was Granted unto Margaret Bouquet the Executrix in the said last Will and Testament named Chiefly of well and truly Administering the same and of making a true and perfect Inventory of all and Singular the Goods Chattells and Credits of said Deceased and Exhibiting the same into the Registry of the prerogative Court [in the] Secretarys Office at or before the Ninth Day of July next Ensueing and of Rendring a Just and true account when there[unto] Required In Testimony whereof I have Caused the prerogative Seal to be hereunto Affixed at New York this [Ninth] Day of January Anno Domini 1721/2

J H Bobin D. Secry

Albany, New York, Wills, 1721/2 (AB 12). FHL film 481, 436.

In the Name of god Amen I Evert
Bogardus of the Corporation of Kingstowne
in the County of Ulster Marinor being weak
of body but of sound mind memory and
understanding and Considering the uncertainty
of Life and Certainty of Death Doe make
and Declare this my Last will & Testament
as followeth Imprimis I Bequeath my Soul
in to the hands of Almighty god that gave
it mee And my body to the Eart to be Deacently
buryed at the Discretion of my Executors
Herein after Named And as to all my Worldly
Estate with which it hath pleased Almighty
God to bless mee I Give Devise & Bequeath the
Same as followeth (Viz:) I Doe Give unto
my Loving wife all my Estate Reall and
Temporall for Long as She Shall Remaine
unmarried She paying the Legacies Herein
after Given And Bequeathed & Incase my
wife Catie by Name Should againe Marry
after my Decease then She Shall have but
the one Just third part of my said Estate
Real & Temporall Dureing her Naturall Life
& after her Decease it Shall againe Return
[illegible] Herein after Named or all my

In the Name of god Amen I Evert
Bogardus of the Corporation of Kingstowne [Kingston]
in the County of Ulster Mariner. being weake
of body but of Sound Mind Memory and
Understanding and Considering the Uncertainty
of Life and Certainety of Death Doe make
and Declare this My Last will & Testament
as followeth Imprimis I Bequeath my Soul
in to the hands of Almighty god that gave
it mee And my body to the Eart [Earth] to be Deacently
buryed at the Discretion of my Executors
Herein after Named. And as to all my Worldly
Estate wth which it hath Pleased Almighty
God to bless mee I Give Devise & Bequeath the
Same as followeth (Viz:^t^) I Doe Give unto
my Loveing wife all My Estate Reall and
Temporall Soe Long as She Shall Remaine
Unmarried She paying the Legacies Herein
after Given And Bequeathed & In case my
wife Tatie by Name Should againe Marry
after my Decease then She Shall have but
the one Just third part of my Said Estate
Real & Temporall Dureing her Naturall Life
& after her Decease it Shall againe Return
[to My Heirs Herein after] Named or all my

Will, Ulster Co., New York, 13 April 1717 (AB 10). FHL film 481,436.

Sr

Inclosed according to his Excellencys Comission to me directed I have administerd the oath to the Wittnesses to the Last will of Evert Bogardus deceased as by the same may appeare the executors do not think to take administration but think it properley belongs to the widdow one of the same executors comes down with her and the other refers that to his other Collegue and desires that what Nicolas Hoffman may propose for the widdow to have the administration of her husbands Estate may be granted her with due Respects to you & your Coll^o Chambers & all friends is what at present offers from

Your Assured friend
& Verry humble Servt

Kingston october 14th 1717

H Wollingham

S[r]

Inclosed according to his Excellencys Comission to me directed I have administered the oath to the Wittnesses to the Last will of Evert Bogardus deceased as by the same may appeare the Executors do not thinck to take admdrstation [administration] but thinck it properley belongs to the widdow one of the same Executors Comes down with her and the other Refers that to his other Collegue [Colleague] and desires that what Nicolas Hoffman may propose for the widdow to have the administration of her husbands Estate may be granted her with due Respects to you your Coll[a] Chambers & all friends is what at present offers from

Your assured friend
& Verry humble Serv[t]

Kingston [Ulster Co., New York] october 14:[th] 1717

W[m] [William] Nottingham

Will, Ulster Co., New York, 1717 (AB 10). FHL film 481,436.

Marriages

1710

	Mon:	Day	
	5	27	Joseph Harrisson and Katherine Noble
Cohanzy	6	17	Wm Robinson . and Dinah Fortescue of Cohanzy
	7	2	Henry Willoughby and Tamsin Jurdan
		30	Thomas Fluellin and Rebekah Golden
Jamaica	9		William Brown & Eleanor [illegible]
N. York	10	12	

1711

	Mon:	Day	
	2	12	William Snowden & Abigail Woolly
	3	22	John Hepborn . and Mary Warren
	4	12	John Kelly & Mary Spencer
	5	17	Francis Gillion & Elshee Linderman
	6	21	Luke Tuzoe . & Elizabeth Rainier
	7	11	Paulus van-Vleck & Jane Van-Dike
		17	Gabriel Shouler & Margaret Rodes
	9	25	Bernard Tailer and Susanna Beer
	10	31	Francis Johnson and Phebe Ducy

1712

	Mon:	Day	
	1	8	Henry Fords and Esther Linden
	2	20	Shadlock Rivers & Mary Hazen
	3	3	Moses Edwards & Anne Ellis
			[illegible] & Anne Roll

Marriages

	Mon:	Day	1710
	5	27	Joseph Harrisson and Katherine Noble
Cohanzy	6	17	W:[m] Robinson and Dinah Fortescue of Cohanzy
	7	2	Henry Willoughby and Tamsin Jurdan
Jamaica	9	30	Thomas Fluellin and Rebekah Golden
N. York	10	12	William Brown & Eleanor Thomsen
			1711
	2	12	William Snowden & Abigail Woolly
	3	22	John Hepborn and Mary Warren
	4	12	John Kelly & Mary Spencer
	5	17	Francis Gillion & Elshee Linderman
	6	23	Luke Tuzoe & Elizabeth Rainier
	7	11	Paulus van Vleck & Jane van Dike
		17	Gabriel Shouler & Margaret Rodco
	9	25	Bernard Tailor and Susanna Beer
	10	31	Francis Johnson and Phebe Ducey
			1712
	1	8	Henry F...es and Esther Sidden
	2	20	Shadlock Rivers & Mary Haran
	3	3	Moses Edwards & Anne Ellis

Register of Marriages, 1710-1712, First Presbyterian Church, Philadelphia, Pennsylvania. FHL film 468, 374.

No. Carolina ss. By the Honble Depty Govr & Councile

A Proclamation

For dissolving the present Assembly & declaring the speedy Calling another

WHEREAS Severall of the Members of the present Assembly which mett at ye House of Capt Jno Hecklefield in Little river the fifth of November last pursuant to an Act of Assembly and by prorogation Continued to the fifteenth Day of Janry next After many repeated affronts Manifest Contempts and Deceits refused to Qualify themselves by takeing Such Oathes as might make them Capable of doeing the Countrys Business to the great loss of tyme the very great and unnecessary Charge of the Publick and to the great Greivance of the Publick Creditors for Provisions [illegible] Wee have thought fitt to dissolve this present Assembly and wee doe by [illegible] our Proclamation dissolve [illegible] them accordingly.

And wee doe [illegible] hereby make knowne to all the Inhabitants of this Colony that wee have Given directions for the Issueing out of Writts in due Course of Law for the Calling of a New Assembly which Shall begin and be holden at the House of Capt. Jno Hecklefield in Little river on the one & twentyeth day of Janry next Given under our hands and the Seale of the Colony this third day of December Anno Dni 1708

[illegible]

Samuel Swann

Thomas Pollock

John Arderne

Edwd Moseley

N°. Carolina Ss: By the Honble [Honorable] Dep^ty [Deputy] Govr: [Governor] & Councell

A Proclamation

ffor dissolveing this p^rsent [present] Assembly
& declareing the Speedy Calling of
another

Whereas Severall [Severale] of the
Members of this p^rsent [present] Assembly which
mett at ye house of Capt. Jn°: Hecklefield in
Litle river the fifth of November Last
pursuant to An Act of Assembly and by
prorogation Continued to the fifteenth
Day of Jan^ry: next After many repeated
Affronts Manifest Contempts and Deceits
refused to Quallify themselves by takeing
Such Oathes as might make them Capable
of doeing the Countrys Buisness [Business] to the great
loss of tyme the very great and unnecessary
Charge of the Publick and to the great
Greivance of the Publick Creditors for
Preventio [Prevention] whereof Wee have thought
fitt to dissolve this Present Assembly And
wee doe by [this] our Proclamation
dissolve . . . accordingly.
And wee doe [here]by make knowne to all the
Inhabitants of this Collony that wee
have Given directions for the Issueing out
of Writts in due Course of Law for the
Calling of a New Assembly which shall
begin and be holden [held] at the House of Capt:
Jn°: Hecklefield in Litle river on the one
& Twentyeth day of Jan^ry: next Given und^r [under]
our hands and the Seale of the Colony this
third day of December Ano Dni [Domini] 1705 [1708]

Thomas Cary
Samuel Swann
Thomas Pollock
John Arderne [Arderns]
Edwd. Moseley

Colonial Court Records, Miscellaneous Papers, 1677-1775, House of Burgesses and Governor and Council Proclamations, Petitions, and Instructions, 1679-1742, North Carolina State Archives, Raleigh, N.C. Courtesy North Carolina State Archives.

In the name of God Amen

This Sixth of may one thouzand seven hundred and one acording to ye Computation of ye Church of England I Claudius Xigron mariner now Navigating under Capt: Michael Basset Commander of ye: good Brigantein ann of new yorK Being weake in Body but praised be Almighty God of sound & perfect minde and memory doe make and ordayne this my Last will and testament in maner & former fallowing that is to say first & principally I Command my soul into ye hands of almighthy God hoppeing through ye merits death and passion of my saviour Jesus Christ to have full and free pardon & forgiveness of all my sinns & to Inherit Everlasting Life as touching the disposition

In the name of God Amen

This Fiefth of may one thousand Seven Hunderd and one acording
to y^{e}. Computation of y^{e}: Church of England I CLaudius
Aigron mariner now Nauigating under $Cap^{n:}$ Michael
Basset Commander. of y^{e}: Good Briganteen ann of new yorek
Being weake in Body but praised be ALmighty God
of Sound & perfect minde and memory doe make and ordayne
this my Last will and testament in maner & Former Fallowing
that is to Say First & principally I Command my Soul
into y^{e}. hands. of almigthy God hoppeing through y^{e}
merits Death and passion of my Saviour. Jesus Christ
to have full and free pardon & Forgiveness of all my sinns
& to Inherit EverLasting Life as touching the disposition

Albany County, New York, Will, 1701. FHL film 481, 436 (AA3).

(33)

The Court upon Consideration of the whole matter doe See Cause to order that there shall be appoynted Some Sutable persons as Conservators of that Estate untill the Court to be held on the 2d Tuesday of Novemb:r next who shall Take Care that the Estate be not wasted./

And the Court doe appoynt Sam:ll Benton and Thomas Whiples to be Conservators as abovs:d And doe Impower and order them to act in that Capacitie./

And further the Court order that the aboveaid Susannah be Cited to appear at the abovs:d Court in Novemb:r next To give in Such Information of the death of her husband as shall Come to her knowledge

(33)

The Court upon Consideration of the whole matter doe se [see] Cause to order that there Shall be appoynted Some Sutable persons as Conservators of that Estate untill the Court to be held on the 2d Tuesday of Novembr next who Shall Take Care that the Estate be not wasted/

And the Court doe appoynt Samll Benton and Thomas Whaples to be Conservators as above sd : And doe Impower and order them to act in that Capacitie./

And further the Court order that the abov said Susannah be Cited to appear at the abov sd : Court in Novembr Next To give in Such Information of the death of her husband as Shall Come to her Knowledge

Register of Probate, Hartford, Connecticut, 1700-1709, p. 33. FHL film 004, 551.

Memorandum

That it hath been the Constant Customs, and Practice of the Judge & Justices of the County Courts, and Courts of Probates, in this County of Hartford, when any Inventory of the Estate of a deceased person, is Exhibited in Court - To Administer an Oath to the Executor, or Administrator of the person deceas'd or Such person as produceth and Sheweth the Estate to the Apprizers, and doth exhibit the Inventory thereof in Said Court - in the manner and form following, or fully to this purpose - That is to Say -

You, A: B. do Swear, that you have truly and fully presented all, and every part of the Estate of, C:D. deceased, that at person you know of, to the Apprizers thereof, (which is Contained in the Inventory thereof made & now exhibited in this Court) And that if hereafter any more of the Estate of the Said, C:D. deceased - Shall come into your hands or knowledge, You will present a true Account thereof to this Court, that it may be added to the Said Inventory.

Test Caleb Stanly Clerk.

Memorandum

That it hath been the Constant Custome, and Practice of the Judge & Justice of the County Courts, and Courts of Probates, in this County of Hartford, when any Inventory of the Estate of a deceased person, is Exhibited in Court. To administer an Oath to the Executor, or administrator of the person decease[d] or Such person as produceth and Sheweth the Estate to the Apprizers, and doth exhibit the Inventory thereof in Said Court. in the manner and form following, or fully to this purpose- That is to Say-

> You, A: B. do Swear, that you have truly and fully presented all, and every part of the Estate of, C: D. deceased, that at presen[t] you know of. to the Apprizers thereof, (which is Contained in the Inventory thereof made & now exhibited in this Court) And that if hereafter any more of the Estate of the Said, C: D. deceased Shall come into your hands or knowledge, You will present a true Account thereof to this Court, that it may be added to the Said Inventory.

Test Caleb Stanly Clerk.

Register of Probate Records, Hartford, Connecticut, 1700-1709. FHL film 004, 551.

Thomas Dodge the son of Josiah
Dodge & Sarah his wife borne the
30th Day of November anno Dom! 1700

Elizabeth Fiske the daughter of
Samuel Fiske Jun: & Elizabeth his
wife borne the 8th day of December
anno Dom! 1700

Annah Edwards the Daughter of
John Edwards & Annah his wife
borne the 10th Day of Decembr 1700

Sarah the Daughter of Theophilus
Rix by Elizabeth his wife borne the
15th Day of January anno Dom! 1700

Nathaniel Piper the son of Thomas
Piper by Grace his wife borne the
22th Day of January 1700/701

Prudence Dodge the Daughter of
William Dodge & Prudence his wife
borne the 27th day of Januarey 1700/701

Benjamin Killum the son of Samuel
Killum by Deborah his wife borne
the 6th Day of February 1700/701

Israel Trow the son of Tobias Trow
and Mary his wife borne the
Day of Februardy: 1700/701

Nathaniel Kemball the son of
Samuel Kemball Jun & Elizabeth his
wife borne the 4th March 1700/701

Mary Maxey the Daughter
of Allexsander Maxey & Abbigall
his wife borne the 19th Day of
March anno Dom! 1700/701

Abbigall Moulton the daughter
of John Moulton by Sarah his wife
borne the 27th day of March 1701

Abbigall Haggett the Daughter of
Henry Haggett by Elizabeth his
wife borne the 30th Day of March
anno Dom! 1701

Thomas Dodge the Son of Josiah 7. Dodge & Sarah his wife borne the 30th Day of November anno Dom. 1700
Elizabeth Fiske the daughter of Samuel Fiske Junr & Elizabeth his wife borne the 8th day of December anno Dom. 1700
Annah Edwards the Daughter of John Edwards & Annah his wife borne the 10th Day of Decemb^{r}. 1700
Sarah the Daughter of Theophilus Rix by Elizabeth his wife borne the 15 Day of January anno Dom. 1700/1
Nathaniel Piper the Son of Thomas Piper by Grace his wife borne the 22th day of January 1700/701
Prudence Dodge the Daughter of William Dodge & Prudence his wife borne the 27th day of Januarey 1700/701.
Benjamin Killum the Son of Samue[l] Killum by Deborah his wife borne the 6th Day of February 1700/701
Israel Trow the son of Tobias Trow and Mary his wife borne the Day of februarey 1700/701
Nathaniel Kemball the son of Samuel Kemball Junr & Elizabeth his wife borne the 4th March: 1700/701
Mary Maxey the Daughter of Allexsander Maxey & Abbigall his wife borne the 19th Day of March anno Dom 1700/701
Abbigall Moulton the daughter of John Moulton by Sarah his wife borne the 27th day of March 1701
Abbigall Haggett the Daughter of Henry Haggett by Elizabeth his wife borne the 30th Day of March anno Dom 1701

Wenham, Essex Co., Massachusetts, Vital Records, Births, 1700–1701, p. 7.
FHL film 864, 290 (2nd item).

Hartford June 16th: 1698

Honble Sr

I received your Letter of the 2th Instant by the Post Samll Rogers And according to your Comand, I have Communicated the Same to the Councill here, for their advice. And now send to your Honr Inclosed a Copie of Colonll Dongans Letter of November the fift 1683 Containing his Claim upon this Colonie of all the Land lying within twentie miles of Hudsons River. The act of the Generall Assembly holden at Hartford Novembr the 14th following Comissionating Majr Gold, Colonll Allin, And Mr Pitkin to treat with Colonll Dongan About the Dividing Line between York and this Colonie, And their instructions to the Comissioners. A writ termed Articles of agreement, Concluded Novembr 28: 1683: between Colonll Dongan Governr of Newyork with his Councill Robert Treat Governr of Connecticutt. An Account of a Line Runn by persons Comissionated by Colonll Dongan Octobr 10th: 1684. Intended for a dividing Line between the Province of Newyork and this Colonie &c: The Severall Applications of the towns of Rye and Bedford to this Court with such papers as were Given in by their deputies. And the Acts of the Governr and Councill, and Generall Assembly thereupon. Which is all that by the Advice of the Assistants here, is to be found upon Record, of any weight in the Case depending. The Worshipfull Assistants have directed me to Signifie to your Honr, that they are Credibly informed, from the Affirmation of Colonll Dongan that there is nothing sent into England Concerning this Late pretended Aggreement, neither is there any thing thereof in the office of Record in the Governmt of Newyork. I have inclosed also the Order of the Generll Assembly Impowring Comissioners to treat with the Rhodeislanders. I have sent also by the post Copies for the Severall townes in the Countie of Newlondon and for Windham of the acts of the Last Generall Assembly. They Require much writing. but I intend to send them all out this week. I am Required by the Worshipfull Assistants here to send to your Honr A Copie drawn by Called Colonll Allin Intitled a A Copie of Connecticutt first Charter. which is submitted to your Honrs Wise Consideration according to their Order: I am Honble Sr:

Your Honrs Most humble and
Obedient Servant.
Eleazar Kimberly Secr

Hartford June 16th: 1698

Honble Sr

I recieved your Letter of the 13th Instant by the Post Samll Rogers And according to your Comand I have comunicated the same to the Councill here for their advise. And now send to your Honr Inclosed a Copie of Colonll Dongans~ Letter of November the fift 1683 Containing his Claim upon this Colonie of all the Land lying within twentie miles of Hudsons River. The act of the Generall Assembly holden at Hartford Novembr the 14th following Comissionating Majr Gold, Colonll Allin, And Mr Pitkin to treat with Colonll Dongan about the Dividing Line between York and this Colonie, And their instructions to the Comissioners. A writ formed Articles of ag— greement, Concluded Novembr 28:1683: between Colonll Dongan Governr of New york with his Councill Robert Treat Governr of Connecticutt. An Account of a Line RunE [running] by persons Comissionated by Colonll Dongan Octobr 10th: 1684 Intended for a dividing Line between the Province of New york and this Colonie &c: The Severall Applications of the towns of Rye and Bedford to this Court with Such papers as were propeer [proper] in by their deputies. And the Acts of the Governr and Councill, and Generall Assembly thereupon. Which is all that by the Advice of the Assistants here, is to be found upon Record, of any weight in the Case depending. The Worshipfull Assistants have directed me to signifie to your Honr, that they are Credibly informed, from the Affirmation of Colonll Dongan that there is nothing sent into England Concerning this Late pretend— ed Aggreement, neither is there any thing thereof in the office of Re— cord in the Governmt of New york. I have inclosed also the Order of the Genrll Assembly Impowering Comissioners to treat with the Rhode Islanders~ I have sent also by the post Copies for the Severall townes in the Countie of Newlondon and for Windham of the acts of the Last Ge— nerall Assembly. They Require much writing but I intend to send them all out this week. I am Required by the Worshipfull Assistants how to Send to your Honrble Copie drawn by Called Colonll Allin Intitled a A Copie of Conecticutt first Charter. which is Submitted to you Honr Wise Consideration according to their Order: I am Honble Sr:

Your Honr Most humble and
Obedient Servant.
Eleazar Kimberly

Eleazar Kimberly to Fitz-John Winthrop, 16 June 1698, Winthrop Family Papers, Massachusetts Historical Society, Boston, MA. Courtesy Massachusetts Historical Society.

Honoured

Sr:

My father being just going to Plimouth, desired me to inform you that he recieved your letter by the post, and if the Sandwich men are not gon before he gets there he will stop them til April. Sr I have sent a letter which my father recieved from John Bill, & he would desire you to agree with him; his wages are about 3: or 4: pound as my father reckned when he was there. Sr please to to pardon my unhandsome writing. I remaine your dutyful & obedient nephew.

This day the ships sayl'd for England.

J W.

Sr please to remember me to my Cousin.

March 4th. 1697/8

Honoured

S:r My father being just going to Plimouth desired me to
inform you that he recieved your letter by the post,
and if the Sandwich men are not gon [gone] before he gets there
he will stop them till Aprill: S:r I have sent a letter
which my father recieved from John Bill & he would
desre [desire] you to agree with him; his wages are about 3: or 4:
pound as my father reconed when he was there. S:r please to
to pardon my unhandsome writing. I remaine your
dutyfull & obedient nephew.

This day the ship's sayl'd [sailed] for England. JW. [John Winthrop]

S:r please to remember me to my Cousin.
March 7:th 1697/8

John Winthrop to Fitz-John Winthrop, 7 March 1697/8, Winthrop Family Papers, Massachusetts Historical Society, Boston, MA. Courtesy Massachusetts Historical Society.

Sr ye 4. Sept. 97

Having an opportunity of conveyance this serves to acquaint you of our wellfare, & that our friendes are safe come downe, & bring us the acceptible tidings of your wellfare & intention of comeing hither, wch will bee very pleasing if standes wth your conveniencie, Bror Hyde tells mee hath left orders wth Coussen Brookes to make provision for wt your occasions require for supplyes of cash, one of wch is lodged there, ye 8.10. noate on Excheq. that Bror. left wth you, is a ready mony noate, payable on demand, you may exchange wth Coussen Brookes or Mr Hacker for Specie, ye waters will not allow mee writing worke therefore must breake of, only present you wth my best wishes & desires that whether wee meete or not againe heere wee may have a happy meeting hereafter &c

Sr Yr affectionate kinsman
Sam: Reade

SR y^{e}. 4. Septr 97 [1697]

Having an oppertunity of conveyance this serves to acquaint you of our wellfare, & that our friendes are safe come downe, & bring us the acceptible tidings of your wellfare & intention of comeing hither, w^{ch} [which] will bee very pleasing if standes wth [with] your conveniencie, Bro.^{r} Lyde tells mee hath left orders wth Coussen Brookes to make provision for w^{t} [what] your occasions require for Supplyes of cash out of w^{t} is lodged there, ye lb. 10. noate [note] on Excheq. that Bro.^{r} left wth you, is a ready mony noate, payable on demand, you may exchange it wth Coussen Brookes or Mr Hacker for Specie, ye masers will not allow mee writing worke therefore must breake of, only present you wth my best wishes & desires that whether wee meete or not againe heere wee may have a happy meeting heerafter & rest [test]

Sr

Y^{r} [Your] affectionate kinsman

Sam: [Samuel] Reade

Samuel Reade to Fitz-John Winthrop, 4 Sept. 1697, Winthrop Family Papers, Massachusetts Historical Society, Boston, MA. Courtesy Massachusetts Historical Society.

At a meeting of the Select men granting Libertey to the Inhabitants to gitt Timber on the Towne Comon for ther owne use in the Towne Dec. 27 1697

Libertey granted to Benja Edwards for Timber for building an End to his barne of fourteen fett Long,

And for one hundred of Rayles

Mordicha Larkum Two hundred of Rayles and fivety posts: for fencing his land

John Gott six pine Trees for to make board and Shingle for a Leanto to his hous

John Brown. Two hundred of Rayles and fiftey posts and libertey for Gurts for his barne & slepers to lay a floare on in his dwelling hous

Goodman Lue Three score posts & one hundred of Rayles & two pine Trees for boards

Sergt James Friend pine. Timber Trees a nuff to make one Thousand of board for finishing his dwelling hous

& Two hundred of Rayles & fivety posts

Robart Hobbart one hundred of Rayles & fivety posts for fencing his land

Theophilus Rix two hundred of Rayles and fivety posts for fencing his land

Caleb Kemball, one hundred & half of Rayles & fivety posts & two pine Trees

Att a meeting of the Select men
for granting Libertey to the Inhabitants
to gitt Timber on the Towne Com˜on for
ther [their] owne use in the Towne Dec[b]. 27. 1697
Libertey granted to Benj:[a] Edwards for
Timber for building an End to his barne
of fourteen fott [foot] long
and for one hundred of Rayles
Mordichai Larkum Two hundred of Rayles
and fivety posts: for fenceing his land
John Gott six pine Trees for to make board
and Shingle for a Lean too to his hous
John Browne Two hundred of Rayles and
fivetey [fifty] posts and libertey for Gurts for
his barne & Slepers to lay a floare [floor] on
in his dwelling hous
Goodman Cue Thre score posts & one
hundred of Rayles & thre pine Trees
for boards
Sergt. James Freind Pine Timber Trees
a nuff [enough] to make one Thousand of board
for finishing his dwelling hous
& Two hundred of Rayles & fivety posts
Robart Hebbart [Hebbard] one hundred of Rayles
& fivetey [fifty] posts for fenceing his land
Theophilus Rix Two hundred of Rayles
and fivety posts for fenceing his land
Caleb Kemball, one hundred & half of
Rayles & fivety posts & two pine Trees

Wenham, Essex Co., Massachusetts, Town Records, 1697. FHL film 878, 669.

S^r

The Lords Commissioners of the Councill of Trade being prest for a Resolution upon the Subject of the Memorial for uniting the Governments of New Yorke and New England under one Head (whereof I sent You a Copy yesterday) they have againe commanded me to desire — You to dispatch as soon as possibly You can, whatever Observations — You may think fitt to offer them thereupon. I am

S^r

Whitehall
February the 4th - 169 6/7

Your most humble Servant
Wm Popple.

S.^{r}

The Lords Commissioners of the Councill of Trade being prest for a Resolution upon the Subject of the Memorial for uniting the Governments of New Yorke and New England under one Head (whereof I sent You a Copy yesterday) they have againe commanded me to desire You to dispatch as soon as possibly You can, what ever Observations You may think fitt to offer them thereupon. I am

S^{r}

Whitehall
February the 4th - 1696/7

Your most humble servant

W^{m} [William] Popple.

William Popple to Fitz-John Winthrop, 4 Feb. 1696/7, Winthrop Family Papers, Massachusetts Historical Society, Boston, MA. Courtesy Massachusetts Historical Society.

Know all men by these presents that Wee John Metcalfe & Jose Appleton of Boston in New England Merchts are held and stand firmely bound and obliged unto Majr Genll Waite Winthrop of the same Boston Esqr in the full and just summe of Three Hundred and twenty pounds Currant mony of New England To be paid unto ye said Waite Winthrop or to his certaine Attorney Executrs Admrs or assignes To the which payment well and truly to be made Wee bind ourselves and each of us by himselfe jointly and severally for the whole and in the whole our and each of our heires Executors and admrs Firmely by these presents Sealed with our Seales Dated the Eleventh day of November Anno Domi One thousand Six hundred Ninety and five Annoq. RRs Gulielmi Tertii Angliae &c Septimo —

The Condition of this pʳsent obligacon is such that Whereas the above bounden John Metcalfe for value by him recd of the abovenamed Waite Winthrop hath drawne a sett of foure bills of exchange bearing even date with these pʳsents upon Mr Sammell Ball & Company Merchts in London for One hundred pounds sterling payable to the said Waite Winthrop or order in London Twelve dayes after Sight As in and by the said bills reference thereto being had more fully may appeare If therefore the said Bills of Exchange or any one of them being presented doe find acceptance and due payment according to time therein Limited Or in default thereof If the abovebound John Metcalfe and Jose Appleton or either of them their or either of their heires Executors or admrs shall doe well and truly pay or cause to be paid unto ye abovenamed Waite Winthrop or to his certaine Attorney Exects Admrs or assignes in Boston aforesd the full and just summe of One hundred & Sixty Pounds in the present Currant money of New England Upon sight of a protest upon either or any of the said Bills for non acceptance or nonpayment thereof or other certaine Advice of the same without fraud coven or farther delay That then this present Obligacon to be utterly void and of none Effect

Signed Sealed & Delivd
in presence of us

Richard Middlecott

George Elliston

Benjamin Faneuil Jun. John Appleton

Gabriel Bernon

John Metcalfe

Jose Appleton

Know all men by these presents that Wee John Metcalfe &
Jose Appleton of Boston in New England Merch^{ts} are held
and stand firmely bound and obliged unto Majo^{r} Gen^{rll} Waite~
Winthrop of the same Boston Esqr in the full and just summe of
Three hundred and twenty pounds currant money of New England
To be paid unto ye said Waite Winthrop or to his certaine attorney
Executo^{rs} Adm^{rs} or assignes To the which payment well and truely
to be made Wee bind ourselves and each of us by himself joyntly
and severally for the whole and in the whole our and each of our
heires Executo^{rs} and adm^{rs} firmely by these presents Sealed
with our Seales Dated the Eleventh day of November Anno
Domi one thousand six hundred ninety and ffive Annoq^{e} RR^{s} Gulies
Tertij Anglie &c Septimo~ (Annoque Regni Regis Guiliemi Tertii Angliae etc. Septimo)
[And in the year of the reign of King William III of England etc. the Seventh]

The Condition of this p^{r}sent obligacon [obligation] is such that Whereas the
above bounden John Metcalf for value by him rec^{d} [received] of the above named
Waite Winthrop hath drawne a sett of foure bills of Exch^{a} bearenigeoen [bearing one]
date with these p^{r}sents upon Mr Samuele Ball & Company Merch^{ts} [Merchants] in London
for one hundred pounds sterling payable to the said Waite Winthrop or ord^{r}
in London Twelve dayes after Sight As in and by the said bills reference
whereto benig [being] had more fully may appeare If Therefore the said
Bills of Exchange or any one of them benig [being] presented doe find accep~
tance and due payment according to time therein Limited Or in default
thereof If the above bound John Metcalf and Jose Appleton or
either of them their or either of their heires Executo^{rs} or adm^{rs} shall
& doe well and truely pay or cause to be paid unto ye above named
Waite Winthrop or to his Certaine Attorney Exec^{rs} Adm^{rs} or assignes
in Boston afores^{d} the ffull and just Summe of One hundred &
Sixty Pounds in the present Current money of New England Upon
Sight of a protest upon either or any of the said Bills for non
acceptance or non payment thereof or other certaine Advice of
the same without fraud coven or farther delay That then this
present Obligacon [Obligation] to be utterly void and of none Effect

Signed Sealed & Deliv^{d} — John Metcalfe
in p^{r}sence of us
Richard Middlecott [Middleroth] — Jose Appleton
George Ellistone
Benjamin Faneuil J^{nr} John appleton
Gabril Bernon [Bernow, Benrow]

John Metcalfe and Jose Appleton, bond, 11 Nov. 1695, Winthrop Family Papers, Massachusetts Historical Society, Boston, MA. Courtesy Massachusetts Historical Society.

1695 July 4 a

The Deposition of Matthew Salter of Boston Boatman aged about 47 years he testifieth & saith that sometime about the middle of May last past I being imployed by Capt. David Robinson to unload the Ship Swan whereof he was Comander, the sd Robertson spoke to me in particular concerning goods marked P.O and said that when the goods comes to hand Marked PO I would have you carry them to the Crane by Mr. Winsors warehouse and afterward in the same month there came a parcel of Cordage and Sail Cloth to hand marked PO and I carryed them and delivered them at the Crane aforesaid and there Capt. Robertson ordered the Porters to take them out of the boate

Matthew Salter
MS
his marke

Boston July 4th. 1695

Matthew Salter personally appearing before me the Subscriber one of his Majties Justices of the Peace for the County of Suffolk made Oath to the truth above written capt. Robertson having heard it read to him

Jurt. Coram Jno. Eyre

A true Copie Attest. Joseph Webb Cler

The Deposition of Matthew Salter of Boston Boatman aged about 47 yeares he testifieth & saith that sometime about the middle of May last past I being imployed by Capt. David Robinson to unload the Ship Swan whereof he was Comander, the s^d^ Robertson spoke to me in particular concerning goods marked P.O and said that when the goods comes to hand Marked P O I would have you carry them to the Crane by m^r^. Winsors warehouse and afterward in the same month there came a parcel of Cordage and sail cloth to hand marked P O and I carryed them and delivered them at the Crane aforesaid and there Capt. Robertson ordered the Porters to take them out of the boate

Matthew Salter

MS

his marke

Boston July. 4th. 1695

Matthew Salter personally appearing before me the subscriber one of his Maj.^ties^ Justices of the Peace for the County of Suffolk made Oath to the truth above written cap^t^. Robertson haveing heard it read to him

Jur^t^. Coram Jno. Eyre

A true copie Attest ^r^ Joseph Webb Cler[k]

Matthew Salter, Boston, 4 July 1695, Miscellaneous Bound Collection, Massachusetts Historical Society, Boston, MA. Courtesy Massachusetts Historical Society.

Sr

Since we last met about the Narraganset business I have discoursed severall persons concerning it who advise the present prosecution of it thinking this the most proper time to pursue that matter and to prevent others who may have some designe prejudiciall to the Proprietors —

I am still of opinion that we should prefer a petition in order to bring the affair before their Lordships — that so this may have some effectuall care taken in it by their Lordships at the same time, and as well as other New-England Matters, As for the Charges which presume will not be great shall be willing to contribute my part, and I am assured that Mr Sewall will do the like, and there is no reason to doubt of the Rest — — I am Sr Your Most humble servt

Benja. Lynde —

Aprill 13th 1694.

S^r^./

Since we last met about the Narraganssett business
I have discoursed severall psons [persons] concerning it who advise
the present prosecution of it thinking this the most proper
time to pursue that matter and to prevent others who may
have some designe prejudiciall to the Proprietors
I am still of opinion that we should prefer a petition
in order to bring the affair before their Lordships
that so this may have some effectuall care taken in it
[for] by their Lordships at the same time, and as well as
other New–England Matters, As for the Charges
which presume will not be great shall be willing to
contribute my part, and I am assured that M[r] Servall [Sewall]
will do the Like, and there is no reason to doubt of the
Rest ~ ~ I am S.[r] Your Most humble Serv[t] [servant]

Aprill 13th 1694 Benj[a]. [Benjamin] Lynde

Benjamin Lynde to Fitz-John Winthrop, 13 April 1694, Winthrop Family Papers, Massachusetts Historical Society, Boston, MA. Courtesy Massachusetts Historical Society.

Sr

Kingstreet in Bloomsbury Apr. 21: 1694

My obligations to promote ye welfare of our American Plantations Especially in New-England being neither New nor Small I take this liberty to desire your favour to give me a particular in writing of the Several Quotas of Souldiers now insisted upon to be drawn out of ye respective Plantations of Conecticott Matachusets New York Roade Island East & West Jersey Pensilvania & Virginia to be posted at Albany under the Comand of ye Governr of New-Yorke allso that it may be expressed what Powers are urging to be given to ye Governour of New York in Superintendence over ye aforementioned Plantations & their Respective Governours Allso that it may be Exprest wherein ye aforementioned Plantations are contented to Submit & wherein they desire to be Exempted with ye Reasons for ye Same

I beseech you pardon this freedom from him who desires to Expresse Himselfe withall respect to be

Sr

Yr most humble Servant

Edw Harley

Sr Kingstreet in Bloomsbury Apr. 21:1694

My obligations to promote ye welfare of our American Plantations Especially in New-England being neither New nor Small I take this liberty to desire your favour to give me a particular in writing of the Several Quotas of Souldiers now enlisted upon to be drawn out of y^e respective Plantations of Conecticott Matachussets New York Roade Island East & West Jersey Pensilvania & Virginia to be posted at Albany under the Comand of y^e $Governo^r$ of New=Yorke allso that it may be Express'd what Powers are urging to be given to y^e Governour of New Yorke in Superintendence over y^e aforementioned Plantations & their Respective Governours Allso that it may be Exprest wherein y^e aforementioned Plantations are contented to Submit & wherein they desire to be Exempted with ye Reasons for ye Same

I beseech you pardon this freedom from him who desires to Expresse Himselfe with all respect to be

S^r

Yo^r [Your] most humble Servant

EW Harley

Edward Harley to Fitz-John Winthrop, 21 April 1694, Winthrop Family Papers, Massachusetts Historical Society, Boston, MA. Courtesy Massachusetts Historical Society.

This Indenture wittnesseth that John Bowers of medfield in ye County of Suffolk in Newengland hath of his own free will and with ye Consent of his Gardian Benjamin Clark hath put and bound himselfe unto Samuell wight in said Town and County linnin weauer as an apprentice from ye Day and Date hereof untill ye first Day of July in ye year onethousant six hundreed ninety and four. in case any Charges Rise upon his head this year if not then un till ye first Day of June: 1694 to learn ye art and mistery of aweauer: him to searue as a faithfull aprentice During ye whole tearm he shall not absent himselfe by night or by Day from his masters family or businesse: with out his said masters leaue all his masters lawfull Comands he shall carefully obay his secreets he shall keep his goods he shall not imbasell nor inordinately spend nor lend with out his said masters leaue and in all things he shall behaue and Demean himselfe as a faith apprentice to his said master the whole tearm

And his said master Samuell wight shall teach instruct and learn: his said apprentice John Bowers in ye art and mistery of aweauer as farr as he can teach him and he ye said apprentice is capable of learning and also he shall prouide all nessisarys for his said apprentice in sicknesse and in helth the whole tearm victualls Drink washing and lodging and he shall prouide all sort of cloathing linnin and woollin hatts shooes and stockens all said tearm: and two suits of apparrell when said time is out ye one for holy Days and ye other for working Days: and for ye faithfull performance hereof. Each to other we haue interchangeably sett to our hands and seals: this: 23d day of August sixteen hundreed: ninety and two

witnesses: Joseph Bullard
Saml Barbur

Beniamin Clark

iohn bowers

This Indenture wittnesseth that John Bowers of medfield
in ye County of Suffolk in New england hath of his own free
will and with ye Consent of his Gardian Benjamin Clark
hath put and bound him selfe unto Samuell wight in said
Town and County lininn [linen] weauer [weaver] as an apprentice from
ye Day and Date hereof untill ye first Day of July in y^{e}
year one thousant six hundreed ninety and four: in case
any Charges Rise upon his head this year if not then un
till ye first Day of June: 1694 to learn ye art and mistery
of a weauer: him to learne as a faithfull aprentice Dueing [During]
ye whole tearm he shall not absent himselfe by night or by
Day from his masters family or buisiness: with out his
said masters leave att his masters lawfull Comands [Commands]
he shall carefully obay his secreets he shall keep his
goods he shall not imbasell nor inordinately spend nor
lend with out his said masters leine and in all thing[s]
he shall behave and Demean himselfe as afaith appre[n]
tice to his said master the whole tearm [term]

And his said master Samuell wight shall teach in struct
and learn: his said apprentice John Bowers in ye art
and mistery of a weauer as farr as he can teach
him and he ye said apprentice is capable of learnin[g]
and also he shall provide all nessisarys for his said
apprentice in sicknesse and in helth [health] the whole tearm
victuells Drink washing and lodgeing and he shall pro
vide all sort of cloathing linnim [linen] and woollin hatts
Shooes and stockens all said tearm: and two suits
of apparrell when said time is out ye one for holy
Days and ye other for working Days: and for ye faith
full performance hereof: Each to other we have intercha
ngeably sett to our hands and seals: this: 23^{d}: day of August
Sixteen hundreed ninety and two

wittnes^{s} Joseph Bullard | john bowers
Sam^{ll} Barbur | Beniamin [Benjamin] Clar^{k}

John Bowers, Indenture, 23 August 1692, Wight Family Papers, Massachusetts Historical Society, Boston, MA. Courtesy Massachusetts Historical Society.

Nath^ll Brown's Answer to Peter Marshall's Reasons of Appeal given in at Ipswitch August: 24th: 1692.

Imp^r As to Peter Marshall's first Reason he saith that Maj^r Pikes judgment was just, but I say It was not just therefore I appealed from it to the County Court at Ipswitch; & I have the judgement of twelve honest men on oath who reversed the former judgment and gave me cost.

2^ly And as to his second reason he the s^d Marshall saith that I did say there was no ground of action, I judge it is not worth my while to give an Answer to it.

But may it please this Hon^d Court and Gentlemen of ye Jury to consider those few lines as followeth, I Nath^ll Brown was sued by Peter Marshall before Maj^r Pike in an action of the case for charges, for withholding 15^s mony or what shall appear on a trial of the case for charges before Maj^r Pike. Maj^r ~~Pike allowed~~ ~~damage and cost of Court~~, I say consider Marshall hath not proved in this case now before the Court that he was damnified one penny by me or that he any-ways hath been at any expence of mony or time by any default of mine.

Juries are sworn to true trials make, and just verdict give, according to Law and evidence, therfore he that proveth nothing must have nothing.

I hope the Hon^d Court will be carefull not to receive any new testimony but what was given in at Ipswitch Court, because s^d Marshall spake of giving in more I shall not trouble your honours with many words but desire the Lord to direct you. Your humble servant

Nath^ll Brown

Nath^{ll} Brown's Answer to Peter Marshalls Reasons of Appeal
given in at Ipswitch August: 24th: 1692.

Imp^{r} As to Peter Marshalls first Reason he saith that Maj^{r} Pikes judgment was just, but I say It was not just therefore I appealed from it to the County Court at Ipswitch; & I have the judgement of twelve honest men on oath who= reversed the former judgment and gave me cost.

2.^{ly} And as to his second reason he the s^{d} Marshall saith that I did say there was no ground of action, I judge it is not worth my while to give an Answer to it.

But may it please this Hon^{d}. Court and Gentlemen of y^{e} Jury to consider = these few lines as followeth, I Nath^{ll} Brown was sued by Peter Marshall before Maj^{r} Pike in an action of the case for charges, for withholding 15^{s} mony or what shall appear on a trial of the case for charges before Maj^{r} Pike.

Maj^{r} Pike allowed ye damage and ... pray consider Marshall hath not proved in this case now before the Court that he was damnified one penny by me or that he any-wayes hath been at any expence of mony or time by any default of mine.

Juries are sworn to true trials make, and just verdict give, according to law= and evidence, therfore he that proveth nothing must have nothing.

I hope the Hon^{d}: Court will be carefull not to receive any new testimony but what was given in at Ipswitch Court, because s^{d} Marshall spake of giving in more I shall not trouble your honours with many words but desire the Lord to direct you. Your humble servant~

Nath^{ll} Brown~

Nathaniel Brown, 24 Aug. 1692, Miscellaneous Bound Collection, Massachusetts Historical Society, Boston, MA. Courtesy Massachusetts Historical Society.

Know all men by these psents That I John Richards of Boston in ye County of Suffolke in the Province of the Massachusetts Bay in New England, mrchant am holden & firmly bound unto Majo Genll Waite Winthrop of sd Boston Esqr in two thousand pounds lawfull money of New England, to be paid unto the said Waite Winthrop or his Certaine Attorney his heires Executors Admintors or Assignes: to the wch paymt well & truly to be made I the sd John Richards do binde my Selfe my heires Executors & Admintors firmly by these psents. Sealed wth my Seal. Dated in Boston afore sd this fourteenth day of June anno dom. one thousand Six hundred ninety two. Annoq. RRs & Rnae Gulielmi & Mariae Angliae &c. Quarto.

The Condicon of this Obligacon is Such, That whereas there is a Contract of Marriage intended between the above bound John Richards & mrs Ann Winthrop Sister to ye above sd Majo Genll Winthrop, by Gods grace to be Shortly had & Solemnized; In reference to wch Contract, It is Covenanted promised & agreed by the sd John Richards to & wth ye sd Wait Winthrop in the behalfe of his sd Sister Ann Winthrop, That (in case the sd marriage take effect) If the sd John Richards happen to depart this life before the said Ann, then the sd Ann shall have & Enjoy to her owne proper use for Ever, one thousand pounds lawfull money of New England out of the Estate of the said John Richards to be paid unto her or her order by his Executors or Admintors wthin Six monethes after his decease, besides what will accrue to her by law out of my reall Estate, & over and above what I the said John Richards, may or shall give & bequeath unto her the sd Ann by my last Will and Testament, & besides what shall be the portions or Bequests to the Children of the said John & Ann if God graciously give them such a blessing. If then the sd Ann, the Relict of the said John Richards, her heires Executors or Admintors shall & do, in case as above mentioned, receive out of the Estate of the above sd John Richards the full & Just Sume of one thousand pounds lawfull money of New England as is above Covenanted & expressed, then this Obligacon to be voyd & of none Effect otherwise to stand & be in full force power & virtue.

Jno Richards

Signed Sealed & delivered in psence of us

Obadiah Gill

William Gill

John Viall

Know all men by these p^{r}sents that I John Richards of Boston in ye county of Suffolke in the Province of the Massachusetts Bay in New England, m^{r}chant am holden & firmly bound unto Majo^{r} Gen^{o} Waite Winthrop of s^{d} Boston Esqr- in two thousand pounds lawfull money of New England, to be paid unto the said Waite Winthrop or his certaine Atturney his heires Executors Admin^{tors} or Assignes: to the wch paym^{t} well & truly to be made I the s^{d} John Richards do binde my selfe my heires Executo^{rs} & Admin^{tors} firmly by these p^{r}sents. sealed wth my - seal. Dated in Boston afores^{d} this fourteenth day of June anno dom. one thousand six hundred ninety two. Annoq R R^{s} et R^{na} Gulielmi & Mariae Angliae &c. Quarto.
(Annoque Regni Regis et Reginae Gulielmi et Mariae Angliae etc. Quarto)
[and in the year of the reign of King and Queen William and Mary of England etc. the 4th]

The Condicon [Condition] of this Obligacon [Obligation] is such that whereas there is a contract of Marriage intended
between the above bound John Richards & Mrs Ann Winthrop sister to ye above s^{d} Majo^{r} Gen.^{a} Winthrop, by Gods grace to be shortly had & solemnized; In reference to wch Contract, It is covenanted promised & agreed by the s^{d} John Richards to & wth ye s^{d} Wait Winthrop in the behalf of his s^{d} sister Ann Winthrop that (in case the s^{d} marriage take effect) If the s^{d} John Richards happen to depart this life before the said Ann, then the s^{d} Ann shall have & Enjoy to her owne proper use for Ever, one thousand pounds Lawfull money of New England out of the Estate of the said John Richards to be paid unto her or her order by his Executors or Admin^{tors} wthin six months after his decease, besides what will accrue to her by law out of my reall Estate, & over and above what I the said - John Richards, may or shall give & bequeath unto her the s^{d} Ann by my last will and - testament, & besides what shall be the portions or Bequests to the Children of the said - John & Ann, if god graciously give them such a blessing. If then the s^{d} Ann the, Relict of the said John Richards, her heires Executors or Admin^{tors} shall & do, in case as above mentioned, receive out of the Estate of the above s^{d} John Richards the full & Just Sume of one thousand pounds lawfull money of New England as is above covenanted & Exp^{r}ssed, then this obligacon to be voyd [void] & of none Effect otherwise to stand & be in full force power & virtue.

Signed sealed & delivered — John Richards
in p^{r}sence of us
Obadiah Gill
William Gill
John Viall

John Richard's bond, 14 June 1692, Winthrop Family Papers, Massachusetts Historical Society, Boston, MA. Courtesy Massachusetts Historical Society.

Forasmuch as our respective Bills of Sale wch Majr Waite Winthrop hath given to us the Subscribers for one Sixth part apeice of the Ship Concord whereof Symon Eyre is att present mastr, specifie the Summe of One hundred and thirteene pounds three shillings and two pence, to be the Consideracon for a Sixth part thereof as shee is now fitted to ye Sea (which is allready paid by ye Subscribers). Now Know all men by these presents that if should happen that the sd Shipp att any Time hereaftr be Lawfully recovered from us by any person or persons whatsoevr; Then in such Case wee the Subscribrs, for or selves respectively, and for or severall and respective heires Exrs and Admrs doe acquitt exonerate and discharge the sd Waite Winthrop his heires Exrs and admrs of and from any Farther Summe of money then our respective parts of the Summe of Three hundred & fifty pounds, which is the prime Cost of sd vessell with her standing rigging &ca as shee was bought att New London in New England of the sd Waite Winthrop — In Witness whereof wee have hereunto sett or hands and seales ye thirteenth day of Novembr 1691 In the third year of their Maties Reigne —

Signed Sealed Delivd in presence of ye the words (wch is allready paid by the Subscribrs) being first interlined —

John Appleton

Tho. Jackson

Eliezer Moody Scr:

Adam Winthrop

Penn Townsend

Jer: Dummer.

Samuel Lillie

Jeremiah Dummer

Forasmuch as our respective Bills of Sale wch Majo^r^ Waite Winthrop hath given to us the subscribers for one sixth part apeice of the ship Concord whereof Symon Eyre is att p^r^sent mast^r^ [master] Specifie the summe of One hundred and thirteene pounds three shillings and two pence, to be the Consideracon for a Sixth part thereof as shee (which is already paid by ye subscribers) is now ffitted to ye sea. Now know all men by these p^r^sents that it should happen that the s^d^ shipp att any Time hereaft^r^ [hereafter] be lawfully recovered from us by any person or persons whatsoev^r^, Then in such Case wee the subscribers for o^r^selves respectively, and for o^r^ [our] severall and respective heires Ex^rs^ and adm^rs^ doe acquitt exonerate and discharge these Waite Winthropp his heires Ex^rs^ and adm^rs^ of and from any Farther Summe of money then our resepective parts of the Summe of Three hundred & fifty pounds, which is the prime Cost of se [sea] vessell with her standing rigging &c^a^ as shee was bought att New London in New England p[per] the s^d^ Waite Winthrop In Witnesse whereof wee have hereunto sett o^r^ hands and seales ye thirteenth day of Novemb^r^ 1691 In the third yeare of their Maj^ties^ Reigne

Signed Sealed Deliv^rd^
in p^r^sence of us the word
(wch is allready paid by the subscrib^rs^)
being First interlined-

John Appleton

Tho. Jackson

Eliezer. Moody Ser:

Adam Winthrop

Penn Townsend

Jer: Dumer [Dummer]

Samuel Lillie

Jermiah Hearte

Adam Winthrop, 13 Nov 1691, Winthrop Family Papers, Massachusetts Historical Society, Boston, MA. Courtesy Massachusetts Historical Society.

Boston April 1. 1691.

Honoured Aunt.

I am forced to send you a very rude letter because of my hast by reason of a fair wind now offering, But these will tell you that I have received of Mr. Isaac Jones for yor Accompt twenty pounds Cash, and of Mr. Richard Harris Eight pounds; for the whole fitting out of the Pinke comes to £118:06:06 and the quarter part comes to £29 = 08 = ij ½ you will thinke it a very large Accompt, but I am sorry that I am so unhappy as not to be able to kiss Mr. Blagroves hands and to give him a particular Satisfaction; I have sent you by Mr. Jones as yu may see by receipt forty three pounds fifteen shillings paper money wch is the quar. part of £175 the hire of the Vessell. I hope yu will not blame me for the badness of the pay but goe on to love

yr. humble Servant
Thom. Berry.

Superscribed.
To mrs. Eliz: Blagrove
in Bristoll.

A true Copie
= attest Joseph Webb Clerk

Boston April. 1. 1691.

Honoured Aunt.

I am forced to send you a very rude letter because of my
hast by reason of a fair wind now offering, But these will tell you
that I have received of m^{r}. Isaac Jones for yor [your] Accompt twenty
pounds Cash, and of m^{r}. Richard Harris Eight pounds; for the
whole fitting out of the sinke comes to £ 118:06:06 and the
quart^{r} part comes to £29= 08 1½ [s1½] you will thinke it a very
large accompt, but I am sorry that I am so unhappy as not
to be able to kiss m^{r}. Blagroves hands and to give him a particular
satisfaction, I have sent you p[per] m^{r}. Jones as y^{u} [you] may see p[per] receipt
forty three pounds fifteen shillings paper money w^{ch} [which] is the
quar.^{D} part of £175 the hire of the Vessell. I hope y^{u} will
not blame me for the badness of the pay but goe on to love

y^{r}. [your] humble servant

Thom. [Thomas] Berry

Superscribed.
To m^{rs}. Eliz: Blagrove
in Bristoll.

A true Copie
= attest ^{r} Joseph Webb cler[k]

Thomas Berry, 1 April 1691, Miscellaneous Bound Collection, Massachusetts Historical Society, Boston, MA. Courtesy Massachusetts Historical Society.

Ruth daughter of John & Ruth Row Born April ye 2d. 1691 —

Nathaniel Matson & Ruth Row of this Town Joyned in Marriage before the Reverend Simon Bradstreet January ye 18th. 1714/5

Taken out of Charlestown Books for Records of Births and Marriages this 28th of June 1722

Thomas Jenner Town Clerk.

A true Copy Exam ℘ Samuel Phipps Clr

Ruth daughter of John & Ruth Row   Born April ye 2^d. 1691 ——

Nathaniel Matson & Ruth Row of this Town Joyned in Marriage before the Reverend Simon Bradstreet   January ye 18th . 1714/5

Taken out of Charlestowns Books for Records of Births and Marriages this 28th of June 1722

Thomas Jenner Town Clerk.

A true Copy Exam [examined] At [attest] Samuel Phipps Cler[k]

John and Ruth Row, Miscellaneous Bound Collection, 1691, Massachusetts Historical Society, Boston, MA. Courtesy Massachusetts Historical Society.

1 Born unto Benjamin Franklyn & Phebe his wife on the 12 day of September 1692 A Son named John Franklyn
2 Born to them the 3^d of July 1690 a Daughter named Mary Franklyn December 15. 1737.

This is a true Copy taken out of the Book of Records belonging to the Town of Marlborough by me Abraham Eager Town Cler.

a true Copy Exam^d. p. Ezek^l. Goldthwait Cler

1 Born unto Benjamin Franklyn & Phebe his wife on
the 12 day of September 1692 A Son named John Franklyn

2 Born to them the 3[d] of July 1690 a Daughter named
Mary Franklyn December 15. 1737.

This is a true Copy taken out of the Book
of Records belonging to the Town of Marlborough
by me Abraham Eager Town Cler. [Clerk]

A true Copy Exam[d] At [attest] Ezek[l]. Goldthwait Cler[k]

Benjamin Franklyn, 1690-92, Miscellaneous Bound Collection, Massachusetts Historical Society, Boston, MA. Courtesy Massachusetts Historical Society.

Major General Winthrop, and Major Elisha Hutchinson are desired and appointed to take a Survay of the great Artillery in and about the Town of Boston, to see whither there may not be some Guns spared for the better strengthning of the Forts at Salem and Marblehead; Also so soon as they conveniently may to make a Journy to Salem, and to take a view of their ffortifications makeing Report of this Affayre unto the Govr. and Council. —

By Order of the Govr. & Council

Is^a. Addington Secr^y.

Boston, March. 6th.
1690/1.

Major General Winthrop, and Major Elisha Hutchinson are desired and appointed to take a Survay of the great Artillery in and about the Town of Boston to see whither there may not be some Guns Spared for the better strengthning of the Forts at Salem and Marblehead; Also so soon as they conveniently may: to make a Journy to Salem, and to take a view of their ffortifications makeing Report of this Affayre [affair] unto the Govr and Council. — :

By Order of the Govr & Council

= Js^{a} [Isaac] Addington Sec^{ry}.

Boston, March. 6th
1690/1

Major General Winthrop, 6 March 1690/91, Winthrop Family Papers, Massachusetts Historical Society, Boston, MA. Courtesy Massachusetts Historical Society.

No. 4 1690.

Whereas there was a meeting of Commissioners appointed
by the province of New-York & ye Colonyes of ye Massachusets
Plimouth & Connecticott who sate at New york aforesaid
upon ye 1st of may Last & then and there Concluded
Divers matters and things Comprized in a Certain act
subscribed by them as their unanimous Result Re
lateing to forces then Raised & to be Raised for an
expedition against the french and Indian enemies, &
Whereas it was further agreed upon by the said Commis
sioners that the major be appointed by the Levt. Go=
vernour of N. york and att the Instance & speciall
Request of Connecticott as also Massachusets Colony that
major Generall John Winthrop might have ye Conduct of
said forces as before mentioned ye Levt. Governour Leisler
Complyed with the same, subscribeing a Commission un
der the seal of the province aforesaid for said major
Generall Winthrop to Command in Cheife, upon whose
Arrivall with ~~a Considerable~~ one hundred ~~Number of~~ men ~~....~~ more
of the full Complement for Connecticott, agreed upon by ye sd Commissioners ~~designed~~ found the said
Commission sent up by ye sd Levt. Governr Leisler,
very much defective, which occasioned a Debate &
Consultations between those Commissioned by ye said
Levt. Governr Leisler at Albany to settle what Relates
to ye province of N-york and the major Generall Win=
throp for his maties service and the benefit of the
Confederates; and doe Conclude that the said major Gene
rall shall have wth all possible speed a Commission
sent him by Levt. Governr Leisler pursuant to the
Commission Granted him by the Governr of Conne=
cticott In as full and ample manner as the said
Commission is worded to all Intents, constructions, and
purposes and that In the mean time till such Com
mission shall be by him Received we doe engage upon
the Behalfe of sd Levt. Governr Leisler that the
said major Generall shall have as ample power and
Authoritie over the forces of the province of N-york as
if they were Comprehended in the Commission from Con
necticott. And whereas it was agreed upon by the sd Commissioners, that the aforesd Governr Leisler, should appoint
the Commander in cheife, so it is expected that ye said
Levt. Governr or his successor takes Care that a suitable & just Recom
pence be made to ye Commander in cheife for his atten
dence upon the aforesaid service.

Whereas there was a meeting of Commissioners appointed
By the province of New-York & ye Colonyes of ye masachusets
Plimouth & Connecticott who late at New york aforesaid
upon y ^{e} 1st of may last & then and there: Concluded
Divers matters and things Comprized in a Certain act
subscribed by them as their unaminious Result, Re
lateing to forces then Raised & to be Raised for an
expedition against the french and Indian enemies; &
Whereas it was further agreed upon by the said Commis
sioners that the major be appointed by the Leu^{t}: Go=
vernour of N. york and at the Instance & speciall
Request of Connecticott as also Masachusets Colony that
major Generall John Winthrop might have y^{e} Conduct of
said forces as before mentioned Leu^{t}: Governour Leister
Complyed with the same, subscribeing a Commission un
der the seal of the province aforesaid for said major
Generall Winthrop To Command in Cheife, upon whose
Arrivall with a Considerable an hundred men more
the full Complement for Connecticott agreed upon by commission one found, the said
Commission sent up by y^{e} s^{d} Leu^{t}: Govern^{r} Leister
very much defective, which occasioned a Debate &
Consultations between those Commissioned by y^{e} said
Leu^{t}: Govern^{r} Leister at Albany To settle what Relates
to y^{e} province of N-york and the major Generall Win=
throp for his maj^{ties} service and the benefit of the
Confederates; and doe Conclude that the said major Gene
rall shall have wth all possible speed a Commission
sent him by Leu^{t}: Govern^{r} Leister, pursuant to the
Commission granted him by the Govern^{r} of Connec=
ticott, In as full and ample manner as the said
Commission is worded to all Intents, Constructions, and
purposes and that In the mean time, till such Com
mission shall be by him, Received, we doe engage upon
the Behalfe of s^{d} Leu^{t}: Govern^{r}: Leister that the
said major Generall, shall have as ample power and
Authoritie over the forces of the province of N-york, as
if they were Comprehended in the Commission from Con
necticott; And whereas it was agreed upon by the s^{d} Commissioners, that the afores^{d} Govern^{r} Leister, should appoint
the Commander in cheife, so it is expected that ye said
Leu^{t}: Govern^{r} or his successor takes Care that a suitable & Just Recom
pence be made to ye Commander in cheife for his atten
dence upon the aforesaid service.

Report of Meeting, 1690, Winthrop Family Papers, Massachusetts Historical Society, Boston, MA. Courtesy Massachusetts Historical Society.

To the much Hono^rd the County Court now sitting in Boston

The Petition of Margaret Haywood Widow & Relict of Anthony Heiwood late of Boston dec^d.

Humbly sheweth

That your poor, afflicted Petitioner is, by ye Decease of her late Husband, left in a very distressed & desolate Condition, with ffour young Children to bring up, & nothing wherewithall to doe it. And therfore praies y^t you will please to appoint some meet Persons imediatly to set out to her the Thirds of the Houses & Lands [that her late husband died seized of] according to Law, & may she have the Liberty to chuse her Part, & may there be any other way found out, such as in your Wisdome shall seem best, to add something toward her Relief out of the Estate, as it is extreamly needed, so it wilbe most thankfully acknowledged,

And your Petitioner shall ever pray &c.

Boston 29th July 1690.

To the much Honord the County Court now sitting in Boston

The Petition of Margaret Haywood   Widow & Relict of Anthony

Humbly sheweth   Heiwood [Haywood] late of Boston dec^{d}. [deceased]

That your poor, afflicted Petitioner is , by ye Decease of her Late
Husband, left in a very distressed & desolate Condition, with ffour
young Children to bring up, & nothing wherewithall to doe it,
And therfore praies y^{t} you will please to appoint some meek [meet]
that her late husband dced [deceased] joined at
Persons imediatly [immediately] to set out to her the Thirds of the Houses
& Lands
according to Law, & may she have the Liberty to chuse her Part,
& may there be any other way found out, such as in your Wisdome shall
seem best, to add somthing toward her Relief out of the Estate, as it is
extreamly needed, so it wilbe most thankfully acknowledged.

And your Petitioner shall ever pray &c

Boston 29th July 1690

Margaret Haywood, 1690, Miscellaneous Bound Collection, Massachusetts Historical Society, Boston, MA.
Courtesy Massachusetts Historical Society.

N. Y.

Jacob Leisler Esqr Lieut Governor and Commander in Chief of ye Province of New York and dependencyes In america under his most Sacred Majtie King William of England, Scotland, France and Ireland, &c; Defendr of ye faith Supreame Lord of Said Province & dependencyas In america, &ca: To the Honorable John Winthrop Esqr Greeting By virtue of ye authority derived unto mee I do hereby constitute and apoint you to be Majr of all ye forces now raised or to be raised for ye Expedicon of albany out of this Province & ye New England Collonies & Maryland according to ye unanimous result made with Said Collonies against ye ffrench at Canada you are There fore Carefully and diligently to discharge ye duty of a Majr by Excercising ye Same In armes & Keeping them in good order & discipline both officers and Souldjers observing Strictly all ye articles In ye Said Result Expressed here by Willing and Commanding them to observe and follow Such Orders and directions as you Shall from time to time receive from Mee or any apointed by my Selfe and Councill according to ye Rules & discipline of Warr Pursuant to ye trust reposed in you and to Execute all acts of hostility against ye ffrench King his Subiects & their adherents & this Commission to continue during my will & Pleasur Only given under my hand & Sealed with ye Seale of ye Province this [illegible] July in ye Second yeare of theire Majties Reigne 1690

Seale

Past ye office

Jacob Milborne Secry

Jacob Leisler

N.Y.

Jacob Leisler Esqr Lieu^{t}: Gouerno^{r} [Governor] and Command^{r}; in Chief of ye Province of new York
and dependencyes In america under his most Sacred Maj^{tie}; King William of England, Scotland, France
and Ireland &c^{a}; Defend^{r} of ye faith Supreame Lord of Said Province & dependencyas In america &c^{a}:
To the Honorable John Winthrop Esqr: Greeting By virtue of ye authority deriued [derived] unto mee
I do hereby constitute and apoint you to be Maj^{r}; of all ye forces now raised or to be raised for ye Expedicon
of albany out of this Province & ye New England Collonies & Maryland according to ye unanimous result
made with Said Collonies against ye ffrench at Canada you are There fore Carefully and diligently to
discharge ye duty of a Maj^{r}; by Excercising ye Same In armes & Keeping them in good order & discipline
both officers and Souldjers observing Strictly all ye articles In ye Said Result Expressed here by Willing and
Commanding them to obserue [observe] and follow Such orders and directions as you Shall from time to time
receue [receive] from Mee or any apointed by my Selfe and Councill according to ye Rules & discipline of
Warr Pursuant to ye trust reposed in you and to Execute all acts of hostility against ye ffrench King
his Subjects & their adherents & this Commission to continue during my will & Pleasur only given under
my hand & Sealed with ye Seale of ye Province this [31] July in ye Second yeare of there Maj^{ties}: Reigne 1690 ~

Post ye office

Jacob: Leisler

Jacob Milborne Secry

Jacob Leisler to Fitz-John Winthrop, 31 July 1690, Winthrop Family Papers, Massachusetts Historical Society, Boston, MA. Courtesy Massachusetts Historical Society.

1696

To the honored Lieft governour Judge of the probat of wills and for granting of administration:

The petition of Samuell Wight of Mettfeild humbly sheweth, That somtime past my brother Thomas Wight of mettfeild deceased Intestate And left severall children among whom was a son Named: Joshua: Wight who was young, and the estate of my brother being to come to a division, the Honored County Court being pleased to apoint your petitionor a gardien for my brothers son, which was somtime In the year (1690) And your petitionor for the sake of my brother and of his son did accept and att the division of my brothers estate did take into my hands that portion of estate that was divided unto the young man for whom I was gardien and continued in the improvement of sd estate acording to my best abillity. And your honor having been pleased now in this year (1695) to give gardienship unto Joseph Clark of mettfeild over the sd son of my brother, And I being very desirous to deliver over the estate in my hand unto sd Clark that so your petitionor might no longer be envolled in the trouble of the same, And your petitionor having oft tendred the estate to the sd Clark and the sd Clark unto this day refusing to take sd estate into his hands whereby your petitionor is Like still to be envollved in dificullty and trouble your petitionor therfore humbly prayes your honors help herein that the sd Clark may apear before your honor there to render rason of his refusall att which time your petitionor will present his acounts of his doings in and about sd estate unto your honor And your honors help herein shall oblige your petitionor ever to pray

Samuell Wight

1690

To the honored Lifft governour Judge of the probat of wills and for granting of administration:

The petition of Samuell Wight of mettfeild humbly sheweth, That sometime past my brother Thomas Wight of mettfeild, deceased Intestate, And Left sevarall ^children^ among whom was a son Named: Joshua: Wight who was young, and the estate of my brother being to come to A division, the honored County court being pleased to apoint your petitionor A gardien for my brothers son, which was somtime In the year (1690) And your petitionor for the sake of my brothr and of his son did accept and att the division of my brothers estate did take Into my hands that portion of estate that was divided unto the young man for whom I was gardien and continued in the improvement of s[d] estate acording to my best abillity. And your honor having been pleased Now in this year (1695) to give gardienship unto Joseph Clark of mettfeild over the s[d] son of my brother, And I beeing very desirous to deliver over the estate in my hand unto s[d] Clark that so your petitionor might No Longer be envolled in the ~ Trouble of the same, And your petitionor having oft tendred the estate to the s[d] Clark and the s[d] Clark unto this day refusing to take s[d] estate into his hands whereby your petitionor is Like [shall] to be envollved in dificullty and trouble your petitionor therfore humbly prayes your honors help herein that the s[d] Clark may apear before your honor there to render rason of his refusall att which time your petitionor will present his acounts of his doings in and about s[d] estate unto your honor And your honors help herein shall~~ oblige your petitionor ever to pray

Samuell Wight

Samuell Wight, Petition, 1690, Wight Family Papers, Massachusetts Historical Society, Boston, MA. Courtesy Massachusetts Historical Society.

Plimouth March 12th 1690/91

Honoured Sr After my harty service to
yor selfe these are to Request you that If my
pattent be past & signed, to send it to me by this —
Barer Robert Ransom: (Inclosed) with a few Lines
from yor selfe (& what I am Inddebted to you) & I
will send yor Mony by the Next Oportunity ~ & please
to present my humble service to his Excelly: & Aquaint
him: that my Brother William Clarke Cannot [illegible]
Acomadate his Excelly with sheep fitt for his turne soe
quickly as is Desired, But If itt may sute his Excelly —
for some Longer time: he will Gladly & Readily serve
him, for he tells me this is the worst time for itt
having noe more att present but wishing you health &
prosperity I Rest yor Assured humble servtt —

Nath: Clarke

Plimouth March:12 1687/8

Honoured Sr After my harty Service to
yor [your] selfe: these are to Request you: that If my
pattent be past & signed, to send it to me by this
Baren Robert Ransom: (Inclosed) with a few Lines
from yor [your] self (& what I am Indebted to you) & I
will send yor [your] Mony by the Next Opertunity ~ & please
to p^rsent my humble service to his Exelly: [Excellency] & Aquaint
him: that my Brother William Clarke Cannot
Acomadate his Exelly with sheep fitt for his turne soe
quickly as is Desired, But If itt may sute [suit] his Exelly [Excellency]
In some Longer time: he will Gladly & Readily serve
him, for he tells me this is the worst time for itt
haveing noe more att p^rsent but wishing you health &
prosperity I Rest Yo^r [your] Assured humble Serv^tt [Servant]

Nath:^ll Clarke

Nathaniel Clarke, Miscellaneous Bound Collection, 1687/8, Massachusetts Historical Society, Boston, MA. Courtesy Massachusetts Historical Society.

Boston March 5th: 1667/8 — 11. 4

Wee whose names are Underwritten: Inhabitants of Sudbury Streett in Boston, Understand yt ye sd Streett is not appointed by ye Justices, to be paved. doe make it our Request to be Added, to the said Order. ~~doe make it our Request~~ being very Willing & ready to fall upon the same.

Tho: Cooper

James Hawkins

William Paine

Stephen Minott

This Petition is granted by the Justices, paying fees.

Boston March 5th: 1687/8

Wee whose names are Underwritten. Inhabitants. of ——
Sudbury Streett. in Boston Understand y^{t} [that] o^{r} [our]: Streett is not
appointed p^{r} [per] ye Justices. to be paved. doe make it our Resquest
to be Added; to the Said Order;
being very Willing & ready to fall upon the same.

Tho: Cooper

James Hawkins
William Paine
Stephen Minott

This Petition is granted
by the Justices paying fees

Thomas Cooper, Miscellaneous Bound Collection, 1687/8, Massachusetts Historical Society, Boston, MA. Courtesy Massachusetts Historical Society.

At a Genall Court held In Boston ye. 15.th October 1684

Upon ye Motion & desire of Maj: Genall Daniel Gookin Capt Thomas Prentice & Daniel Henchman this Courts Comittee for ye setling of a new plantation neare Quansikomon pond

1 Humbly desiring yt. ye Court will please to name ye Town Worcester, & yt ye brand marks for cattle there may be thus 

2 That one of sd Comittee being deceased yt. ye Court will pleas to appoint a fitt man to supply his place, for to help in ye further setling of sd Town to all intents & purposes as formerly Ordered; & do humbly propound to ye Hond. Court yt Mr Adam Winthrop may be ye person, being one interested in sd Town.

At a Gen^{all} [General] Court held In Boston ye 15th October 1684

Vpon [Upon] ye Motion & desire of Maj^{o} Gen^{all} Daniel Gookin Capt Thomas Prentice & Daniel Henchman this Courts Comittee for ye setling of a new plantation neare Quansikomon pond [Quinsigamond Pond]

1 Humbly desireing y^{t} [that] y^{e} [the] Court will please to name ye Town Worcester, & y^{t} [that] ye Brand marke [marks] for cattle there may be thus

<pre>
 +
+ +
 +
</pre>

2 That one of sd Comittee being deceased y^{t} ye Court will pleas to appoint a fitt man to supply his place, for to help in ye further setling of sd Town to all intents & purposes as formerly ordered; & do humbly ppound [propound] to ye Honrd Court y^{t} Mr Adam Winthrop may be ye person, being one interested in s^{d} Town.

Francis E. Blake, *Incidents of the First and Second Settlements of Worcester* (Worcester, Mass.: Franklin P. Rice, 1884), pp. 13-14.

The Deputys Judge meete to graunt all the above mentioned particulars & desire o[ur] hon[oure]d magists consent hereto

William Torrey Cleric

17th of October 1684 Consented to by the magists Edward Rawson Secrety

21 octob 84 The magists Judge meete to add Capt Wing to the rest of this Committee there being then the deputys here to consenting. Edward Rawson Secrety

Consented to by the Deputys

William Torrey Cleric

The Deputs [Deputies] Judge meete to graunt [grant]
all the aboue [above] mentioned pticulers [particulars] & desire
o^{r} honrd Magists Consent thereto

William Torrey Cleric

Consented to by the magists Edward Rauson Secret
17th of october 1684.

The magists Judge meete to Add Capt wing to bee of this Comittee their
21 octob 84 brethren the Deputyes hereto Consenting=Edward Rawson Secret

Consented to by the Depts

William Torrey Cleric

Francis E. Blake, *Incidents of the First and Second Settlements of Worcester* (Worcester, Mass.: Franklin P. Rice, 1884), pp. 13-14.

Copy

In the name of ye Lord amen, Appeared before me Pelgrom Clock Clarke appointed by ye worshipfull Constable and overseers of Boswick, Joost Adriaens, being sick abedd, but having his memory and understanding and using ye same, as outwardly appeared, and clearly could be seen, whoe declared, to Consider the life of men upon earth to be nothing else but a Shadow, transient. and therefore nothing more certaine then death and ye Contrary nothing more uncertain then the time thereof, First recommanding his immortall Soul, when shee shale be departed out ye body in the hands of God Almighty, and his Corps a Christian buriall. So it is that ye appearant, for Considerable reasons in his Sickness, as likewise out of greate love, bearing to his beloved wife, for her attendance in his Sickness bequeathed to a dowery all his Cattle, and houshold Stuffe wch shee used dayly, to his beloved wife Mary hay, as likewise ye timber for ye windows not willing or desiring that any after his decease shale oppose the premisses, in Courts or else out, in any manner, to to permitt his Said wife peacable possession thereof, to keep & use the same as should be, desiring from me Clarke to make thereof an act in due forme tot be & use the Same for an evidence as is required, done and past also ~~ye~~ at ye dwelling house of ye appearant living in ye Jurisdiction of Boswick ye 27th July 1673. — the originale under my Clerkes hands with ye witnesse underSigned

Concordat quod attestor
P Clocq Clerk

Copy

In the name of ye Lord Amen. Appeared before me
Pelgrow Clock Clarke [clerk] appointed by ye worshipfull Con=
Stuble [constable] and overSeers of Boswick [Boswich], Joost Adrians, being Sick
a bedd, but having his memory and understanding and
using ye Same, as outwardly appeared, and Clearly Could be
Seen, whoe declared, to Consider the life of men upon
earth tobe nothing else but a Shadow, transient, and
therefore nothing more certaine then death, and ...
ye Contrary nothing more uncertain then ye ...
time thereof, First recommanding his immortale
Soul, when Shee Shall be departed out ye boddy in the
hands of God Almichty [Almighty], and his Corps a Christian burial
So it is that ye appearant, for Considerable reason[s]
in his Sickness, as likewise out of greate love, bearing
to his beloved wife, for her attendance in his Sickness
bequeched [bequeathed] to a dowery all his Cattle, and houshold
Stuffe wch [which] Shee used dayly, to his beloved wife
Mary hay, as likewise ye timber forye windows
not willing or desiring that any after his de=
cease Shall oppose the premisses, in Courts or with
out, in any manner, to to permitt his Said wife
peacable possession there of, to keep & use the Same
as Should be, desiring from me Clarke [clerk] to make
there of an act in due [one] forme tot [to] be & use the
Same for an evidence as is required, done and pon [upon]
also as ye dwelling house of ye Appearant living in
ye Jurisdiction of boswick ye 27th July 1683.
the originale [ ] under my Clerkes hands with
ye wittnesse underSigned

Concord at quod attestor
P. Clocg [Clocq] Clerk

Record of wills proved at Albany, New York, Surrogate's Court, Albany County, New York (AA2). FHL film 481, 436.

1678
11 Apl.

To the Hono^ble Govern^r and Councill now sitting in Boston
April 11th: 1678

The Petition of Elizabeth Morse Relict widdow of John Morse
in the behalfe of her selfe and Children

Humbly Sheweth that whereas your Petition^rs Late deare husband
hath served the Country in the present [illegible] the space
of Three yeares; of which time he served the Country at Mount Hope
and Narragansett about fourteene weeks, for wch fourteene weeks service
he hath had paym^t: Now for the rest of the Time he hath not had any
Satisfaction: Notwithstanding frequently his whole time was taken up in
makeing provisions for the severall partyes of souldiers that were
sent out and in sending provisions to them abroad and at their returne
in takeing care of an acco^t of the Countryes Armes, as I doubt not is
sufficiently knowne by yor Hono^rs &c. And he being now taken away
by the wise disposing hand of God hath left yor Petition^r a [illegible]
[illegible] with [illegible]

Yo^r Petition^r therefore doth humbly Intreat ye favor of
yor Hono^rs to Consider her desolate Condition; & grant her
and poore Children some Compensation for her s^d husbands
service (whome I hope hath approved himselfe to yor Hono^rs
faithfull and serviceable in his place) So shall shee and
and her Children be ever Obliged to pray &c

Elizabeth Morse

1678
11 Apl.

To the Hono^{ble} Govern^{r} and Councill now sitting in Boston April 11th: 1678 ~ ~ ~

The Petition of Elizabeth Morse Relict Widdow of John Morse in the behalfe of her ~ selfe and Children ~

Humbly sheweth that whereas your Petition & Late deare husband
hath served the Country in the yeare of C...ss for neare that
of Three Yeares; of which time he served the Country at Mount hope
and Narragansett about foureteene weekes for w^{ch} [which] fourteene weeks service
he hath had paym^{t}: Now for the rest of the Time he hath not had any~
Satisfaction : Notwithstanding frequently his whole time was taken up in
makeing provisions for the severall partyes of souldiers that were
sent out and in sending provisions to them abroad and at their returne
in takeing Care of an acco^{t}: [account] of the Countryes Armes, as I doubt not is
sufficiently knowne by Yo^{r} [Your] Hono^{rs} And he being now taken away
by the wise disposeing hand of God hath Left Yo^{r} [Your] Petition a ~
Desolated Widdow wth Eight Children

Yo^{r} Petitio^{r} therefore doth humbly Intreate ye favor of
Yo^{r} Hono^{es} to Consider her desolate Condition; & grant her
and poore Children Some Compensation for her s^{d} husbands
service (Whome I hope hath approved himselfe to yor hono^{es}
faithfull and serviceable in his place) so shall shee and
and her Children be ever Obliged to pray &c ~ ~

Elizabeth Morse

Petition of Elizabeth Morse, 11 April 1678. Accession 1336, original document in NSDAR Americana Collection, National Society Daughters of the American Revolution.
Courtesy National Society Daughters of the American Revolution, Washington, D.C.

There being a full appearance of the Inhabitants of the Towne of Norwalk meett together at a Legall Towne meetting the 17 of Decemb 1678 for the Consulting Agitatting and obtaineing of a Comfortable meeting house that soe the holy ordinances of our Lord Jesus Christ might be Decently and Comlely attended upon but there appearing playnly a great obsticle in the way by Reason of a strong Diversities of apprehensions about the place of the setting downe the sayd meetting house one part of the Inhabitants probably amounting to the moitie of them being strongly for the sayd house to be sett downe upon that place of ground neere the old meetting house the other part of the Inhabitants to have the house sett downe upon the hill usually calld goodman Hoyts hill wheare fore for the Resolveing of the sayd Difference and that the sayd obsticle may be removed to the end that such a Honnorable worke may be carryed on with unanimitie peace and love we the sayd Inhabitants Consisting of both parties doe unanimusly and mutually elect and make choyse of the Honnoured Deputie Govournor Majo Treat the Honnoured Majo Gold and the Reverend Elder Buckingam all whome we humbly Crave that you would be pleased soe farr to Condesend for to Come over unto us and to view the scituation of the Towne and the Inhabitants thereof, and to heare what arguments and light shall be Presented unto you by foure persons Deputed by the two sayd parties and then what Determination Conclusion and appointment of ye the sayd three Elected persons or two of you given under yo hands for the setting downe the sayd meetting house either neere the old meeting house or upon the hill we the sayd Inhabitants doe firmely and faithfully Engage and promise to abide by and sitt downe & acquiesse in wittness wheare of we have sett to oure hands the day and yeare above written

Rich Olmstead
Tho: Fitch senr
Thomas Bennydick Sr
Walter Hoyte
John Platt
Tho Fitch jun
Mark Sention
Richard Holmes
Samuell Hayes
John Hoyt
Judah Gregory
James Sention
Zerubbabel Hoyt
Samuel Keller
Ephraim Lockwood
John Gregory jun
Nathaniel Hayes
George Abbott
John Bennedick
Thomas Tayler
Samuell Campfield
John Keeler
Ralph Keeler

Thomas Hanford
John Gregory Sr
nathaniel Richards
Mathew Marvin Sr
James Olmsted
Thomas Betts sen
Samuell Keler
Samuel Kelloge
James Pickitt
Samuell Bennydick
William Lees
John Fitch
Mathew Sention
Samuell Sention
John Belden
Samuel Smith
John Olmsted
John Bouton
James Bennedick
Tho Bennydick
Richard Holmes
Daniel Benedick
Joseph Gregory
John Nash
James Beebe

edward nash
John Rusco
Tho Graniss
Christopher Cumstock
Thomas Hyatt
John Crampton
John Whitney

There Being afull, apeareance of the Inhabitants of the Towne of Norwalk 49
meett together at Legall. Towne meetting the 17 of Decembr 1678, for the Consulting Adgitatting and obtaineing of a Comfortable meeting house that for the holy ordinances of our Lord Jesus Christ might be Descently and Comly-ly attended upon but there appeareing playnly a great obsticle, in the way by Reason of a strong Diversities of apprehenssions about the place of the setting Downe the sayd meeting house one part of the Inhabitants probably amounting to the moittee [majority] of them: being strongly for the sayd house to be sett downe upon that place of ground neare the old meetting house the other part of the Inhabitants to have the house sett downe upon the hill usually cald goodman Hoyts hill whearfore for the Resolveing [Desolveing] of the sayd Differance and yt the sayd obsticle may be removed to the end that such a Honno^{r}able worke may be carryed on with uninimitie, peace and love. we the sayd Inhabitants Consisting of both parties. doe unanimusly and mutually elect and make choyse of the Honnoured Deputie Governo^{r} Majo^{r} Treat the Honnoured Major Gold and the Reverend Elder. Buckingham: all whom we Humbly Crave that you would be pleased soe farr to Condesend. for to Come over unto us. and to view the scituation of the Towne: and the Inhabitants therof, and to heare what arguments. and Light. shall be Presented unto you. by foure persons Depute-ed. by the two sayd. parties and then what Determination. Conclusion and appoy-ntment of ye the sayd three. Elected persons or two of you. given under yor hands for the setting downe the sayd meeting. house either neere the old meeting house or upon the hill we the sayd Inhabitants. doe firmely and faithfully Engage and promise to abide by and sitt downe Accquiesse in wittness whearof we have sett to oure hands the day and yeere above written

Rich. Olmsetd
Tos. Ffitch, Senr.
Thomas Bennydick, Sr.
Walltar Hoyte
John Platt
Tho. ffitch Jun.
Mark Sension
Robard Stuard
Samuell Hayes
John Hayt
Judah Gregory
James Sention
Zerubbabel hayt
James miller
Ephraim Lokwood
John gregory, jun.
Nathanill Hayes
George Abbott
John Bennedict
Thomas Taylor
Samuell Canfeld
John Keeler
Ralph Keeler

Thomas Hanford
John Gregory: Sr.
nathaniell Richards
Mathew Marvin Sr
James Olmsted
Thomas Betts Jun
Samuell Keler
Samuell Belden
James Pickitt
Samuell Bennydick
William Lees
John Ffitch
Mathias Sention
Samuell Sention
John Bellden
Samuel Smith
John Olmsted
John Bouton
James Bennedick
Tho Bennydick
Richard Holmnes
Daniell benedick
Joseph greogorie
John nash
James Beebe

edward Nash

John Ruscoe
Thos Seamur
Crytopher Cumstock
thomas hyat
John Crampton
John Whitnee

Norwalk, Connecticut, 1678, Petition. Copy in possession of Kip Sperry.

John Hull
agt
John Radford

Whereas John Hull hath Arrested John Radford to this
Court & doth not declare agt him The Court doth Orde
that ye said Hull shallbe nonsuited & pay unto ye said
Radford 50 lb Tobo for a nonsuite forthwith with
Charges of Court else execution

John Hull	Whereas John Hull hath Arrested John Radford to this
ag^{t} [against]	Court & doth not declare ag^{t} [against] him The Court doth Ord^{r}
John Radford	that y^{e} [the] said Hull shalbe nonsuited & pay unto ye said
	Radford 50 ^{lb} [pounds] Tob^{co} [Tobacco] for a nonsuite forthwith with
	Charges of Court else execucon [execution]

Northumberland County, Virginia, Order Book, 1652-1665, p. 23 (1653). See Kent P. Bailey and Ransom B. True, *A Guide to Seventeenth-Century Virginia Court Handwriting* (Richmond, Virginia: Association for the Preservation of Virginia Antiquities, 1980), p. 57. Courtesy Association for the Preservation of Virginia Antiquities.

An Attachmt: is granted unto Bartholomewe Hoskins agt soe much of
the Estate of John Piggott Marchant as shallcome satisfaction for the
some of One Thousand & fower hundred pounds of tob: wth Caske unto ye
sd Hoskins or his assignes beinge made appeare to be due uppon bill
together wth Cost Chardges: /

An Attachmt: [Attachment] is granted unto Bartholomewe Hoskins agt [against] soe [so] much of
the Estate of John Piggott Marchant [merchant, his occupation] as shalbecome satisfactory for the
some of One Thousand & fower [four] Hundred pounds of tob: [tobacco] wth [with] Caske unto y^{e}
sd [said] Hoskins or his assignes beinge made appeare to be due uppon bill
together wth [with] Co^{rt}: [Court] Chardges: [charges] /

Norfolk County, Virginia, Wills and Deeds C, 1651-1656, p. 171a (1652). See Kent P. Bailey and Ransom B. True, *A Guide to Seventeenth-Century Virginia Court Handwriting* (Richmond, Virginia: Association for the Preservation of Virginia Antiquities, 1980), p. 55. Courtesy Association for the Preservation of Virginia Antiquities.

Memorandum That Edward Lilly doth acquitt release and
discharge Henry Robinson of and from all debts dues and
demaunds reckonings and accompts or from any parte or
parcell of the estate of the said Robinson which was formerly
in the custody of mee the said Edward Lilly wittnes my hand
this sixth of December 1647 Edw: Lilly: Wittnes at
present Thomas Allen Tho: Kirkby.

Memorandum That Edward Lilly doth acquitt release and
discharge Henry Robinson of and from all debts dues and
demaunds Reckonings and accoumpts or from any parte or
parcell of the estate of the said Robinson which was formerly
in the custody of mee the said Edward Lilly wittnes my hand
this sixth of December 1647 Edw: Lilly: Wittnes at
present Thomas Allen   Tho: Kedby./

Norfolk County, Virginia, Wills and Deeds B, 1646-1651, page 61 (1647). See Kent P. Bailey and Ransom B. True, *A Guide to Seventeenth-Century Virginia Court Handwriting* (Richmond, Virginia: Association for the Preservation of Virginia Antiquities, 1980), p. 51. Courtesy Association for the Preservation of Virginia Antiquities.

whereas it appeares to the Court that Sauill Gaskin is indebted upon ballance of accompts fforty pounds of tob unto William Capps the Administrator of James Smith deceased Payment is ordered to bee made thereof with Court Charges als execution /

Whereas it appeares to the Court that Sauill [Savill] Gaskin is indebted
upon ballance of accompts fforty pounds of to^{b} [tobacco] unto William Capps
the Administrator of James Smith deceased Payment is ordered to
bee made thereof with Court Charges als execucon [execution] /

Norfolk County, Virginia, Wills and Deeds B, 1646-1651, p. 62 (1647). See Kent P. Bailey and Ransom B. True, *A Guide to Seventeenth-Century Virginia Court Handwriting* (Richmond, Virginia: Association for the Preservation of Virginia Antiquities, 1980), p. 49. Courtesy Association for the Preservation of Virginia Antiquities.

m^r Peter Ashton } his Cer^t for Land }

These are to Certifie that according to sufficient proofe made before this Court there is due to m^r Peter Ashton 200 acres of Land for the transportation of 4 persons into this Country (vizt:)

Charles Hoyle } Edward Dyer }
Edward Rogers } W^m fflorence }

Mr Peter Ashton)
his Cer^{t} for Land)

These are to Certifie that according to sufficient proofe made before this Court there is due to Mr Peter Ashton 200 acres of Land for the transportacon [transportation] of 4 psons [persons] into the Country (vizt:) [namely:]

Charles Hoyle) Eduard [Edward] Dyer)
Edward Rogers) W^{m} fflorence)

Northumberland County, Virginia, Order Book, 1652-1665, p. 94 (1658). See Kent P. Bailey and Ransom B. True, *A Guide to Seventeenth-Century Virginia Court Handwriting* (Richmond, Virginia: Association for the Preservation of Virginia Antiquities, 1980), p. 53. Courtesy Association for the Preservation of Virginia Antiquities.

We whose names are Underwritten
being mett together in behalfe
of the towne & for ol Select to
Settle the Bounds betwixt mr
Smiths farme & the towne &
other persons who gave lands
Adjoyning to the said farme have
Agreed as followeth; viz:
that that stake with a heape of
stones Southwards about foure
Rod from the meettinghouse is
the Corner Bounds of said farme
from wch stake Eastward the
Country Road is settled fowre
Rod wide taking the fence on
the north & the stakes on the
South till it Cometh to Richard
Huttns house hereby declaring
that ~~on~~ the north side of said high
waye is late in ffelmingham
Bounds ~~& on~~ the South side are the
bounds of the afforesaid mr
Thomas Smiths farme &
from thence the high waye
is Staked till it Cometh to the
north Corner of Goodman
mappys fence & from thence
to Ipswich Lyne as the fence
formerly stood on the East
side of the roade & on the
west syde of the Roade as the
fence nowe standeth & on the
west syde of the Country roade
from Richard Huttns house
to Ipswich ~~Roade~~ Lyne is by his

18th: 4th [month, June]: 1680 [page] 54

Wee whose names are underwritn
being mett [met] together in behalfe
of the towne & for o^{r} selves [ourselves] to
setle [settle] the Bounds betwine [between] M^{r}
Smiths farme & the town &
other psons [persons] who have lands
Adjoyning to the said farme have
Agreed as followeth viz: [namely]
that that [the] stake with a heape of
stones South wards about fowre [four]
Rod from the meetting house is
A [the] Corner Bounds of said farme
from w^{ch} [which] Stake Eastward the
Country road is settld fowre [four]
Rod wide takeing the fence on
the north & the Stakes on the
South till it Cometh to Richard
Huttns howse [house] hereby declareing
that the north side of said high-
waye is late Mr felmingham^{s}
Bounds the South side is the
bounds of the afforesaid M^{r}
Thomas Smiths farme &
from thence the high waye
is Staked till it Cometh to the
north Corner of Goodman
Maxeys fence & from thence
to Ipswich lyne [line] as the fenc [fence]
formerly stood on the East
sid [side] of the roade & on the
west syde of the Roade; [as] y^{e} [y^{r}]
fence nowe stand; & on the
west syd [side] of the Country roade
from Richard Huttns house ...

Wenham, Essex Co., Massachusetts, Town Records, p. 54. FHL film 878,669.

19: 1 mo: 1660 : (535)

Know all men By these
presents that whereas mr
Saml Smith of wenham
Deceased did Give to the
towne ten acres of land to
the towne neare the old meeting house; the Select men
in behalfe of the towne & mr
Thomas Smith haue &
Doe Jointly Agree that the
land from the grade of mr
Saml: field Call the fifty acres
wch the towne haue Disposed
of & is within fence as the
fence now stands Downe
to pond by mr Gerishes house
is settled for the bounds of the
ten acres always provided
if mr Thomas Smith shall see
Cause to remove the northeast
Corner two lengths of fence
inwards it shall be lawfull
for him soe to doe allowing
two lengths ~~outwards~~ outward
at the other end: & further
the aforesaid mr Thomas Smith
doth Jointly Graunt & Confirme
all that land Between the lower

18th: 4th: mo. [June] 1680 [page] (55)

Know all men By these
p^r sents [presents] that whereas
Sam^ll [Samuel] Smith of Wenham
Deceised [deceased] did Give to the
towne ten acres of land: to
the towne neare the old meeting howse [house]; the Select men
in behalfe of the towne wth [with]
Mr Thomas Smith have &
Doe hereby Agree that the
land from the heade of ye [the]
Gen^ll field Cald [called] the fifty acres
wch [which] the towne have Disposed
of & is within fence as the
fence nowe stands downe
to ye pond by Mr Gerishes howse [house]
is setld [settled] for the bounds of sd [said]
ten acres alwayes provided
if Mr Thomas Smith shall see
Cause to remove the northeast
Corner two lengths of fence
inwards it shall be lawefull
for him soe to doe alloweing
two lengths outward
at the uper end: & further
the aforesaid Mr Thomas Smith
doth hereby Grante & Confirme
all that land Betwin [between] the lower

Wenham, Essex Co., Massachusetts, Town Records, p. 55. FHL film 878,669.

Cause to ...

Canar ...

inwards ... he ...

let him ... allowing

... amd

at the upper end ... further

the aforesaid Mr Thomas Smith

doth hereby ... & Confirme

all that land ... between the lower ...

Wolham, Essex Co. ... Massachusetts ... Records ... 56 ... PH ...